Five Kohutian Postulates

Five Kohutian Postulates

Psychotherapy Theory from an Empathic Perspective

Ronald R. Lee, Angie Rountree,
and Sally McMahon

JASON ARONSON

Lanham • Boulder • New York • Toronto • Plymouth, UK

Published in the United States of America
by Jason Aronson
An imprint of Rowman & Littlefield Publishers, Inc.

A wholly owned subsidiary of
The Rowman & Littlefield Publishing Group, Inc.
4501 Forbes Boulevard, Suite 200, Lanham, Maryland 20706
www.rowmanlittlefield.com

Estover Road
Plymouth PL6 7PY
United Kingdom

British Library Cataloguing in Publication Information Available

Library of Congress Cataloging-in-Publication Data

Lee, Ronald R.
Five Kohutian postulates : psychotherapy theory from an empathic perspective / Ronald R. Lee, Angie Rountree, and Sally McMahon.
p. ; cm.
Includes bibliographical references and indexes.
ISBN-13: 978-0-7657-0633-1 (cloth : alk. paper)
ISBN-10: 0-7657-0633-4 (cloth : alk. paper)
eISBN-10: 0-7657-0635-0
eISBN-13: 978-0-7657-0635-5
1. Psychoanalysis. 2. Empathy. 3. Kohut, Heinz. I. Rountree, Angie, 1958- II. McMahon, Sally, 1960- III. Title.
[DNLM: 1. Kohut, Heinz. 2. Self Psychology. 3. Empathy. 4. Psychoanalytic Therapy. WM 460.5.E3 L479f 2008]
RC506.L423 2009
616.89'17--dc22 2008034874

Printed in the United States of America

∞™ The paper used in this publication meets the minimum requirements of American National Standard for Information Sciences—Permanence of Paper for Printed Library Materials, ANSI/NISO Z39.48-1992.

Contents

Acknowledgments

I am very appreciative of the contributions of my coauthors, Angie and Sally, without whose talents and efforts this project may never have been completed. My heartfelt thanks extend to patients, supervisees, students, and friends for keeping me anchored in the reality of "living documents." Acknowledgments go to the untiring support of Dr. Brian James, the former principle of St. Hilda's College of the University of Melbourne, to the suggestions of Dr. Colby Martin (Naperville, IL), to the stimulating Professor Sid Bloch of the University of Melbourne Department of Psychiatry, to the staff of the Melbourne St. Vincent Hospital's Mental Health Service, and to the remarkable Paul Stepansky, who used editorial knowledge and skills to exemplify Kohut's "selfobject of creativity." Last, but not least, I have special thanks for the loving support of my indefatigable wife, Maggie.

Ronald R. Lee
The Gurdies, Victoria, Australia

CHAPTER ONE

Self Psychology

A Healing Research Program

Since the death of Heinz Kohut in 1981, a plethora of books have explained the changes he made to classical psychoanalytic theory, changes now recognized as an empathy-based theory called "self psychology." Although initially Kohut did not intend to challenge Freud's general theory of neurosis, his revision of Freud's theory of narcissism developed into a new psychotherapy theory that has been extensively written about during the last three decades. We now have access to Kohut's books (1971, 1977, 1984), published papers (Kohut, 1978a, 1990, 1991), much of his correspondence (Cocks, 1994), a biography (Strozier, 2001), and transcripts of his lectures to the students at the Chicago Institute (Kohut, 1996). Perhaps, however, the most telling feature of this empathy-based psychotherapy theory, has been the extensive publications of many of his former colleagues (Basch, Goldberg, and Wolf, as examples), explicating and extending his ideas. So, why another book on self psychology?

Our project attempts to shape Kohut's major theoretical constructs into a "research program," or a "cohesive organization of propositions" (Hartmann, 1939, p. 6). This undertaking was heavily influenced by the ideas of Imre Lakatos, one of an important generation of philosophers of science who challenged the reigning objectivism of the philosophy of science and provided a powerful new framework for understanding the evolving of science. These philosophers, who included Thomas Kuhn and Paul Feyerabend, thought science had both "normal" periods of evolutionary growth and periods of revolutionary change. Lakatos contributed to the growth of scientific theory by proposing that the primary reason for changes to a significant scientific theory—Kuhn's "paradigm"—was a theory's increasing inability to generate new hypotheses. Kandel's (2006) ideas coincide with Lakatos's point when he says that psychoanalysis "had exhausted much of its novel investigative power" (p. 365). So, Lakatos's emphasis on a theory's ability to generate new hypotheses offers a useful guide for the further development of Kohut's self-psychology theory. As Lakatos's ideas are not broadly known, however, we explore them in more detail in the next section.

In viewing Kohut's psychotherapy theory as a "research program" we hope to encourage practitioners who use Kohut's ideas in their psychotherapeutic work to generate extensions of his ideas. Importantly, his emphasis on a "field-based" research means a theory's value comes from its ability to help practitioners of long-term, empathy-based psychoanalytic psychotherapy in their work with patients. By psychoanalytic we mean that the major purpose of the psychotherapy is to resolve repetitive and narcissistic transferences (see Kohut 1978b, pp. 344–50). In a useful psychotherapy theory, competent practitioners, not laboratory experts, test the viability of new or modified auxiliary postulates to see if they help facilitate the empathic experiences of patients.

We have also styled the text for advanced students. Influenced by the philosopher Quine, we have excursed into many allied fields other than psychotherapy to generate hypotheses for testing to see if they enhance a patient's experiences of empathic understanding. And influenced by the historically minded philosopher Hesse (1974), we believe that support for Kohut's postulates comes from analogy, metaphor, and imagination. Positive responses from seminar attendees have also encouraged us. In content, we present Kohutian theory as complementary to the dynamic psychotherapies of the analytic tradition. In the larger perspective, we see empathy-based, long-term, psychoanalytic psychotherapy as a major component in treating mental illness, where it complements and is complemented by short-term EST (empirically supported therapy), also called EBT (evidence based therapy), and bio-based therapies (medication).

We undertook this project, believing an empathy-based long-term psychoanalytic psychotherapy theory is needed more than ever in the arsenal of treatments for mental illness. Admittedly, the modern social milieu favors seemingly low-cost EST, or biotherapy, especially as longer, empathy-based, intensive psychotherapies are discouraged by insurance companies and government agencies in an effort to stem the financial drain on mental health services. So, a shift toward EST and biotherapy has occurred despite growing evidence that their contributions to mental health, while significant, are limited. For example, a study by the Research Branch of the National Institutes of Mental Health (Elkin et al., 1989) randomly assigned 250 depressed patients to four different treatments for sixteen weeks. They found that for the severely depressed patients, treatment with imipramine and clinical management (treatment 1) or with interpersonal psychotherapy (treatment 2) were more effective in relieving their depression than cognitive behavior therapy (treatment 3) or a placebo and management (treatment 4).

More recently, a meta-analysis of thirty-four EST studies of two and a half thousand patients, Westen and Morrison (2001), found a "*lack of sustained efficacy* [italics added] of treatment for depression and general anxiety disorders" (p. 887). They conclude that compared with "what most consumers would reasonably expect, . . . 'empirically supported' sustained efficiency rates of 25 percent to 30 percent over 12–24 months are poor by almost any standards" (p. 887). These results suggest that the 70 percent whose improvements from EST could not be sustained, need to consider longer forms of psychotherapy. As Eric Kandel (2006), the Nobel prize researcher of cellular memory points out,

> The long-term effects of the new psychotherapies are still uncertain. . . . Although they often achieve results, both therapeutically and in terms of basic understanding, within five to fifteen sessions, the improvement is not always long-lasting. Indeed, it would appear that for some patients to achieve sustained improvement, therapy must continue for one or two years, perhaps because treating symptoms of their disorder without addressing the underlying conflicts is not always efficacious [p. 370].

A shift toward biotherapy has occurred despite no compelling evidence of its general efficacy and with evidence that its heavy long-term use involves considerable risks of creating harmful, permanent neural damage. Admittedly biotherapy is necessary in treating extremely destructive and intractable forms of mental disturbances, and undoubtedly its use in conjunction with psychotherapy helps some patients develop a therapeutic bond, when without it the patient's fear does not enable a bond to get established. Yet there is a general lack of acceptance outside the medical–pharmaceutical complex, about biotherapy's general effectiveness as a viable long-term treatment for all forms of mental illness. For example, in a study of 20,000 patients in the FDA (Federal Drug Administration) trials, Breggin (1991) found only 20 percent improvement in depressed patients who were given the serotonin selective reuptake inhibitor (SSRI) fluroxitine (Prozac), compared with 17 percent efficacy for patients given a placebo. The results of this influential study were supported a decade later from a meta-analysis by Kirsch, Moore, Scoboria, and Nicholls (2002) using the efficacy data of forty-seven trials submitted to the FDA for the six most widely prescribed SSRIs (fluroxitine, paroxetine, sertraline, venlafaxine, nefazadone, and citalopram). As the difference between patients treated with medication or a placebo was less than two points on the fifty-one point Hamilton depression scale, the authors claim that the significance of a pharmacological effect is "dubious."

So, evidence of useful but temporary effects of short-term psychotherapy, and a valuable but limited role for biotherapy in combating mental illness, points to the need for long-term, empathy-based psychoanalytic psychotherapy to play an important complementary role in fostering and maintaining mental health. In general it may be said, that the more the limitations of all treatments, including long-term psychotherapy, are acknowledged, the more obvious becomes the need for further extensive research and theoretical development, and mental health strategies that include empathy-based long-term psychoanalytic psychotherapy.

The chapters that follow examine five postulates of Kohut's self psychology theory. We refer to Kohut's key ideas as "postulates" because, like Euclid's five postulates of plane geometry—for example, "two points determine a line"—they cannot be proven by reference to more basic statements within a theoretical system. They can only be valued by the results that accrue from using them as basic assumptions. Using five Kohutian postulates retains a firm, theoretical identity in self psychology, and yet allows the inclusion of complementary ideas from other theories. In what follows we discuss these Kohutian postulates in three sections as (A) shaped by a Lakatosian system, as (B) orienting stars in theoretical space, and as (C), emerging from the concept of empathy as the patient's point of view.

A. Self Psychology Postulates as a Lakatosian System

We find Lakatos's (1970, 1974) ideas about "research programs" useful for continuing the development of an empathy-based long-term psychoanalytic psychotherapy theory such as self psychology. His program centers on a core belief that is surrounded by a belt of auxiliary beliefs. He makes the strong case that it's irrational to abandon a research program that is generating "dramatic, unexpected, stunning" predictions merely because some "facts" seem incompatible with the program's core belief. The central postulate of a research program needs to be jealously protected against falsifications—as long as it continues to be fruitful (Passmore, 1985, p. 111). So, auxiliary postulates collectively form a "protective belt" around a core belief (Lakatos, 1970, p. 133).

In a Lakatos's research program the core belief remains unchanged, but modifying auxiliary beliefs aims at making a research program more predictive in gaining greater general knowledge. Increasing predictability, Lakatos's key to a regenerating theory, means that if a theory's beliefs lead to failed experimental predictions, the program alters its auxiliary beliefs. However, as psychotherapy theory is a "science of the unique," regeneration in a subjective theory does not increase general theoretical predictions; instead it aims at giving greater support to psychotherapists treating a diverse range of patients. Schon (1983) makes a similar point with his concept of "reflection-in-action," where the practitioner engages in "reflective conversation with a situation that he treats as unique and uncertain" (p. 163). In response, it may be protested that it isn't science if the results aren't generalizable. Yet science has traditionally neither been defined by its method nor its outcome, but by its field of inquiry. Science uses methods appropriate to the field under investigation. Kohut claims that his empathy-based, long-term psychoanalytic psychotherapy theory is scientific because it uses empathy as a method for understanding human subjectivity and intersubjectivity.

As will be outlined in the empathy chapter that follows, a theory of science aiming at general knowledge is entirely different than a theory that increases the capacity of psychotherapists to understand the uniqueness of each patient. Much hinges on the meaning we ascribe to the word "science." The concept comes from the Greek word "logos" which means "knowledge or study of." Geology, for example, is "geo"—"logos," the study of the earth. This means that a scientific approach to psychotherapy theory as a study of the subjectively unique through participation (Chessick, 2007, p. 63) is entirely different from the traditional approach of developing general knowledge based on attempts at non-involvement and abstraction. Traditional science attempts to maximize the reliability (consistency) and validity of the constructs used in forming generalizations. With the science of the unique, however, the central organizing focus is not on generalizations, but on the generation of consistent and validating experiences for persons who interact and communicate in relationships. This distinction between a generalizable science and a science of unique personal experiences is illustrated in the development of the Diagnostic and Statistical Manual of Mental Disorders (DSM). Horwitz and Wakefield (2007) describe how in the last quarter of the twentieth century the DSM III and IV diagnosis of depression became based on a standardized list of symptoms, to strengthen the reliability of construct measurement in research and epidemiological studies, but did so by weakening the validity of what is measured. The shift was from an "unreliable clinical approach" to an "objective" scientific approach. Modern psychiatry shifted away from validity toward reliability as it focused on a science of knowledge that applies to the majority, including more pharmacology, and less a science of understanding the unique story of each patient. The psychotherapy that follows in succeeding chapters reflects the stance of the science of the unique.

These two forms of science use dissimilar strategies. In using a Lakatosian-like system for psychotherapy theory, we are not aiming at gaining greater general knowledge. This is because empathy-based, long-term psychoanalytic psychotherapy theory does not aim to make predictions based on abstractions, as Lakatos would, but functions as a proximal guidance system for the study of each unique patient. And although psychotherapy theory functions differently to a traditional general knowledge theory, we have found it useful to compare this science of the unique with the development of a scientific theory of general knowledge. But in doing so, why use a Lakatosian theoretical framework?

Lakatos (1970) reminds us that "proof" (justification), the identification of knowledge with proven knowledge, has been "the dominant tradition in rational thought throughout the ages" (p. 94). As the classical rationalists asked the question, "How can knowledge be proven as true?" the seventeenth century philosophers such as Descartes furthered the sciences of generalized knowledge by privileging "reason" as a major way of gaining proven knowledge. In contrast to this need for justification, however, skeptics claimed that not only had the classical rationalists not proven their theories to be true, there was no way they could. They ridiculed the idea of objective knowledge and thought that scientific integrity demanded the assertion that rational knowledge could not be objectively proven.

In modern philosophy of science, Karl Popper (1934 [2002], 1957) answered the skeptics by saying that rationality accumulates as a result of surviving attempts to rigorously falsify it. Falsification to Popper was not certain proof, but the closest we could get to it, because if a belief survives rigorous attempts to experimentally and intellectually discredit it, it is worth retaining. Popper's method was known as "methodological falsificationism" (Lakatos, 1970, p. 105). Then, following the classical rationalists and Popper, but in contrast to them, Kuhn (1962) strongly advocated the idea of nonlinear progress in scientific theory and divided a theory's development into normal and revolutionary phases. According to Kuhn, during normal science the dominant paradigm is neither questioned nor rigorously tested and there is little, if any, theoretical growth. Members of a scientific community, in accepting a dominant paradigm, use it as a means of solving outstanding problems. Any problems a paradigm cannot solve are considered, at first, to be minor anomalies. But if these minor anomalies accumulate, says Kuhn, they eventually create a crisis of confidence in the paradigm and trigger a surge of new theoretical growth and a revolutionary phase of paradigm change.

During this revolutionary phase principles behind the paradigm are debated until an alternative paradigm is persuasive enough to become the dominant one. Kuhn's description is one way to see the emergence of Kohut's self-psychology paradigm out of classical psychoanalysis, as indicated in an earlier work (Lee and Martin, 1991). But we don't believe that Kuhn's concept of a dominating paradigm adequately describes the relationships among the three major streams of treating mental illness: short-term EST, biotherapy, and empathy-based, long-term psychoanalytic psychotherapy, where each is needed to complement the functions of the others in curbing modern mental illness. Their complementary relationships suggest the need for a nonlinear model of dynamic theoretical organization to understand their optimal functioning in treating mental illness.

Empathy-based, long-term, psychoanalytic psychotherapy theory has been viewed as nonscientific because it is not empirically validated, despite the view in philosophy that "empiricism of the classical British sort is now at a low ebb" (Passmore, 1985, p. 19). How can so much emphasis be placed on equating science with empiricism when, as Hesse, Duhem, and Quine have convincingly argued, there is an "underdetermination of theory by empirical data," and the observation that there are always "an infinite number of theories that fit the observed facts more adequately" (Passmore, 1985, p. 114). And the view that anything not empirically validated is nonscientific, ignores the contradiction that most of traditional scientific theories have never been fully empirically validated. As Chessick (2007) articulates,

> Witness the plethora of contemporary theories and arguments in such traditional sciences as physics and astrophysics about quantum theory, about the so-called "cosmological constant" and whether it is necessary to postulate an inflationary phase in the origin of the universe, and the curious difficulty in locating proton decay, determining neutrinos, and finding gravitational waves predicted by the various theories but so far not possible to demonstrate empirically. Some very elaborate hypotheses such "string theory" have never produced a single testable prediction [p. 81].

So why in the name of science, is long-term psychotherapy theory supposed to have strict randomized, treatment versus control group design and empirical validation, when so much traditional science has loose empirical underpinnings at best? And, why is such a research project as conducted by the Menninger Foundation (Wallerstein, 1986)—which followed forty-two treated patients for three decades—not an appropriate empirical underpinning of the effectiveness of empathy-based long-term psychoanalytic psychotherapy?

Surely its results are far more compelling than those obtained from experiments run with randomized treatment and control groups, where the treatment lasts a few weeks?

As a philosopher of science, Lakatos knows that the issue of empirical underpinning is never simple and clear. "Empirical studies" are more like a military struggle with attacks and counterattacks on the auxiliary beliefs of the protective belt. Few, if any, such attacks are decisive. For Lakatos what is essential is not the empirical underpinnings per se, but whether a theory is regenerating or degenerating. If changes to auxiliary beliefs based on empirical studies do not increase a theory's predictability, it is "degenerating," despite the "purity" of the empirical data. If alterations lead to novel predictions, then the research program is "regenerating." Lakatos judges a good research program by its capacity to regenerate alterations to the auxiliary beliefs and increase its general predictions. In placing this emphasis on a program's ability to generate new predictions, Lakatos shifted away from a scientific strategy of naïve falsification. He thinks that in any strong research program, experiments whose results do not support a prevailing, entrenched principle are either ignored or trigger off other experiments to counter the results that are not consistent with the prevailing beliefs. So much for the value of empiricism!

Lakatos illustrates with a hypothetical story of a new planet, P, being observed when Newton's laws of gravitation were the prevailing major theory for calculating its projected path. He conjectures what would probably happen if the planet does not take the calculated path. He (1970) says,

> Does the Newtonian physicist consider that the deviation was forbidden by Newton's theory, and therefore that, once established, it refutes the theory [of gravitation]? No! He suggests that there must be a hitherto unknown planet P1 which perturbs the path of P. He calculates the mass, orbit, etc., of this hypothetical planet and then asks an experimental astronomer to test his hypothesis. The planet P1 is so small that even the biggest available telescopes cannot possibly observe it: the experimental astronomer applies for a research grant to build yet a bigger one. In three years' time the new telescope is ready. Were the unknown planet P1 to be discovered, it would be hailed as a new victory for Newtonian science. But it is not. Does our scientist abandon Newton's theory and his idea of a perturbing planet? No [p. 101].

And so the story goes on, with Lakatos pointing out how negative empirical results don't knock out the prevailing major postulate of Newtonian theory, and if they did, it would not be without a long protracted struggle. All that happens says Lakatos is "Either yet another ingenious auxiliary hypothesis is proposed or . . . the whole story is buried in dusty volumes of periodicals" (p. 101).

Examples of core postulates in the history of thought are Newton's laws of motion for classical mechanics; the principles of gradualism and plate tectonics for geology; and adaptation through natural selection for biology (Ketelaar and Ellis, 2000, p. 4). For evolutionary psychology, the core postulate is the adaptive value of the functional characteristics of the human mind (Panksepp and colleagues, 2002). To Lakatos (1970), awareness of a core theoretical postulate helps prevent errors, raises questions about explanations, and suggests lines of research.

Lakatos's emphasis on scientific theory embedded in research programs can be perceived to have parallels in the development of self psychology theory. We believe it has not been just Kohut's theory of narcissism, nor his concept of the selfobject that have given so much impetus to self psychology, but the way in which his key ideas have been linked into a system of postulates with empathy as the nuclear postulate. A feature of the Lakatosian understanding of theory is that auxiliary postulates emerge to supplement or support already existing postulates that are becoming increasingly overloaded and inadequate as they are used to overexplain the psychotherapeutic process. With Kohut, for example, his search for ways narcissistic patients experience him as empathic, led to the formulating of selfobject theory. This development of a new postulate to obviate the necessity to overextend an old postulate illustrates the way a significant research program in psychotherapy regenerates. In comparison, says Lakatos, the overuse and stretching of a theoretical construct suggests a degenerating theory. Theoretical degeneration is illustrated by Lampl-De Groot's (1983, p. 9) complaint about the overuse of mourning theory for explanatory purposes, and Goldberg's (1988, p. 24) insight that when conflict theory stretches to include all opposition, it undermines the theory by trivializing it.

A psychotherapy theory can be judged as regenerative by its capacity to support exploratory attempts to understand patients. It functions as a selfobject for the psychotherapist. Psychotherapy theory for psychotherapists is experienced as supportive, not predictive. On hearing Kohutian postulates first enunciated, psychotherapists sometimes have an "aha! experience," as if they were already familiar with the theory as unformed thought. Consistent with Lakatos's notion of a regenerating research program, Kohut's theory will generate new ways of guiding psychotherapists so that their explorations may be experienced as empathic by a larger range of patients than is now the case.

The guiding/supportive function of Kohut's empathy-based theory of psychotherapy is illustrated by Michael Basch's (Cape Cod lecture) answer to a question about the relationship between classical analysis and empathy. He thought many patients had benefited from traditional psychoanalysis because the analyst had mobilized a covert empathic connection while claiming allegiance to the classical analytic theoretical beliefs of neutrality, interpretation, and a regressive transference neurosis. In another example, an analyst well-known for his pronouncements on strict "analytic neutrality," once said to his patient after a session, "Just a minute." He pulled out a bottle of whisky from his filing cabinet, poured two glasses, handed one to the patient, and said, "God that was rough. I don't know about you, but I needed this."

If only half such stories are true, classical psychoanalysis may have been successful because of empathic experiences, and its overt theory may have functioned more as a test of tribal allegiance than gaining good therapeutic results. So, it seems that the less supportive a theory is to therapeutic engagement in the consulting room, the less regenerative it becomes. Stated another way, a widening gap between the theory and practice of psychotherapy may indicate a degeneration of the theory. Sandler (1983) seems to be saying something similar when he says, "psychoanalysts develop implicit theories, concepts and definitions that differ from the 'official' or 'public' formulations" (p. 43). Once Kohut overtly recognized the empathic method as the key ingredient in psychoanalytic psychotherapy, his development of auxiliary hypotheses to guide further the practitioners of this method enabled his theory to be regenerative.

Although we have placed Kohut's postulates in a Lakatosian-like theoretical frame, we recognize that Laudan's ideas about a research tradition are also useful when thinking about an empathy-based, long-term psychoanalytic psychotherapy theory. To Laudan (1984), the value of a theory lies with its research tradition more than with its capacity for theoretical regeneration. He thinks we should accept a tradition that will solve more problems than its predecessors. It is a simple concept that avoids the issue of Kuhn's description of theory as nonlinear development, or Lakatos's idea of empirically supported auxiliary beliefs. Kohut was acutely aware that by eventually rejecting classical analytic theory, he had begun the enormous task of building a research tradition in a science of the unique, beginning with the introspective concepts of Titchener. We hope that this project helps clarify and strengthen the need for a research tradition in the subjective science of psychotherapy theory. Rather than depending on expert researchers in their laboratories, this tradition depends on experienced practitioners testing the empathic consequences of their guiding theories in their consulting rooms. As Chessick (2007) assures, "Just as science is dead without innovations, so it is lost without its traditions and fundamental body of acquired knowledge" (p. 2).

Consistent with Lakatos's views of theory, Kohut made empathy his nuclear postulate, and then developed a belt of auxiliary postulates as extensions of this central postulate (see figure 1.1). Kohut's self psychology, understood as a Lakatosian system, supports its practitioners because it facilitates growth in both the theory and in those who use it. The central postulate is the empathic method. The auxiliary postulates—selfobject experiences, the self-organizing supraordinate self, the importance of feelings, and internalization/structuralization—extend and facilitate this core belief to enable more effective psychotherapy. In our view, these four Kohutian auxiliary postulates are linked to the nuclear postulate of empathy and to each other. For example, even though the internalization/structuralization postulate was an important theoretical construct for Kohut, the explanation of how this internalization/structuralization took place was broadened after Kohut died. Kohut believed that it occurred as a result of optimal frustration by an idealized object (1971, p. 45), but post Kohutian self psychology included optimal responsiveness (Bacal, 1985) and other ways of self-structuralization

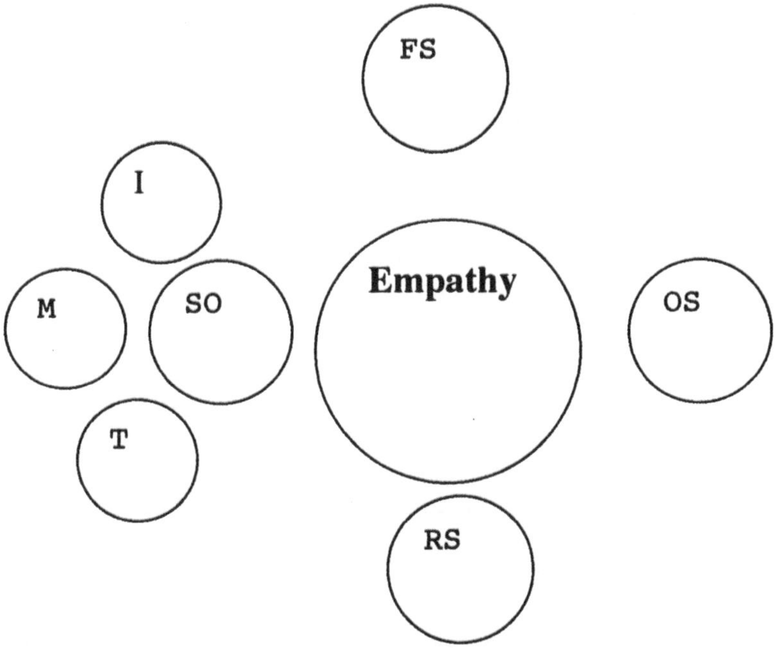

Figure 1.1. ***Self psychology diagrammed in a Lakatosian Framework***
[Empathy is the central postulate; SO (selfobject), FS (feeling self), OS (organizing self, and RS (remembering self [structuralization]) are secondary postulates; I (idealization), M (mirroring) and T (twinship) are the experience-near concepts that concretize the selfobject postulate.]

besides internalization. These changes in understanding internalization/structuralization not only did not undermine the structuralization postulate or the centrality of the empathic method, they demonstrate self psychology's openness to further changes if these produce better clinical results.

B. Postulates as Orienting Stars in Theoretical Space

The initial impetus for this project arose from attempting to present the ideas of Kohut in the Australian context. In Chicago, self psychology had emerged from classical psychoanalysis after Kohut proposed a new theory of narcissism, and then self psychology struggled to differentiate itself from classical psychoanalytic theory. U.S. audiences were sometimes enthralled by the freshness of self psychology's change in perspective, compared with the classical position. Following the death of Kohut, the teaching of self psychology continued this contrast as it increased its dialogue with advocates of such theories as Mitchell's (1988) relational theory or Stolorow and his colleagues' (Stolorow and Atwood, 1979, 1984, 1992; Stolorow and Lachmann, 1980; Stolorow, Brandchaft, and Atwood, 1987; Orange, Atwood, and Stolorow, 1997; Stolorow, Atwood, and Orange, 2002) intersubjective theory.

By the early 1990s, however, changes in psychotherapy theory made the teaching of self psychology more difficult. First, there was a significant decrease in those thoroughly grounded in classical Freudian theory. This decrease made the pedagogy of comparing self psychology with classical psychoanalysis increasingly ineffective, as Kohut noted a few days before he died. He said (1981a) that because his colleagues didn't "know psychoanalysis so well. . . . they don't even know anymore what I am arguing about" (p. 529). If Kohut thought this in the 1980s, it was certainly so by the mid-nineties. By then, using the approach of contrasting classical analysis and self psychology (Lee and Martin, 1991) had become increasingly a process of moving from one relative unknown to another unknown, and an increasingly ineffective way to teach a self psychology approach to psychotherapy.

A second change came from an increased theoretical eclecticism among psychotherapy practitioners. Although eclecticism reflects a healthy openness to new ideas, excessive openness helps create uncertainty, confusion, and increases exhaustion among practitioners conducting empathy-based, long-term intensive psychotherapy with difficult patients. True, rigid theoretical orthodoxy can stultify the creativity of the psychotherapeutic engagement, but, on the other hand, a loose form of eclecticism generates a "confusion of tongues" (Chessick, 2007) that leaves psychotherapists feeling theoretically unsupported in a sea of "potentiality," and runs the risk of weakening therapeutic interaction out of hesitation, theoretical uncertainty, and confusion about the therapeutic story. Just as Descartes formulated his "x" and "y" mathematical co-ordinates as a way of locating an object in space, so psychotherapy needs to be located in theoretical space. Using theory to orient clinical practice reflects a functional objectivity rather than the idea of objectivity as Truth or Reality.

In the past, Freud's ideas functioned as orienting stars. We knew what we believed theoretically by comparing our position with his, and how much we agreed with or rejected his concepts. Freud's theories acted as a reference point that enabled divergent psychotherapy theorists to communicate with each other. Now that Freud's star has faded, how can psychotherapists orient themselves amid a surge of theories within the field of psychotherapy from many other disciplines, especially from the discoveries in the neurosciences? And how can such ideas be integrated into an empathy-based, long-term psychoanalytic psychotherapy theory that retains insights derived from valuable, often heroic, experiences of psychotherapists over the last century?

A third challenge to an empathy-based psychotherapy came from "postmodern psychoanalysts" such as Aron, Benjamin, Hoffman, Mitchell, and Renik (Teicholtz, 1999, p. 7). These theorists, with some exceptions, tend to reject Kohut's postulates because they think it reflects a one-person model. They not only think his concept of empathy is based on a one-person model, they see his selfobject function as too one dimensional, his self construct too bounded, rigidly fixed, and static; they ignore his emphasis on feelings, and they see his ideas on internalization and structuralization as no longer relevant for a two-person theory. Importantly, postmodernists see therapeutic change occurring as a result of psychotherapists revealing their subjectivity, not in functioning as a selfobject. More significantly, as Teicholtz (1999) convincingly demonstrates, the postmodern analysts misrepresent Kohut's theory. These misrepresentations are presented in more detail in the main chapters.

A fourth challenge to empathy-based psychoanalytic psychotherapy arose from the increasing influence in mental health of short-term EST, such as CBT (Cognitive Behavioral Therapy) and biotherapy, supported particularly by research studies in the neurosciences. The short-term empirically supported therapies, however, have not been effective for sustaining treatment results of self-disorders (Westen and Morrison, 2001). What is urgently needed is an assessment of the extent to which a culture oriented toward biotherapy—and party drugs—may be creating new forms of mental illness from biochemically induced neural damage. If the medical research tradition increasingly points to serious "side effects" (neural damage), biotherapy may need to be restricted to specific, limited roles in treating mental illness (Laudan, 1984). Empathy-based, long-term psychoanalytic psychotherapy does not challenge the value of cognitive and bio-based therapies as resources for the treatment of mental illness. It only seeks to challenge an over-reliance on them as dominant paradigms and as general cures for all mental illness. For example, the extreme biotherapy position is criticized by Chessick (2007) and by Laughlin's (2005) convincing argument against a strategy of reductionism (p. 36).

In response to a perceived need for a complementary role for an empathy-based, long-term psychoanalytic psychotherapy theory in mental health, our project offers a cluster of postulates as orienting stars for teaching and conducting an inclusive, self-psychologically informed, empathy-based psychotherapy. We selected the five postulates based on our view of Kohut's theory and clinical experience. Others with different clinical experiences using Kohut's ideas may see different or additional postulates as stars. We also believe there is nothing sacred about them, just as Erikson's eight stages of development were not sacred to Vaillant (2002), who reformulated them as ten. What we do claim, however, is that empathy-based psychoanalytic psychotherapists need "orienting beliefs" to assist in helping mentally damaged patients undergo changes that bring to them a new breath of life. We also believe that the approach of this book

> presents a scientifically subjective, humane approach to understanding and treating emotional problems and demonstrates good results when used by practitioners who are willing to undergo the arduous training to use it well. [Dr. Colby Martin, personal communication]

In applying a Lakatosian-type frame to psychotherapy theory, we began with Kohut's view of empathy in his paper "Introspection, empathy and psychoanalysis" (Kohut, 1959). Although this view resonated with some audiences, it left others wondering what the "fuss" was all about. They accused him (and us) of "preaching to the converted" as "they had heard about empathy before." Such an initial undervaluing of Kohut's concept of empathy is not surprising, as it paralleled his own experience of taking "many years after he wrote the empathy paper . . . to grasp its implications" (Strozier, 2001, p. 143). Encouraged by Kohut's (1981a) highlighting of his concept of empathy at the Fifth Self Psychology Conference a few days before his death, we found that by comparing it with other empathic theories, particularly the theory of Carl Rogers, it evoked new audience interest. Furthermore, when emphasizing Kohut's portrayal of empathy as having roots in Titchener's philosophy of introspection, and elaborating his definition of empathy as vicarious introspection, Kohut's idea of empathy could be constituted within a philosophical and academic tradition.

An even deeper appreciation of self psychology ensues when we accepted that Kohut's starting point for a concept of empathy *is the experience of the patient*. This focus on the patient's experience precipitated many of Kohut's theoretical changes that followed. His views on empathy, for example, contrasted with the views of Carl Rogers and the culture generally, which assumed empathy was predominantly a capacity of the psychotherapist. After we emphasized the distinctiveness of Kohut's theory of empathy, we found that self psychology workshops attracted psychotherapists who wanted to understand the implications of empathy as the experience of the patient.

From the prominence of his empathic method in his last paper (1981a), it is clear that Kohut made empathy his nuclear postulate. This postulate assumes that if a patient experiences a psychotherapist as empathically understanding him, feelings of aloneness and psychological deadness are diminished, and new structural patterns of thinking, feeling and behaving occur in the patient. So, in what follows, after explicating empathy as Kohut's nuclear postulate, we discuss auxiliary postulates that assist a psychotherapist to understand a patient, foster the patient's experience of empathy, and help gain consistently successful outcomes in a self-psychologically conducted psychotherapy. The four auxiliary postulates are linked to the empathic method's assumptions. They function as further organizing points in self psychology's theoretical field. And even though all five postulates are necessary for an appreciation of self psychology, the theory assumes that a theoretical whole is more than the sum of the parts. These five postulates, guiding posts rather than discriminating barriers—to shift the metaphor from the stars to the earth—allow for the inclusion of many other theoretical ideas, as will be demonstrated in the chapters that follow.

In organizing material around these five postulates, we seek to demonstrate that self psychology theory is "open-ended and capable of change under the impact of new data" (Kohut, 1981b, p. 540). But the open-endedness is not absolute. These five self psychology postulates represent a firm but flexible theoretical identity, with as much openness to other theories as possible. In self psychology other theories only influence it peripherally if they completely reject the empathic method and the core assumptions of this method. This developing of an inclusive theory, retaining a clear but evolving identity, may be illustrated by the analogous problem of defining medieval towns and modern cities. Medieval towns, with high walls and locked gates at night, were known by their fixed boundaries. In contrast, modern cities can't be defined by boundaries, but by the patterns of the inhabitants, including shopping and transportation patterns. Similarly, Kohutian postulates are a way of defining self psychology theory by its central ideas, rather than by boundaries that determine which ideas fall inside or outside. In this way the theory minimizes attitudes that foster rigid boundaries and orthodoxy.

A Theory from an Empathic Point of View

As will be readily apparent, self psychology, as a psychotherapy theory, is also unlike a "scientific" paradigm of general knowledge as described by Lakatos (1970, 1974), Popper (1934), Kuhn (1962), or Laudan (1984). Scientific knowledge has been presented as moving from specific experiments to generalized knowledge, following a "nomothetic method" (Stolorow and Atwood, 1992, p. 242). Such generalized knowledge is valuable in the traditional scientific fields but has restricted use in psychotherapy theory. A direct imparting of this general knowledge to patients is usually unsuccessful in inducing long-lasting change in self-organization, revealed by the failure of so much CBT to gain permanent improvements. A self psychology theory of psychoanalytic psychotherapy does not seek ever-increasing accuracy in objective knowledge, but maintains an empathic resonance with the subjective experience of one patient—the emphasis being on the "ideographic" method (Stolorow and Atwood, 1992). Psychotherapy theory, then, uses postulates to help understand the subjective experiences of two persons whose "relationship" constitutes an intersubjective field, where at least one functions as a selfobject for the other. In such an intersubjective field, psychotherapy theory takes the form of a science appropriate to its subject matter, the science of unique intersubjective experiences. For this science, "The observational stance is always within, rather than outside, the intersubjective field" (Atwood and Stolorow, 1984, p. 41).

It could be claimed that by shifting the focus from empathy to an intersubjective field experience, Kohut made a selfobject experience the nuclear postulate of his system and not an auxiliary postulate, a view that does not match the nuclear and auxiliary postulates as outlined in the previous section. We agree that Kohut's selfobject concept could be the nuclear postulate of a research program if the program is confined to researching narcissistic disorders only, because in experiencing the psychotherapist as a selfobject such patients also experience him/her as empathic. However, unless it can be demonstrated that all patients who experience the psychotherapist as being empathic are also experiencing the psychotherapist as a selfobject, empathy needs to be the nuclear concept of a more general theory of self psychology that covers more than narcissistic disorders. For a theory to understand a broad range of pathology, the empathic nuclear postulate may need to accumulate further auxiliary postulates than the four proposed in this project.

Psychotherapy theory does not offer objective knowledge, but specific hypotheses to explore in psychotherapy with patients. It helps create an initial understanding of a psychotherapeutic relationship, and then modifies this understanding with further psychotherapeutic explorations. Modifications in understanding a patient come from effective intersubjective responding between patient and psychotherapist, not from more accurate general psychological knowledge. It may be pointed out that two friends can experience effective understanding and real healing. But friendships usually cannot sustain selfobject experiences long enough to produce significant structuralization. As will be argued in chapter 7, self psychology theory emphasizes the necessity for maintaining consistent attuned experiences, which are best sustained by a professional intersubjective relationship.

Therapeutic modifications of patients also don't occur from research generalizations in the neurosciences, unless they are tested for enhancing a patient's experience of empathy. Self psychology's position is that theory—whether empirically supported or not—can only be a guide to psychotherapy, because healing results from constructive intersubjective relating, experienced by a patient as empathic attunement. Psychotherapy theory may be valuable in empathic exploration by reducing the number of trial and error iterations necessary for a psychotherapist to tune into a patient and be experienced as being empathically understood. But it is the empathic experience, not any general psychotherapy theory of knowledge that leads to the experience of healing.

Psychotherapy theory provides a framework, then, for empathic exploration and eventually, a cocreated explanation (narrative) of the patient's life that is experienced by the patient as being empathically understood. This means that although the nuclear postulate of self psychology theory is the method of empathic understanding, eventually the empathic experience mobilizes the need for explanation to make sense of the empathic experience, and thus helps increase a patient's sense of cohesion. This means that changes in the nonsymbolic memory structures of a self-organization (the procedural memory, for example) can be consolidated further by changes in the symbolic structures of self-organization located in the memory systems of the higher areas of brain functioning that use the hippocampal circuits.

Kohut thinks that both levels of structuralization (symbolic or procedural) take place in an empathy-based, long-term psychoanalytic psychotherapy. He refers not only to the possibility of long periods of empathic immersion, but also to psychotherapy as both understanding and explaining (see, for example, Kohut, 1970, pp. 524–25), because his patients responded positively to narratives that make sense out of unformed thoughts or confusions. This is a similar view to the experimentalist Kelso (1995) who insists, "Explanation demands theory" (p. 33). Except that, as self psychologists, we don't see theory ultimately tested by experimentation, as does Kelso, but in a patient's experience of an empathic therapeutic relationship that leads to a more adaptive, deeply satisfying life.

When psychotherapy theory is seen as helping patients experience empathic understanding, it is less prone to develop into an "orthodoxy" that determines true or false beliefs and that assumes a correspondence between theory and reality. Underlying the development of theoretical orthodoxy is the assumption that theory represents objective knowledge, and that only through exact objective knowledge can healing occur. In contrast, Kohut (1977) believes "all worthwhile theorizing is tentative, probing, provisional—[and] contains an element of playfulness" (p. 206). Kohut uses the word playfulness to contrast the attitude of the sciences from that of dogmatic religion (i.e., the world of absolute values). For those who live in such a serious, absolute world, their joyful search has ended—they have become guarantors of Reality and valiant defenders of Truth. For Kohut the world of creative science consists of playful people who believe their surrounding reality is essentially unknowable (1977, p. 207). By accepting that psychotherapy theory is neither true nor false, self psychology affirms that its value rests on the extent to which it helps a psychotherapist engage patients around their subjective experiences. As Goldberg (1988) says, "I believe we can profit from relinquishing a preoccupation with [theoretical] correctness in favor of one of usefulness" (p. 21).

Self psychology can easily incorporate theory by seeing it, as did the French philosopher Deleuze, as "a box of tools . . . It must be useful. It must function. And not of itself. If no one uses it . . . the theory is worthless" (Bouchard, 1972). The psychoanalyst Kubie (1975) held a similar view when he wrote on "The language tools of psychoanalysis," and the German philosopher Proust echoed this idea when he said, "Treat my book as a pair of glasses directed to the outside, if they don't suit you, find another pair, I leave it to you to find your own instrument" (Bouchard, 1972). William James took the interesting step of likening theory to religious beliefs, where the crucial question is not whether it is true but whether these beliefs improve the quality of a person's life. James (1902) says, what "we believe [religious beliefs] bring us good consequential fruits for life" (p. 15). So self psychology, with empathy as its core postulate, asks, "Does the theoretical construct increase the effectiveness of a psychotherapist through enhancing empathic understanding?" If not, it will eventually atrophy as a result of intellectual degeneration, a process similar to "parcellation" (Edelman, 1987; the dying off of synaptically unconnected neurons in the first year of life).

Kohut believed humans are theory-generating animals whose thinking helps them to act in ways that enhanced their chance of survival. Psychotherapists need theory as a guide to empathically understand their patients. Those psychotherapists who, for whatever reason, reject a need for theory, are more likely from unconscious and unexamined theory to function less effectively. Stolorow and Atwood (1992) think that psychotherapists who reject theory, actually function from a "prereflective unconscious." Ultimately, however, there is no such thing as psychotherapists who don't use theory, only psychotherapists who are aware of, or not aware of the theory they are using.

Patients eventually need a cohesive narrative (theory) to explain their lives. They usually experience theory indirectly through empathic understanding, as narrative that helps cohere their functioning as a co-agent and that takes into account their contextual network of relationships and environmental processes. Patients present for treatment with their own narrative explanations of their problems, and these explanations are to be respected because they have helped them to get this far with their lives despite their inadequacies. Schlesinger (2005) points to the very act of seeking therapy as representing an ending as well as a beginning. The seeking signals the end of patients being willing to rely on their own "narrative" and the solutions it provides. These solutions have often come at a cost that has become increasingly unacceptable, such as an inability to regulate feelings that are expressed in socially destructive ways. Patients may experience increasing maladaptiveness from attempts at self-healing that have actually aggravated their problems, or may experience healing attempts as fruitless because of inadequate beliefs and ineffective strategies, often vague or unconscious. Seeking psychotherapy represents a resolve to begin a new relationship, to revise a narrative understanding of themselves and their problems, and hopefully to provide more adaptive solutions. Self psychology offers a healing research program to assist in an empathic exploration of these patients' old narratives and, by so doing, leads to more adequate narratives.

Kohut often used the terms "experience-near" and "experience-distant" theorizing. These concepts are a response to the view that ideas about objective theory assist in the conduct of psychotherapy, only if they increase a patient's experience of being empathically understood. Psychotherapy helps create a patient's personal narrative that is "experience-near" and matches the patient's experience. Although auxiliary postulates help form a research program, they are not intended as a direct explanation to a patient. Auxiliary postulates—selfobject experiences, self-organizing supraordinate self, feelings as affects, and internalization/structuralization—use experience-distant terms. On the other hand, specific descriptions of a selfobject postulate, such as idealizing, mirroring or twinship, are closer to patient experiences, which if explained non-technically in a session and, if done at the appropriate time, can be readily understood and experienced as helpful.

Just as a patient's personal narrative develops during psychotherapy, so self psychology theory evolves. We have found that the idea of a theory shaped by evolutionary processes is more appropriate than a general idea such as "psychotherapeutic openness." Some sense of semipermanent theoretical structure is necessary if psychotherapists are not to be overwhelmed by therapeutic relationships. Although psychotherapists and psychotherapy theorists are challenged to be open to new ideas (for example, Goldberg, 1990), theories that are too open can be just as susceptible to extinction as those that are too rigid. We think "openness," although necessary to counter the assumption of theoretical orthodoxy may, in creating an "openness compensatory ideal," lead to a loss of identity. Kohut could be seen as a postmodernist who accepted the plurality of experience and "truths" that are connected to a point of view and rejected not only theoretical orthodoxy but also the opposite extreme of openness. He believed that theory was important because it helped determine what we experienced, and lead to adjustments in theory, which in turn lead to new experiences and further adjustments in theory in a never-ending process. This dialectical view can be applied to both the patient's narrative story and to a self psychology research program.

As mentioned earlier in this chapter, theory may be experienced as a selfobject. Chapter 3 explores this selfobject concept in depth, but here it is used in relation to theory—theory functioning as an extension of the psychotherapist. When theory is used to aid the psychotherapist in empathically understanding a patient, it functions as an extension of the psychotherapist, and helps keep a psychotherapist's self-organization more cohesive in a psychotherapeutic relationship. This is especially so where psychotherapists work with difficult or poorly organized patients, where feelings are tense, or where beginning psychotherapists feel easily overwhelmed. Under these circumstances, a flexible but structured theory provides guideposts for the intersubjective field of the consulting room; the psychotherapist is, therefore, less stressed, less exhausted, and better able to maintain a healthy personal life style. A psychotherapist using theory as a selfobject gains an orienting point from which both patient and psychotherapist can explore what is happening between them.

Unfortunately, psychotherapists who cling to theory as absolute truth that can never be wrong, use it as an archaic selfobject. Theory under these circumstances no longer serves to enhance a psychotherapist's healthy self-cohesion; instead, it becomes an extremely defensive attempt to prevent a psychotherapist's self-fragmentation. Under such circumstances, the dynamics of the therapeutic relationship are more dominated by the needs of a desperate psychotherapist than the patient. The psychotherapist loses the professional stance, and begins to "sell" the patient on correct theoretical ideas like a preacher of religious dogma as Ferenczi's patient, RN, apparently did to Ferenczi. Instead of theory being an extension of the psychotherapist, the psychotherapist functions as if he or she is a servant of the theory and not a selfobject for the patient. When this occurs, psychotherapy theory functions like a formal religious belief system that seeks to turn patients and psychotherapists into "true believers" and "disciples" to maintain the psychotherapist's cohesiveness, self-esteem, and sense of competence. This is a reverse selfobject experience for the patient (R. Lee, 1988)—a potentially destructive relationship where the patient is primarily used for the psychotherapist's needs rather than the other way around.

The idea of Kohut's postulates as orienting stars in theoretical space, as mentioned earlier, conjures up images of celestial maps with reference points. When theory is seen as a map, it is useful for exploring space, but it is not the space itself. A map as a symbolic representation is not absolutely accurate, but an approximation. Yet a simple mapping system reduces the energy used in foraging for food, for example, by reducing searching to a local area. Riley and colleagues (2005) found that the waggle dance of bees at a hive sends other bees on food search flights not directly to a location, but signals approximate direction and distance, so that once they reach this area they need to conduct a specific search. Such a simple system reduces the time and energy used, but does not obviate the necessity of some local searching. Similarly psychotherapy theory maps issues that need more detailed exploration and understanding. And just as theory suggests starting points to psychotherapists, it also offers a guide to explore a patient's journey. Ultimately, however, it is only by the psychotherapist and patient walking and searching together that a meaningful therapeutic experience becomes possible.

There is not one psychotherapy theory adequate enough to assist in treating all types of psychopathology. Psychotherapy theories have developed in specific cultural contexts and have been shaped by specific dysfunctions. For example, Freud's theory of neurosis, which developed for treating wealthy patients in nineteenth century Vienna, is vastly different from Kohut's theory of narcissism for patients in twentieth century Chicago. Because of the time and place specificity of psychotherapy theory, Deleuze's reference to theory being like a box of tools earlier is a useful analogy. To illustrate, there are many ways to take a nut off a screw. One can use one's fingers, an open-faced spanner, a socket spanner, an adjustable wrench, a pair of pliers, or if desperate enough, a hacksaw to cut a slot in the nut and a screwdriver inserted into the slot and tapped with a hammer. This last method gets the nut off, but what a long, tedious, time-consuming process! The point? There are many tools with which to take off a nut, but some are more effective than others, depending on circumstances. All theories that have survived (been "selected") serve some purpose, and may be preferred in certain situations because they are more effective and less costly than others, depending on the task at hand.

Just as there are such general tools as a hammer or a screwdriver, there are specialized tools for a special task. So it is with psychotherapy theory. And just as there are broad-spectrum antibiotics and those with more powerful but a narrower range of effectiveness, similarly, some psychotherapy theories cover a broad range of psychopathology, and others are designed for a special purpose. For example, as a specific theory, Roger's theory of short-term counseling demonstrated effectiveness with young students in university counseling centers throughout the United States after World War II, when there was a huge influx into tertiary education. This specific theory worked, especially as the more severely disturbed were referred to departments of psychiatry. Roger's theory especially fitted the transitional problems of late teenage students living away from home for the first time. Similarly, recognizing the impossibility, and perhaps undesirability of developing a general theory of psychotherapy, self psychology maintains that its theory, with its core assumption of empathy, gives psychotherapy a relatively broad base, especially as it is able to incorporate into its auxiliary postulates many of the key ideas of other psychotherapy theories and the neurosciences. In chapter 2, we explore at greater length the core postulate that, for the self psychologist, illuminates the therapeutic journey: empathy.

CHAPTER TWO

Empathic Understanding

At the 1957 Paris International Psychoanalytic Congress, Heinz Kohut (1959) delivered a brief version of "Introspection, Empathy, and Psychoanalysis," his methodological manifesto for a modern self-psychologically-oriented psychoanalytic psychotherapy. As the paper evoked no more than mild interest from a modest audience, many may have overlooked its revolutionary import. Kohut apparently did. His biographer (Strozier, 2001) says, "The irony is that Kohut was not fully aware, or was not yet prepared to face fully, how at odds he was with the existing 'metapsychology' of psychoanalysis. It took many years after he wrote his empathy paper for Kohut himself to grasp its implications" (p. 141). Self psychology had an inconspicuous birth.

Kohut's ideas about empathy have been underappreciated, as indeed, have the ideas of many creative thinkers. With Kohut, at least, his views on empathy had been encouraged by the faculty of the Chicago Psychoanalytic Institute, which he joined in 1953 and where he began asserting that an empathic form of knowing was central to the survival of psychoanalysis. So, for the twenty-fifth anniversary of the Chicago Institute in 1957 Kohut was invited to present a paper on a theory of empathy. After its delivery, the Institute's founder, Franz Alexander, predicted that the paper "would have a dramatic impact on the future of psychoanalysis."

Kohut submitted a revised version of his empathy paper to the Journal of the American Psychoanalytic Association, for publication consideration. Although Kohut was a member of the Board, the Journal editors rejected Kohut's paper because it posed "too basic a challenge to the theory [of psychoanalysis] and therefore was not appropriately psychoanalytic" (Strozier, 2001, p. 143). However, after the influential analyst Maxwell Gittleson insisted that the editors not engage in ideological censorship, the editors changed their minds and accepted the paper for publication. Since then, Kohut's concept of empathy has weathered many rigorous challenges to its central function in psychotherapy.

We now present two sections, section A where we explore Kohut's theory of empathy as vicarious introspection, and section B where we discuss criticisms of his theory.

A. Empathy as Vicarious Introspection

Kohut's empathy paper raises the epistemological question of what it means to "know" in psychoanalysis in the context of a world of "objective" scientific knowledge. In claiming that empathy is a different kind of knowing than "objective" knowledge, Kohut began with the ideas of Titchener (1912), who made a distinction between inspective and introspective methods of observation. Titchener says, "The introspective methods do us the same service in psychology that inspective methods—'observation and experiment' is the more usual phrase—do in natural science" (p. 485). This differentiation reflected Titchener's reaction to the experimental psychologists of his day, who claimed that tachistoscopic studies demonstrated the unreliability of the introspective method. These experimental psychologists showed how responses to a brief tachistoscopic exposure added to, subtracted from, or distorted objects to the eye, because persons see what is not there, and fail to see much of what is there. They were describing an analog to the transference phenomena that Freud had found in conducting psychoanalysis.

Answering the experimentalists, Titchener argued that the tachistoscopic experiments didn't invalidate introspection as a method in general, but only invalidated introspection as a method for accurately observing tachistoscopic stimuli. He did not challenge their study, but questioned their generalizations from it. In doing this, Titchener understood that science is not just empirical, but consists of extrapolations and extensions that are empirically supported, but not directly confirmed. To study consciousness in contrast to measuring stimuli, Titchener says, "it is not whether the reports tally with the stimuli, but whether they give accurate descriptions of the observer's experiential consciousness" (p. 487). To Titchener, whether the introspective method is effective or not depends on the focus of the observer—on the stimuli or on consciousness. He claims, "The observer is trying to describe consciousness; not certain objective letters or figures, but the consciousness which a brief exposure of these stimuli induces" (p. 487). He reinforces his point with a story of a geologist, a farmer, a landscape gardener, and a psychologist, who give differing reports on the same piece of country (Steinthal, 1881). Even though these reports vary, Titchener thinks "all four . . . may be equally true, but . . . each one plainly implies a particular attitude, a special point of view. It is the attitude and point of view, not the method, which must henceforth serve to distinguish the introspecting from the inspecting man of science" (p. 487).

Of course, Titchener's distinction, which was important to Kohut, has not been without its critics. The contemporary philosopher Searle (1999) claims there is a philosophical flaw with Titchener's division between inspection and introspection because introspection "works on the presupposition that there is a distinction between the thing seen and the seeing of it," as does the concept of inspection. Searle thinks that with "'introspection' there is simply no way to make this separation . . . [so] the standard model of observation doesn't work for conscious subjectivity. . . . [and] the idea that there might be a special method of investigating consciousness, namely 'introspection,' was doomed to failure from the start" (p. 97). Yet, although he discredits introspection's claim to access a person's subjectivity, Searle accepts the pragmatic metaphor of feelings, such as "I feel fear." "In short," Searle says, "If by 'introspection' we mean simply thinking about our own mental states, then there is no [philosophical] objection to introspection" (p. 144).

Despite the philosophical criticism of introspection, Kohut made empathy central to his psychotherapy theory because he was interested in developing a way to understand a patient's mental state. He avoided the narcissistic solution of making empathy a special attribute of the therapist—an issue that concerned Searle—by focusing on the experience of the patient as a result of interactions in the therapeutic relationship. Kohut thought such interaction was initiated and facilitated by "vicarious introspection." So, although he was influenced by the ideas of Titchener and Dilthey to inspect his physical surroundings with senses and know his inner world through introspection, Kohut did not lock himself into a static concept of introspection, but used it as an entry point into an intersubjective field with a patient.

Kohut begins a therapeutic relationship by shifting the emphasis from the patient's sharing of introspective associations to the psychotherapist's understanding of a patient's mental state by means of vicarious introspection (1959, p. 206). He says, "We speak of physical phenomenon when the essential ingredient of our observational methods includes our senses, we speak of psychological phenomena when the essential ingredient of our observation is introspection and empathy" (p. 206). Kohut gives an example of a tall man. "Only when we can think ourselves into his place, only when we, by vicarious introspection, begin to feel his unusual size as if it were our own and thus revive inner experiences in which we had been unusual or conspicuous, only then have we observed a psychological fact" (pp. 207–8). Vicarious introspection is the first step in establishing an intersubjective field where the patient feels understood. It seeks to understand the patient from the patient's point of view. This leads to an unfolding "conversation" during which both patient and therapist influence each other and eventually "construct" a relationship that includes the patient's point of view.

The concept of empathy incorporates both the "scientific" and humanistic trends in psychoanalysis. Kohut viewed psychoanalysis as predominantly presenting itself as a science in order to be accepted by the "physical and biological sciences" (Kohut, 1981b, p. 565), at the same time as it preserved a humanistic interest in facilitating therapeutic change. He claimed to follow the scientific tradition of using a method that was appropriate to the subject matter—in this case, the patient's subjectivity, and eventually, intersubjectivity. In his concept of empathy, he sought to bridge the physical/biological sciences and the humanities by making psychotherapy theory the "science of the subjective." Therefore, in defining empathy as vicarious introspection, Kohut supported psychoanalysis' rejection of the repetitive measurement strategies of the inspective empirical sciences and confirmed sharing experiences of subjective states in a therapeutic relationship as a type of knowing. To Kohut, psychotherapy relies on a "science of inner experience" rather than a "science of outer observation." Psychotherapy focuses on the quality of experience, not its quantity.

Kohut also recognized that inspection covers a range of observations, from the complex task of conducting experiments using randomization, control groups, and statistical levels of significance, to the relative simplicity of eyewitness accounts. In developing empathy's role in healing as perceiving from a patient's point of view, Kohut soon realized that he needed to distinguish between "extrospection" and introspection. Extrospection involves a patient's point of view, using the patient as an eyewitness to events (Kohut, 1980, p. 493). Through extrospection, a psychotherapist can envisage the patient's situation. To illustrate this, one of Wolf's (1983) patients shared the experience of being at the large mass conducted by Pope John Paul II in Chicago, and Wolf tried to imagine what it would have been like to be there. Placing himself in the shoes of his patient/eyewitness, Wolf imagined a great deal of noise, but when he verbalized this, the patient said the crowd had been remarkably quiet. Wolf had vicariously extrospected—not vicariously introspected. Even though Wolf placed himself in his patient's shoes, he imagined himself seeing the external event rather than experiencing the patient's internal state. In contrast to extrospection, vicarious introspection understands a patient's feelings and thoughts as an extra step beyond a vicarious extrospection of an event. Vicarious extrospection, obviously not vicarious introspection, may contribute to psychotherapy as a step in facilitating vicarious introspection.

Kohut (1981b) illustrates the value of vicarious extrospection from the preparations for the first landing on the moon. Using extrospection, the project's scientists imagined themselves into various scenarios that could confront the astronauts and suggested "what to look for, what materials to gather, and how to report about what they saw" (footnote, p. 543). So, vicarious extrospection is not vicarious introspection, even though both involve the psychotherapist adopting the point of view of a patient. Vicarious introspection is not only placing oneself in the shoes of another, but *understanding the other person's feelings and thoughts in such a situation.*

Defining empathy as vicarious introspection would be meaningless without an implicit assumption that using this method leads to increased effectiveness in psychotherapy. Questions about Kohut's understanding of vicarious introspection are not fruitful for the purposes of healing if they come from "essentialist" attempts to investigate "true" empathy; such attention would be better focused on therapeutic results. Kohut once answered a doubter with, "Why spend your time arguing about a better definition [of empathy] when you can see if it results in the better treatment of patients?" What results? As studies of the effectiveness of psychotherapy are costly to organize and difficult to measure, Kohut simply pointed out that patients, formerly unsuitable for treatment in psychoanalytic institutes, were now able to be successfully treated using the empathic method. He considered this a significant, concrete result. So, in defining empathy as vicarious introspection, Kohut is claiming that the experience of being empathically understood leads to significant, positive changes in a patient's life.

Under Kohut's definition of empathic understanding, failure to achieve therapeutic results is either evidence against the viability of his empathic method, or indicates something in the non-matching of therapist and patient voided the patient's experience of empathic understanding. Kantrowitz (1996), for example, concludes from a study of the responses of 399 psychoanalysts to questionnaires, that if the life circumstances of psychotherapist and patient are far apart, they create a "bad match" and make an empathic connection difficult. Patients' empathic experience may be voided because of a psychotherapist's ineffective understanding of the empathic method, despite significant efforts to examine the epistemological roots of empathy.

Before turning to epistemology's influence on empathic understanding since Dilthey and Titchener, we illustrate how Kohut's approach may significantly influence the initial phase of psychotherapy.

In the initial phase we present a self psychological point of view that assumes a psychotherapist's nonjudgment is impossible. There is always a judgment, because there is always a point of view. In an empathic approach, a psychotherapist does not avoid judging; he discloses the stance from which the judging will be undertaken—the point of view of the patient. After explaining this, it is then possible to explain further that any such judgment does not emphasize a diagnostic category, but a story, tentative and incomplete, always open to further understanding. The ultimate test for this emerging self-story will not be "Is it true" but "Does it make you feel understood?"

B. Major Criticisms of Kohut's Theory of Empathy

Criticism of Kohut's concept of empathy as vicarious introspection, come from psychoanalysis, philosophy, and the neurosciences, which may be summarized as not appreciating Kohut's distinction between empathy as the experience of the patient and empathy as a special quality of the psychotherapist, and thinking that his empathic idea is too static. These general criticisms are explored under the following headings: empathy as (1) old idea, (2) postmodern rejection, (3) constructed experience, (4) hermeneutical process, and (5) affective/cognitive complex. To round out the chapter, there is a final section (6) on empathy for purposes other than healing.

(1) Empathy is an Old Idea

In response to Kohut's emphasis on the empathic method, critics of self psychology take pains to point out that empathy has been a clinical construct since the days of Freud. For example, Freud used the German word "*Einfuhling*" (empathy) twenty times in the Standard Edition of his writings, evidence that it was of some importance to him. In their claim that Kohut overvalued his contribution to a theory of empathy, his critics failed to grasp the importance of Kohut's clarifications based on the ideas of Dilthey and Titchener. Their criticisms also seem to ignore Kohut's numerous acknowledgements that a concept of empathy existed in early psychoanalysis, and particularly Kohut's (1968, p. 83) recognition of Freud's reference to empathy: "A path leads from identification by way of imitation to empathy, that is, to the comprehension of the mechanism by means of which we are enabled to take up any attitude at all towards another mental life" (Freud, 1921c, p. 110).

Kohut also noted Ferenczi's idea of empathy as "tact" and Ferenczi's (1928a) comment on Freud:

> [Freud] discovered that it is just as possible to obtain new knowledge through scientific ordering of the data of inspection as it is through the utilization of the data of external perception derived from observation and experiment . . . by simply viewing the introspected material from a new vantage point Freud created a system of psychology; this system contains [not only ascertained facts but also] a number of hypotheses; but the same situation prevails in the natural sciences . . . thanks to psychoanalysis we now possess the systematic knowledge concerning a series of data which had been neglected by the natural sciences—[analysis] demonstrates to us the influence of internal forces, which can only be discovered through introspection [1928a, p. 3].

And as Kohut's critics point out, another early psychoanalyst, Theodore Reik (1937), actually defined empathy similarly to Kohut, as the analyst's sharing of the patient's experience as if it were his own. These and other early psychoanalytic theorists, with whom Kohut was familiar, reveal that psychoanalytic pioneers used a concept of empathy in psychoanalysis

These early psychoanalytic views on empathy include Robert Knight, who wrote an article on "Psychotherapy of an adolescent catatonic schizophrenic with mutism: A study in empathy and establishing contact" (1946). Also prominent was Fromm-Reichmann (1950), who believed that empathy was crucial for psychotherapy with schizophrenic patients, as did the British analyst Balint (1952). Furthermore, Sullivan (1953) used the term "empathic linkage" to mean "a situation in which two people are linked in such a way that one induces a feeling in the other" (Chessick, 1999, p. 350). As well, Schafer (1959) coined the phrase "generative empathy," and Friedman (1978), concluded that in the struggle between insight and empathy for supremacy as a method, empathy has been seen historically as the more primary therapeutic agent. There were many others (Read, 1996, p. 185ff). Clearly, the concept of empathy has had a long history in psychoanalytically oriented psychotherapy, which Kohut acknowledged.

The person who did more to popularize the concept of empathy in modern psychotherapy was Carl Rogers (1961). In his "person-centered" psychotherapy, "empathy" and "unconditional positive regard" were seen as qualities essential for therapeutic change. Although those familiar with the empathic method in psychotherapy may resonate with Rogers' statement, and although his empathic approach was effective in brief counseling with college students, his ideas about empathy are susceptible to being misused, especially in long-term psychotherapy aimed at permanent changes in self-organization. In emphasizing it as a property of the psychotherapist, Roger's concept of empathy clearly diverged from Kohut, who saw empathy not as a quality of the psychotherapist, but as the experience of the patient. Schwaber (1992) holds a similar view. She says, "It is from the point of view of the patient that exploration and elucidation [of the psychotherapy] assume the central focus. This is in contrast to an interpersonal position which draws upon the analyst's or other outside observer's vantage point" (p. 357).

A personal experience of Jane, a psychotherapist, illustrates the difference between Rogers' empathic approach and Kohut's. One day her young son, jealous of the attention Jane was giving his sister, became angry and hit his sister in front of Jane. Jane did not angrily berate her son, or respond with a stereotypical "You feel angry!" or "How do you feel?" Instead, she tested her insight with the question, "Do you want mummy to give you some attention?" When he said "yes," she gave it to him. Jane had empathically put herself in his shoes, recognized the lack of her attention as the reason for his anger, and then responded by addressing the underlying need, which melted his anger and stopped him hitting his sister.

Karl Bonhoeffer, father of the famous Lutheran theologian/martyr Dietrich Bonhoeffer, preceded Carl Rogers' in his view of empathy. In 1912 Karl Bonhoeffer accepted a professorship at the University of Berlin, a leading position in German psychiatry and neurology, and, until his death in 1948, resisted the invasion of the interpretive approach of Freudian and Jungian psychoanalysis into the German capital. In contrast to an interpretive analytic approach, Karl Bonhoeffer thought that empathy, as an intuitive quality of the practitioner, was the key to healing. Bonhoeffer's view of empathy is confirmed by Robert Gaupp (Professor of Psychiatry in Heidelberg), who says that Karl was "a sensitive psychiatrist with a remarkable gift for empathy, and who did outstanding work on the nature of hysterical formation," and "in intuitive psychology and scrupulous observation . . . had no superior" (Bethge, 1967, p. 22).

Kohut's position differed with Bonhoeffer's and Rogers'; he saw empathy not as a quality or act (including verbal response) of the psychotherapist but the patient's experience of the psychotherapist's response. In such an emphasis, Kohut (1981a) made empathy an intersubjective concept and a step beyond his 1959 definition of "empathy as a definer of a field . . . a field that relates to the inner life of man" (p. 526). Furthermore, in contrast to both Rogers and Bonhoeffer, Kohut's empathy was not antithetical to interpretation, but led naturally to interpretations where a patient could experience being empathically understood.

The unfortunate prevalence in psychoanalysis of empathy as a quality of the psychotherapist is evident in the clinical study of suicide cases by Maltsberger and Buie (1974, 1980). Buie (1981) describes patients who "killed themselves when, on the basis of "*empathic assessment*" [italics added], they were believed to be safe and were permitted to visit home, were discharged, etc.," and were "actively suicidal even though empathically (and descriptively) appeared to be stable" (p. 281). How could this be? Certainly these results demonstrate the inadequacy of "empathy" as a means of assessing patients, but it was Kohut's position that empathy is never an outside (objective) assessment by a psychotherapist, but a knowing of the patient from the patient's point of view, that requires the patient's active participation. That these patients committed suicide suggests that they did not feel empathically understood, and the negative results actually support Kohut's view that empathy should not be used for assessing patients. So, although the Maltsberger and Buie study demonstrates the ineffectiveness of an empathic theory as an objective evaluative capacity of a psychotherapist, it does not refute a Kohutian theory of empathy, which emphasizes the experience of the patient, albeit some psychotherapists are more skilled in inducing this experience than others.

Kohut's empathic theory is also supported by a study of fifty-nine suicide attempters. Heller and Yaynal (1997) wanted to see if psychiatrists could predict which of these patients would reattempt suicide. The psychiatrists made written predictions based on videotaped interviews that focused on the faces of both the psychiatrists and their patients. Twelve months later, after ten patients had made a further suicide attempt, they found the psychiatrists' written predictions had been only 29 percent accurate, whereas a silent videotape analysis of their faces, (blind to which patients made further suicidal attempts), correctly classified 81 percent of the patients.

As there was no written or verbalized patient point of view about the interview, the researchers substituted reading the face of the patient. They looked for feelings of distress, disgust, or anger, expressed on the patients' faces. These patient faces turned out to be a better predictor of a further suicidal attempt than the psychiatrists' evaluations, but even more significantly, *the most accurate predictor of the repeat suicidal attempt was the expression on the psychiatrists' faces*. In the presence of repeat suicide attempters, "the psychiatrist frowned more, showed more head-and-eye orientation, and showed more overall facial activation and increased speech" (Beebe and Lachmann, 2002, p. 41). These results suggest that the feelings of the nuclear selves of these patients were "read" by the psychiatrists nonverbally. This Beebe and

Lachmann study points to the intersubjective field in which the empathic experience of the patient takes place.

Intersubjective field theory could be construed as correcting a Kohutian noninteractive view of empathy. The original presenters of intersubjectivity however, did not intend this. For example, Atwood and Stolorow (1984) define intersubjectivity as "an intersubjective field—a system of differently organized, interacting subjective worlds" of patient and analyst (p. 119). Their observational stance is from within and not outside the intersubjective, field, and they aver that intersubjectivity "guarantees *the centrality of introspection and empathy as methods of observation*" (p. 41). Stolorow and Atwood (1992) then clarify how empathy is necessary for the healthy functioning of an intersubjective system that consists of patient and analyst, because "an intersubjective field is a system of *reciprocal mutual influence*" (p. 3). So, in an adaptive, well-functioning relationship, both parties have the capacity to generate an empathic experience in the other, through vicarious introspection. So, intersubjective theory does not negate the concept of empathy but reminds us that a healthy relationship is built on a capacity for each party to generate reciprocal experiences of empathy.

Understandably, the more maladaptive, dysfunctional patients either lack the capacity to generate an empathic experience in others, or may refuse to vicariously introspect because they resent the fact that others do not empathically understand them. They are stuck in static relationships that lack empathic experiences and make psychological survival a struggle. As portrayed by intersubjective theory, any attempt by a psychotherapist to develop a therapeutic relationship with such a patient may degenerate into a struggle whether the patient influences the psychotherapist to become more dysfunctional, or whether the therapist influences the patient to be more adaptive. Kohut sees vicarious introspection as tilting the odds in favor of the therapist influencing the patient. With severely disordered patients empathy initially can only be a one directional means of understanding, paving the way for new experiences, and eventually leading to experiences of reciprocal empathy. Mutual empathic experiences generate interaction effects such as joy, as a result of feeling empathically understood by the other party.

A danger with an intersubjective view of the psychotherapeutic relationship is that it focuses on interactions rather than the patient feeling understood. Empathy that uses vicarious introspection as its method enables patients with little inclination to look at a relationship from another's viewpoint, to experience others as being empathic. The crucial issue for psychotherapy is how to proceed if patients can only initially tolerate a static relationship and do not take into account the point of view of others. Under these circumstances, Kohut is saying that by looking at an experience from the patient's point of view, the psychotherapist begins a one-way approach as a way forward. By beginning psychotherapy using vicarious introspection, Kohut reached patients and enabled the development of a mutual capacity for empathic experiences. In effect, a psychotherapist helps cocreate an intersubjective relationship with patients by establishing a specific psychotherapy context to meet the needs of the patient. Understood intersubjectively, the psychotherapist's initial "passivity" in accepting the patient's need to be understood from his/her point of view, contributes to the growth of a reciprocal empathically-experienced, intersubjective relationship. Under these conditions the therapeutic relationship may look to be static from the outside, but from the inside, is not experienced this way.

We have discussed empathy and intersubjectivity maintaining that in the context of a healing paradigm, empathy is primarily the patient's experience of being understood. In doing so we take seriously the role of the past in a therapeutic relationship. A major danger is that an intersubjective perspective's focus on the "here-and-now" does not allow sufficiently for past influences, especially repetitive transferences. Chessick (2007), for one, is concerned that in "the centerpiece of [the intersubjectivist] approach, the focus on the here and now, tends to place the transference and the childhood experiences of the patient in the background, rather than in the foreground where, in my opinion, it belongs" (pp. 10–11). On this issue, we think Kohut's focus on empathy as the experience of the patient helps to keep transference issues in the forefront in the initial stages of the psychotherapy.

Kohut's treatment of narcissistic patients exposed the unexamined assumption of many analysts—that empathy is a quality of the psychotherapist. Once Kohut defined empathy of a healing paradigm as the experience of the patient, he diluted the privileged position of the psychotherapist as the arbiter of reality and shifted the therapeutic relationship toward a shared experience. Kohut's definition was in contrast to a vague concept of empathy and its widespread misuse as a quality of the psychotherapist. The confused meanings of empathy can be seen in Buie's study (1981, p. 282), where he lists six different usages as (1) between two persons, (2) separateness between self and object, (3) intrapsychic experience, (4) human capacity, (5) knowing, and (6) transient experience. Kohut had earlier responded to the challenge of this kind of confusion by linking empathy's definition to issues of epistemology addressed by Titchener and Dewey. In doing this, Kohut also showed that privileging the patient's experience and not the psychotherapist's had the potential to transform severely damaged, narcissistic patients, a task for which classical psychoanalytic theory had been inadequate.

In making empathic understanding dependent on the experience of a patient, Kohut successfully negated privileging a psychotherapist's narcissism, but in doing so, he increased the possibility of reinforcing a patient's archaic narcissism. As Gabbard (1997) is clearly aware, the danger in privileging a patient's subjectivity is that the patient may not be able to separate the psychotherapist as a person from the psychotherapist as a selfobject. This leads to the realization that whereas a psychotherapist understands and accepts the patient's point of view based on a patient's developmental experiences, the psychotherapist retains the prerogative to disagree with the patient's contemplated behavior, based on another point of view. If the timing is right, even though the patient may get angry or distressed, and as long as the patient is not expected to behave according to the therapist's point of view, he/she may experience a beneficial growth in the relationship, where the patient experiences the psychotherapist as less of an archaic selfobject and more a person with his/her own center of initiative and a point of view. This is a key point in postmodern theory (Teicholtz, 1999) that will be discussed in a later chapter.

Patients who experience their point of view privileged in psychotherapy may expect to be empathically understood in a social setting. Patients who expect empathy as socially normative may be hurt when they don't experience it in social situations. An archaic narcissistic experience of being privileged in the psychotherapeutic relationship is designed to foster a regeneration of archaic narcissistic needs, and then, in time, enable structural changes in arrested or undeveloped sectors of the self. These structural changes come from the gradual emergence of different points of view in the sessions and an exploration of the feelings associated with these divergences. To Kohut, psychotherapy's method of understanding the patient's point of view is not intended as normative for social functioning, because adaptive social functioning requires a reasonable degree of assertiveness. Harmonious social interactions incorporate an obligation to take the initiative, sometimes make unpopular decisions, and recognize and accept that one doesn't always get one's own way.

To illustrate, a beginning psychotherapy student requested admission into an advanced course and was refused by the teacher. She left the teacher's office hurt and distressed, and returned some time later to confront the teacher with her "unempathic" experience of him. He responded that he understood her disappointment, was sorry she had been hurt by the experience, and encouraged her to further explore her feelings with her training psychotherapist. The teacher realized he had narcissistically wounded the student because of her idealized expectations of being empathically understood in the classroom. The student, who had read Kohut, had equated Kohut's concept of empathy as getting her own way outside of the psychotherapy relationship. She had assumed that any empathic person would know she hurts easily and would not say "no" to her. So a problem with Kohut's concept of empathic understanding arises when the patient's point of view is taken without making it clear that this empathic experience takes place in the context of psychotherapy for the purpose of making structural changes. Psychotherapy is radically different from a social relationship. Empathy can be experienced in social contexts, but it should not be expected in a group seeking to achieve goals that involve the competing interests of others.

With the defining of empathy as the patient's experience, the unsuitability of some severely disturbed patients for treatment using the empathic method becomes an increasing possibility. Some persons have been so traumatized by negative experiences in the past, that they have strong, bitter transference feelings toward the psychotherapist, almost from the moment of meeting. Such a repetitive transference is triggered because the psychotherapist inadvertently looks like, behaves like, or says something similar to, a person in the patient's past, someone who abused the patient or helped create a strong negative experience. This triggering can be from a bad match (Kantrowitz, 1996). With such a specific, powerful negative therapeutic relationship, a psychotherapist's attempt to understand the patient may result in persistent empathic failure, and it is better for the patient to find another psychotherapist who does not trigger such a negative response and can reach the patient through empathic understanding. In an extreme situation, it is theoretically plausible, and has been clinically experienced, where a negative transference is so pervasive and so generalized to every therapist, that the patient is untreatable in an empathy-based psychotherapy. Once empathy is understood as the experience of the patient, the method is recognized as open to limitations with severely damaged patients unless a good-enough therapeutic match between patient and psychotherapist can be found. Extreme examples of the limitations of the empathic method are the serial killers discussed in chapter 5. Less extreme, but psychologically damaged patients are mostly unreachable by the empathic method, although, undoubtedly, there will be exceptions.

(2) Empathy and Postmodern Rejection

Kohut's emphasis on empathy as the experience of the patient diminishes the idea of empathy as a quality of the psychotherapist, and rejects the idea of empathy as intuition. The popular idea that "intuition" is a special, instantaneous, magic-like form of empathy, increases the risk that it does not match the patient's experience and will be experienced by the patient as non-empathic. Kohut (1981a) is especially critical of intuitive psychotherapists who wrongly believe "about curing through love, through empathy, through kindness, through compassion, [and by] . . . just being there and being nice" (p. 527). Despite Kohut's efforts to distance himself from this intuitive approach, postmodern analysts such as Hoffman (1983) equated Kohut's empathy with a "friendly, naturally responsive attitude" (p. 398), even though Kohut (1971) clearly states "that unusually friendly behavior from the side of the analyst, . . . *is no more advisable in the analysis of a narcissistic personality disturbance than it is in the analysis of transference neuroses*" (pp. 88–89). A decade later Hoffman (1994) had still not grasped Kohut's intersubjective view of empathy as the patient's experience of interactions with their therapist. Hoffman claims that Kohut "introduced a new kind of institutional disguise for personal, countertransferential tendencies" (p. 196). The self psychologist Teicholtz (1999) counters, "Do [Kohut's and Loewald's] theories express countertransferential tendencies to a greater degree than do, for instance, those of the postmodern analysts, whose theories are concerned with issues of the analyst's self-expression, authenticity, and self-disclosure" (p. 64)?

Having misunderstood Kohut's development of empathy into an intersubjective concept, Hoffman (1994) continued to see empathy as a psychotherapist's "friendliness" and as a benign ingredient in the therapeutic relationship (p. 191). Of course, if "friendliness" was all there is to Kohut's concept of empathy, we would agree with Hoffman. But it isn't. Hoffman, citing Slavin and Kriegman (1992), in a caricature of empathy, portrays it as a mechanical "technique," ironically, almost the opposite to Kohut's idea of a patient's experience of feeling understood from his/her point of view. Hoffman's almost complete reversal of Kohut's meaning only confuses the debate about what is therapeutically mutative. Hoffman's critique of empathy, as Teicholtz (1999) points out, is equivalent to an inaccurate critique of postmodernists that says "every analyst writing about the analyst's subjectivity or self expression is a veiled narcissist, unable to focus attention on anyone outside himself" (p. 65).

Teicholtz (1999) focuses also on contemporary analysts such as Slavin and Kriegman, who emphasize negotiation as an aspect of a therapeutic relationship. She is tempted to criticize them as "aggressive egotists exploiting the vulnerability of their patients in dealings that are rigged from the start owing to the analyst's relative position of power" (p. 65), but recognizes that

> such assertions are sustainable only by removal of the author's original words from their original contexts and an almost willful distortion of their author's

intent; they involve ludicrous exaggeration of an author's central point through the portrayal of a mindless and perseverative execution of a recommended stance [p. 65].

Yet, this is precisely what postmodern authors have done with Kohut. This stance of postmodern analysts is discussed in later chapters.

While postmodern theory may not have sufficient safeguards against narcissistic analysts, self psychology made it clear it did not condone the narcissistic misuse of empathy by psychotherapists who thought of empathy as intuition and were tempted to directly intervene in the life of the patient based on intuition, rather than indirect change resulting from a patient's feeling understood. The price paid for direct intervention is the undermining of a patient's sense of self-agency, which is antithetical to what psychotherapy seeks to achieve with self-disordered patients. More importantly, Kohut thinks that psychotherapists who rely on "intuition" are more vulnerable to archaic forms of grandiose thinking. The mistake of the intuitionists lies in using intuition as a substitute for empathy rather than using intuitive "hunches" as starting points for empathic exploration that then lead to inferences and the uncovering of the assumptions that both patient and psychotherapist bring to a therapeutic relationship. Thus, psychotherapists whose archaic grandiosity focuses on "brilliant intuitions" are less able to help narcissistic patients transform their archaic forms of narcissism because of their own.

From supervising, we have noted that psychotherapists who believe empathy is a personal quality trigger more disjunctions in the long-term treatment of self-disordered patients than those who see empathy as the experience of the patient. When disjunctions occur, intuitive psychotherapists experience intense shame because a therapeutic failure is a failure of "their" empathy. Interestingly, intuitive psychotherapists with a belief in their own magical capacities are often able to function well in brief counseling, but if shamed by their failures with long-term psychotherapy, find it increasingly difficult to repair their disjunctions with patients. If they are to sustain long-term work, they do so at the price of becoming utterly exhausted.

Narcissism is not only involved in an overconfident intuitive quality of psychotherapists and their insensitivity to the subjective state of patients, it may also show as the opposite, as a hypersensitivity to a patient's subjective state. The difficulty with a hypersensitive psychotherapist is not an inability to walk in the shoes of their patients—they do this well—but a difficulty responding helpfully because of their inadequate, easily fragmented or chaotic self-organization. These psychotherapists are like the mother in Kohut's example (1996) who, "instead of . . . empathy with the child's anxiety leading to enfolding the child in her calmness, . . . [the child's anxiety] led to the mother's panic; and this makes even the correct empathy of the mother useless for the child and the child has to withdraw" (p. 112). Hypersensitive psychotherapists, who can't help rejecting their patients because they are so fearful of therapeutic failure, are experienced by the patient as unempathic, despite their ability to understand the subjective state of the patient.

Mrs. S is an example of a psychologist who, after graduation, attempted private practice for several years, but whose practice never developed beyond a small number of once-weekly patients. Despairing, she sought twice-monthly personal psychotherapy, and when the psychotherapist explained she needed twice-weekly sessions in order to develop self-structures that would sustain her therapeutic work, she reluctantly agreed to once-a-week personal psychotherapy. In the beginning, as Mrs. S shared details of her two previous psychotherapies, conducted with fortnightly sessions, it soon became evident that neither of these had gone beyond addressing issues of the peripheral self, and had barely touched the issue of an increased structuralization of her hypersensitive nuclear self.

Mrs. S had experienced considerable rejection from her parents as a child, especially from a firm, authoritarian father, and had been date-raped as an adolescent. The adult Mrs. S had a pattern of easily being offended and a heightened capacity to place herself into her patient's shoes. After she went through a training program that "required" a small number of sessions of personal psychotherapy for graduation, she began seeing a trickle of patients. Eventually a suicidal, low-fee patient, who needed at least twice-weekly psychotherapy in order to prevent fragmentation, was referred to her. As this patient shared his distress, Mrs. S had no trouble placing herself in his shoes, or understanding his sense of loneliness, shame, and terror. This empathic understanding, however, created an enormous problem for her because she lacked the internal structures to contain her terror and chaotic feelings as a result of twinning the patient. Mrs S's fear triggered the amygdala/hypothalamic/brain stem freeze response, she became extremely passive, and this passivity inhibited her ability to respond helpfully to him (LeDoux and Gorman, 2001). As the despairing patient sensed Mrs. S's emotional unavailability, he became more desperate, sought to archaically merge with her. She then felt powerless to stop increasing panicky telephone intrusions, was too ashamed to refer him for medication or to another psychotherapist, and was too fearful to terminate him. The situation became dangerous for both of them.

To make matters worse, as a result of fragmenting fears her patient stirred in her, Mrs. S began to grossly identify and archaically merge with the patient, which in turn made the patient even more fragmented. This cycle was eventually broken when Mrs. S became too exhausted to continue and, feeling defeated, eventually referred her archaic, merger-prone patient. The failure in this case did not lie in Mrs. S's empathic insensitivity to her patient, rather it came from her lack of sufficiently robust nuclear self-structures with which to respond to her patient's need. Empathy as data gathering alone is generally insufficient to bring about structural therapeutic change—as will be discussed in later chapters. Empathy is not the magic some wish it to be.

(3) Empathy is a Constructed Experience

The common meaning of "experience" in the Oxford English Dictionary is of something encountered or undergone. We *have* an experience. A shift in modern philosophy, however, has led to the idea that experience is not something we have, that is, passively receive, but something in which the receiving person also participates and therefore helps to construct. Yet, as the passive meaning of empathy has been ingrained into Western culture after long usage, the idea of empathy as a constructed experience may be difficult to accept.

The notion of constructed experience is in contrast to Freud's "associationistic" views that see experience as consisting of a series of discrete mental entities and concepts arising from various combinations or associations of these entities (Donnel Stern, 1983, p. 78). These associational views led Freud to conceive of nonconscious thought as repressed rather than as unformed objects, because Freud assumed that new experiences were perceived as fully formulated intellectual objects and then added to a store of memories like a crate being stacked in a warehouse. At stake in these differences between constructionist and associational views is the distribution of power between psychotherapist and patient. In the constructionist view, the psychotherapist loses his/her privileged position as the arbiter of reality and has a relationship that is much more balanced, so that the psychotherapist and patient cocreate this relationship (Donnel Stern, 1992, p. 331).

Donnel Stern, a psychotherapy theorist who takes the philosophical stance that experience is always constructed, thinks that empathy must also be constructed. In holding a constructionist view, he rejects a concept of empathy as a direct, unmediated perception. While we believe there is room for special moments of direct, unmediated empathic communication (as discussed in a later section), we also think that a self psychology concept of empathy can comfortably incorporate and mainly functions within a constructionist view of reality. Donnel Stern (1992, p. 331) broadly defines contructionism by quoting Watzlawick (1984): "Any so-called reality is—in the most immediate and concrete sense—the construction of those who believe they have discovered and investigated it" (p. 16). So Stern claims that knowledge comes, not from the gradual accretion of "objective" facts that "then tumble into [a] new understanding of their own weight" (1992, p. 330), but from a creative new hypothesis that reveals the existence of facts previously unformulated. Earlier, Atwood and Stolorow (1984) thought that such unformed thought indicates a "prereflective" unconscious (p. 42), an idea that follows William James' idea that each of us "sculpts" conscious experience from a block of unformulated experience, where meaning becomes created, not discovered. (Donnel Stern, 1983, p. 71).

From a constructionist view of epistemology, Donnel Stern is critical of Kohut's concept of "empathic immersion." Stern (1991) says, "The analyst who believes he has no choice but to work from a position of embeddedness cannot trust his own intention to enter the patient's inner world, to learn through empathic immersion" (p. 91). The problem of "empathic immersion" for Stern is how to enter another person's world if that world is constantly changing (being constructed), because for Stern, one can only enter another's world if it is preconceived and static. But Stern's criticism of Kohut is not accurate, because a careful reading of Kohut's one reference to empathic immersion refers to a field generated by patient and analyst. Kohut (1977) states, "with regard to clinical phenomena, of [the analyst's] long-term, empathic immersion *in the transference* [italics added]" (p. xxii). So, in the context of this immersion statement, Kohut refers to the transference relationship and not just the patient, even though he acknowledges he is "trying to observe and explain [the] inner experience" of the patient (xxii).

Is Kohut the "static" theorist of empathy depicted by Stern? We don't think so. But whatever the answer to this question, ultimately, the more important issue is whether Kohut's concept of empathy can accommodate a constructionist view. We think it can if we do not confine co-construction to the "here and now material" of the therapeutic session. As Chessick (2007) points out, a patient's character patterns are brought into the psychotherapy, not created by it (p. 19). Stolorow and his colleagues (1994), who brought an intersubjective perspective to self psychology, take a constructionist view of empathy, and avoid the language of "immersion" by referring to a "sustained empathic inquiry" (p. 44) (see also Stolorow et al., 1987, p. 10). They say, "[This inquiry is] an attitude that consistently seeks to comprehend the meaning of a patient's expressions from a perspective within, rather than outside, the patient's own subjective frame of reference" (1994, p. 44).

(4) Empathy is Hermeneutical

Modern views in epistemology challenge a static theory of empathy in yet another way. Once we abandon the position that empathically knowing a person means discovering an idea that already exists and awaits discovery, and accept that knowledge is a co-determined construction, we face questions of how this co-construction takes place. To do this, modern philosophy has turned to the ideas of the father of hermeneutic thinking, Frederick Schleiermacher, who developed the hermeneutical pattern as a way to interpret passages in the New Testament. Prior to Schleiermacher it was assumed that a text's meaning would be self-evident to the reader; understanding was taken for granted; misunderstanding was the exception that needed explaining.

Once scholars of the New Testament began abandoning a literal interpretation of biblical texts, rules evolved to uncover the truth buried behind one's reading of the text. As Donnel Stern (1991) explains, Schleiermacher had reversed the order taken by biblical literalists. Schleiermacher found it more reasonable to

> assume misunderstanding than understanding . . . because intervening between the text and the reader are time, history, custom, changes of language, etc. The reader is faced with a document encrusted and obscured by the debris of change. . . . the truth lay behind one's reading of the text, and had to be reconstructed. If that could be accomplished, one could read the text from within the vantage point of the writer, and it would then be possible to grasp its original meaning" [p. 57].

In practice Schleiermacher's hermeneutic method meant that after reading a group of connected verses in a New Testament book, a hypothesis would form about the purpose of the book as a whole. Assuming this general hypothesis, some of the specific sections could be read with a different meaning. And the process would continue of interpreting the whole from the parts and then the parts from the whole in a "hermeneutic circle," until there were no more shifts in meaning. In effect, this process is the reverse of composition; it begins with the finished work and seeks to understand the processes that created it. It assumes that the bias of someone saturated by the present-day culture interferes with encountering the writer's original intention, and that truth appears when such error is removed.

Schleiermacher's hermeneutics was reconstruction. For Gadamer, a modern hermeneutic writer, the problem of understanding is not reconstruction, but construction, a construction that occurs as a result of interaction between a reader and a text, or between two participants in a relational "conversation." A conversation needs the full participation of both parties, and depends on here-and-now attitudes. Such a conversation is not interested in recreating the past, even though tradition is very much involved in the here and now. Tradition consists of many prejudices of which a person is an embodiment and the carrier for the culture. Gadamer thinks that our nuclear selves consist of assumptions, that is, prejudices, and that these prejudices need to be engaged through dialogue and genuine conversation if understanding is to occur in a relationship. Successful relating, however, not only needs understanding but the willingness to contain or sacrifice emerging prejudices so as to receive another's communication.

Gadamer (1993) points out that the Enlightenment, in rejecting the traditional authority of the priestly ecclesiastical structures of religion, or Scripture, made "Reason" the final authority. But in setting up a system of rationality, the Enlightenment had, in effect, set up a "prejudice against prejudices" (p. 272), which is a contradiction in terms. Gadamer reminds us that it was only after the ideas of the Enlightenment were widely accepted that prejudice acquired a negative connotation. Prior to the enlightenment, "prejudice" meant a temporary judgment before all the elements that determine a situation have been finally examined (p. 270). As Gadamer indicates, "In German legal terminology, a 'prejudice' is a provisional legal verdict before a final verdict is reached" (p. 270). With his meaning, prejudice can have a positive or negative value.

Gadamer's modern version of hermeneutics rejects Schleiermacher's assumption that the meaning of a text is hidden and pre-existing and only available through empathic communion with the writer. Gadamer's point is that our embededness in tradition, and therefore our prejudices, often prevent empathic understanding from occurring. To Gadamer, meaning comes from an articulation and selection of possibilities. We often have glimmers of understanding, which we attempt to extrapolate to the whole, and as we work with these extrapolations, new parts emerge that were previously unformulated. And so the circle continues. When these hypotheses are projected, the analyst adopts a degree of uncertainty. He says that each piece of uncertainty is surrounded by "the infinity of the unsaid."

Gadamer's ideas on hermeneutics and on prejudice are obviously pertinent to a theory of empathy. They suggest that where a patient has an inability to experience empathic understanding, the major reason may be the underlying prejudices of either or both patient and psychotherapist. The problem with a theory of empathy for psychotherapy, therefore, is that only after the relational interaction uncovers prejudices and unformulated thought, is it possible for empathic experiences to become a part of psychotherapy interactions. As Gadamer (1993) says, "Every experience worthy of the name runs counter to expectation. . . . Insight is more than the knowledge of this or that situation. It always involves an escape from something that had deceived us or held us captive" (p. 356). Gadamer's hermeneutics does not undermine or invalidate the use of empathy in a self psychological psychotherapy; it ends up supporting Kohut's concept. In so doing it offers the possibility that patients who have failed to be understood "from their own point of view," despite the attempt at empathic understanding, may be reached through an exploration of the presumptions and prejudices that both patient and psychotherapist bring to the relationship.

As it can be quickly pointed out, patients with severe self-disorders don't usually have a disposition toward exploring their prejudices, and may only do so if they have developed a trusting relational bond with the psychotherapist. But how does a trust develop if the patient brings a negative transference in the psychotherapeutic relationship? Is the point of view of Gadamer and those who talk about examining prejudices a comforting pipe dream to encourage psychotherapists in their attempts to engage such patients? Kohut did not think so.

Kohut very early in his professional career realized that a way for a psychotherapist to break the negative transference of distrust and unexamined prejudices is to commence with the patient's point of view. This empathic stance neither assumes objective reality for the patient's position, nor for the psychotherapist's own. In genuinely exploring the patient's position first, without making demands that the patient conform to the psychotherapist's reality, the psychotherapist offers a way for the relationship to proceed. The psychotherapist also sets an example that the patient can imitate by seeking to understand the psychotherapist's point of view. One of the major values we see in Kohut's view of empathy as the experience of the patient is its ability to slowly dissolve logjams that prevent nourishing and enlivening interactions and eventually uncovering prejudices.

(5) Empathy is Affective/Cognitive

Goldberg thinks that empathy is theory-laden. He (1983) agrees with Kohut's idea of empathy as vicarious introspection and extrospection, but points to the indirectness of the actual data gathering. Goldberg is critical of the view of empathy that consists of placing oneself in the shoes of another as a direct form of knowing, which as Basch (1981) reminds us, was the view of Freud (Eccles, 1970). To Goldberg, all observations, whether inspection, vicarious introspection, or vicarious extrospection, are theory-laden. He thinks we never begin "de-nova," with Locke's "tabula rasa" (clean slate). Therefore, there is no capacity to perceive directly without the filter of preconceived beliefs (Gadamer's "prejudices"). Goldberg believes that one does not see anything unless one already has a general idea of what to look for. He (1983) says, "Students who look into a microscope for the first time usually see nothing until they are given a theory and a set of logical steps to follow" (p. 156). So understanding a patient's point of view inevitably involves understanding the patient's assumptions and temporarily suspending one's own, by taking an "as if" position.

Goldberg (1983) thinks that empathic understanding is not gained directly. He claims that a psychotherapist makes inferences in order to place himself/herself into the shoes of the patient. He believes, furthermore, that using inferences in empathic understanding ought not to present epistemological difficulties to the positivistic philosophers of science because, as Goldberg emphasizes, inference is heavily involved in the inspective processes of science. He points out,

> The path of the electron or any sub-atomic particle is inferred from the tiny markings resulting from a high-energy accelerator. Chemical reactions that result in new compounds are derived from a process of inference. The claim of verifiability by direct perception enjoyed only a brief heyday in the philosophy of science before it was seen that this was not only unreasonable, but an unnecessary requirement [1983, p.159].

Having said this, Goldberg takes pains to say that "Theory guides, but does not determine, our perceptions which are fundamentally empathic" (p. 161). In contrast to Goldberg's view, Feiner and Kiersky (1994a) think that emphasis on an indirect form of perception results in a constructed cognitive theory of empathy that misses the affective component. They think that empathy's affective component enables the subjective state of the patient to be immediately accessible, at times, to the psychotherapist. So they present a two-phase model in which "the empathic process consists of an initial perceptual phase that generates affective resonance, and a second phase in which complex cognitive-affective operations contribute to the construction of meaning" (p. 425). In this first phase there is direct access to the feeling states of others. Their second phase is in line with Goldberg's (1983) emphasis on inference in a theory of empathy and also with Buie (1981) who says,

> Empathy . . . ultimately depends on inference. The empathizer never directly perceives the inner state of the object. Instead he finds a reference that could if expressed reasonably be manifested by cues similar to those he observes in the object. The empathizer infers that congruence between the inner experience of the object and his own internal referent actually exists [p. 303].

In this second phase Feiner and Kirsky (1994a) call "upon the analyst's interpretive and imaginative facility and his theoretical and technical understanding as well as his view of the particular 'moment' in treatment" (p. 426).

With the increasing importance of cognitive theory in modern psychology and the ideas of constructed perception, cognition, and memory, Feiner and Kiersky realize that their idea of the capacity for a direct experience of empathy is against the main stream of opinion and needs supportive evidence. They support their claim by appealing to gestalt theory (Kohler, 1947; Arnheim, 1949) and to the clinical experiences of those who practice psychotherapy from a psychoanalytic self-psychology-oriented empathic approach that focuses on a patient's feelings. Moreover, it is the experimental work of infant researchers that makes it difficult to dismiss their claim that a psychotherapist may, at times, "directly" perceive the inner feeling state of a patient.

In advocating that direct perceptions of feelings help shape a theory of empathy, Feiner and Kiersky especially point to the work of Basch (1983), who refers to the "autonomic . . . imitation of the sender's bodily states and facial expression by the receiver" (p. 108) based on the work of affect theorist Silvan Tomkins (1962, 1963, 1991, 1992; discussed in chapter 5). A direct perception theory is also supported by the research of Ekman, Levenson, and Friesen (1983), who asked actors to make a face to portray a primary emotion—fear, for example—then measure their changes in heart rate, hand skin temperature, and skin resistance, as autonomic nervous system indices. The results of this study showed different autonomic patterns between negative emotions (fear, anger, disgust) and positive ones (startle, joy). This experiment demonstrates that imitating another's face can change the imitating person's internal affective state.

In a follow-up paper, Feiner and Kiersky (1994b) support the role of direct perception in empathy with the experimental work of Field and colleagues (1982), who used trained actors to make joyful, sad, or startled faces to infants thirty-six hours old, and found that the infants imitated the actor's facial expressions. This suggested that a matching capacity is innate. And the adaptive value of matching and sharing feelings was demonstrated in the "visual cliff" experiments with ten-month-old children. In the classic study (Gibson and Walk, 1960), crawling babies avoided crossing a gap with a visual vertical drop-off, even though this "chasm" was covered with a strong, rigid, piece of plexiglass. When infants reached this "chasm" they stopped, uncertain, looked at their mother's faces, and read the feeling content. Campos and colleagues (1983) found that if the mother, as instructed, showed facial pleasure by smiling, the infant crossed the visual cliff. If the mother showed facial fear, the infant turned back from the "cliff."

Feiner and Kiersky also claim that the discoveries of Meltzoff (1990) supports their contention of direct perception. From his research into facial imitation he says

> that infants can relate the gestures they see on another's face to their own unseen facial behavior. The fact that infants imitate the expressions they see suggests that they can detect similarities, at least at the behavioral level, between the action of the self and the other.

Meltzoff thinks that infants "have the information necessary to appreciate that the other has emotional states similar to their own" (p. 161). Feiner and Kiersky think that Meltzoff's evidence is significant for believing that babies detect "cross modal equivalents between those movements-as-felt and movements they see performed by others" (Meltzoff and Gopnik 1993, p. 336). Beebe and Lachmann (2002, pp. 90–100) give a detailed review of studies of facial mirroring that includes most of the important researchers in the infant development field. The evidence is compelling that through the facial interactions of mothers and infants, infants form pre-symbolic representations.

This growing experimental evidence from early mother-infant behavior demonstrates the possibility of a non-inferential form of knowing in empathic experiences. One difficulty with the Feiner and Kiersky two-phase theory, however, is that Tomkins' theory of affects, which accepts the innateness of eight (or nine) primary affects (interest, distress, fear, etc.), also points to the limbic system's affect circuits being linked to the cognitive circuits of the prefrontal lobes. Tomkins thinks that to conceive of affects or cognitions in isolation sets up an artificial dichotomy between them—really a form of dissociation. From his point of view, neural firings in the affect circuits are modified by the cognitive circuits, just as cognitive circuits need affective circuits to form long-term memories. So, although there may be short, direct experiences of empathic understanding in early infancy and more importantly, for brief moments in psychotherapy that are referred to as empathic attunement (Daniel Stern, 1985), the cognitive component, involving inferences, theories, and different self-organizing developments, soon generates explanations as part of the empathic experience. Ultimately, the inferential form of empathy plays a major role.

Both direct and indirect ways of knowing empathically are reflected in Kohut's thinking. In elucidating the innate component, he (1966) says,

> The groundwork for our ability to obtain access to another person's mind is laid by the fact that in our earliest mental organization the feelings, actions, and behavior of the mother had been included in our self. The *primary empathy*

> with the mother prepares us for the recognition that to a large extent the basic inner experiences of other people remain similar to our own [p. 451].

And a decade later, he (1977) states, "the empathic understanding of the experiences of other human beings is as basic an endowment of man as vision, hearing, touch, taste, and smell" (p. 144). In view of the work of Field, Ekman, Daniel Stern, and other infant researchers, Kohut's retention of an innate "direct" capability as an important component in his theory of empathy cannot be easily ignored or rejected.

Those who criticize Kohut for not jettisoning a belief in a direct noninferential experience of empathy may overlook Kohut's view that interpretation also becomes involved in empathic perception. Kohut always held that explanations were necessary to achieve relatively permanent structural change. What he was originally uncertain about was whether to see explanation as a "step beyond" or as a part of the empathic process. He (1971) says, "The scientific psychologist, in general, and the psychoanalyst in particular, not only must have free access to empathic understanding; they must also be able to relinquish the empathic attitude. If they cannot be empathic, they cannot observe and collect the data they need; if they cannot step beyond empathy, they cannot set up hypotheses and theories, and thus ultimately achieve explanations" (p. 303).

A decade later, however, Kohut is including explanation as a part of the process of empathy. This may be because, unlike his critics, he has recognized the problem of casting direct and indirect modes of empathic perception as conflicting opposites, and now sees them as complementary processes at different levels of empathically understanding another person. So Kohut (1981a)

> claims that analysis cures by giving explanations—interventions on the level of interpretation; not by "understanding," not by repeating and confirming what the patient feels and says, that's only the first step; but then [the analyst has] to move on and give an interpretation. . . . And the next step of giving interpretations is a move from a lower form of empathy to a higher form of empathy [p. 532].

This shift suggests that even though the model of Feiner and Kiersky reflects ideas of Kohut, and portrays these as stages with direct and indirect ways of empathic understanding, the model's problem for understanding patients may be because it too readily dichotomizes affects and cognitions. We opt for a flexible model in which some empathic experiences have feeling elements front stage and cognitive components back stage, and other empathic experiences where the staging for affects and cognitions is more balanced or reversed.

In view of growing neurological evidence, it is easy to believe that, except for beginnings and special moments in a session, empathy is mostly cognitive, inferential, and indirect. In brain laterality studies, for example, the empathic experience has been linked to the imaging functions of the right frontal brain (Gazzinga and LeDoux, 1978). More recently, Stuss and colleagues (2001) report experimental findings to support the idea that empathy is mainly inferential. They studied thirty-two brain-damaged patients in an experiment where the patients had to infer what the experimenter's assistants were thinking. Patients with right prefrontal lobe lesions were less able to infer what the assistants were thinking, compared with patients whose lesions were in other parts of the brain, so suggesting that inferential empathy is more a right-brain function than anything else. Eslinger (1998), who studied two cases where prefrontal lesions occurred during childhood, confirmed these results. Cozolino (2002) interprets these findings to mean that the right prefrontal circuits are activated when empathy is experienced because "empathic thinking requires . . . cognitive flexibility and affect regulation [from cognitive modifiers (Tomkins)] to pull back from the environment, put our needs aside, and imagine the feelings of others" (p. 132). Similarly, Schore (2003) takes the view that "the interactive regulation of right brain attachment biology is . . . the substrate of empathy" (p. 44).

The relationship between empathy and the prefrontal lobes was also suggested by a study of twenty-two prisoners accused of murder (Raine and colleagues, 1994). Murderers, of course, are not known generally for their empathic capacities. When these murder suspects underwent PET (positron emission tomography) scans while performing a standard task, they had a lower glucose metabolism (hence less neural firing) in the prefrontal lobes compared with twenty-two matched controls. This result pointed to deficits in the neural circuits of the prefrontal lobes and supports the idea that empathy utilizes this area of the brain. Also affirming this conclusion were studies by Nauta (1971) and Meyers and colleagues (1992), which indicated that damage to the prefrontal lobes was correlated with "anti-social" behavior. The research suggests that persons with what self psychology describes as severe "narcissistic behavior disorders" (Kohut and Wolf, 1978) may have underdeveloped or damaged neural circuits in the precortex, and hence, less control of their affect circuits.

Neuroscience's discovery of "mirror" neurons is very relevant to the empathic experience. Gallese and colleagues (1996), in studying the brain of two macaque monkeys, discovered a special subset of ninety-two neurons in the F5 region, the inferior premotor cortex—Brocca's area in human brains (Nishitani, Schurmann, Amunts, and Hari, 2005)—which fired either when the monkeys performed the action of grasping an object, or when the monkey saw the experimenter perform the same act. After a further decade of studies, Gallese and colleagues (2007) have gone beyond monkeys to demonstrate "the existence in the human brain of a mirror neuron system matching action perception and execution" (p. 134). For example, they point to empirical evidence that the first-person experience of being touched on one's own body stimulates the same neural networks that are activated by observing the body of someone else being touched. They suggest "that our capacity to experience and directly understand the tactile experience of others could be mediated by embodied simulation" (p. 142).

The Gallese et al. (2007) concept of "embodied simulation" raises important issues about a theory of empathy. It is different from simulation theory (Jung, W., 2003) where "simulation requires the subject to empathize, that is, 'to put himself in the shoes of the other'" (p. 215) and relying on vicarious introspection to take the perspective of the other. Simulation theory is more of a conscious, cognitive process of empathy. With "embodied simulation" Gallese et al. (2007) point out, "we do not 'see' an action, an emotion, or sensation. Side by side with the sensory description of the observed social stimuli, internal representations of the body states associated with these actions, emotions, and sensations are evoked in the observer, 'as if' he or she were doing a similar action or experiencing a similar emotion or sensation" (pp. 144–45). Embodied simulation is "an automatic, unconscious, and noninferencial understanding of another's actions, intensions, emotions, sensations, and perhaps even linguistic expressions" (p. 144). So with research into the functioning of mirror neurons supporting the embedded theory of simulation, we see further support for the Feiner and Kiersky idea of direct and indirect phases of empathy.

The neural architecture activated during empathic understanding has been acknowledged by a neuroscientist of no less stature than V. S. Ramachandran (2006), for whom a sophisticated mirror neuron system provides an evolutionary basis for the concept of empathy. He points to the significant delay after the development of the hominid brain to its present size about 200,000 years ago, and the sudden explosion in technological sophistication, widespread cave art, clothes, and stereotyped dwellings around 40,000 years ago. He speculates that the development of the mirror neurons can account for this gap. Mirror neurons are essential for the development of a Lamarkian or cultural inheritance. So, these neurological findings are consistent with the idea that empathic understanding, which can be directly experienced through the face and the affect circuits, uses inferential and cognitive functions of the brain.

(6) Empathy Used for Non-Healing Purposes

The insights into empathy offered by philosophical constructionism, modern hermeneutics, and neuroscience do not necessitate changing Kohut's idea of empathy or its role as the core postulate in a theory of psychotherapy. His emphasis on the experience of the patient is confirmed by successful therapeutic results with difficult-to-treat self-disordered patients. Even so, empathy's use has a "dark side" (F. Lachmann, 2000). Ornstein illustrates this with Kohut's example of a hoodlum standing on a street corner and imagining himself into the shoes of passing pedestrians to determine who would be a good mugging prospect (F. Lachmann, 2000, p. 11). If empathy is the experience of the patient, clearly the victim does not experience the mugger as having any empathy whatsoever. This is because the act of gaining knowledge about the person to be mugged was used for the advantage of the mugger, not the mugged person, which is the very opposite to the employment of therapeutic empathy in healing, where the professional commitment of the psychotherapist is to use empathy to the benefit of the patient.

Another example of the non-healing use of empathy comes from a clinical setting. A senior psychiatrist at an inpatient hospital unit, aware that a former patient was being readmitted, warned the staff that this patient was very skillful at inducing staff squabbling. Despite this warning, the resident staff soon fought among themselves, with one staff member carrying a lock of the patient's hair, and another wearing a necklace with a cross on it as a gift of this patient. The patient's ability to empathically place herself into the shoes of each staff member enabled her to manipulate her environment. The patient used the empathic method to manipulate the staff, which is the very opposite of the employment of empathy in healing, where the psychotherapist's professional commitment is to use empathy to benefit the patient.

Examples of the non-healing use of empathy clarify the distinctiveness and importance of Kohut's concept of therapeutic empathy. These non-healing examples either point to the need for a meaning of empathy that is more than just gaining knowledge vicariously, or a need to use the term only where the welfare of the empathized is the major reason for the emotional transaction. If the latter strategy is taken, many of the non-healing examples of empathy become pseudo-empathy, looked at from the empathized's experience. The empathic strategy involves taking the empathized's point of view, and also working for the best interests of the empathized.

Perhaps there is always a power issue involved with the concept of empathy. This is the position taken by Nietzche for whom empathy arose not from a desire to heal, but from a wish for power as a defense against fear. Supportive of Nietzche's position is the fact that the Nazis added sirens to their buzz bombs that were dropped on London in World War II, knowing that these sounds would increase the terror and confusion of the people (Kohut, 1981a, p. 529). In military terms, for thousands of years, commanders have used empathy to anticipate the strategies and tactics of an enemy commander. And in Shakespeare's literature, as Lachmann (1999) points out, Iago's empathy enables him to manipulate Othello.

Thus, if empathy developed originally in association with non-healing functions, then empathy's use in healing is a special case where the power needs of the empathizer take a back seat to those of the empathized. If healing is a special case of empathy, then a psychotherapy theory needs to be clear that empathy is not just gaining knowledge about another person, but is a special case where the needs of the patient based on the point of view of the patient take precedence over the needs of the psychotherapist. The healer willingly gives up the power position of using any vicariously obtained knowledge for his/her own personal advantage.

The specialness of the empathic method can't be overemphasized. It is most likely needed when interacting with children, when meeting strangers, when a conflict emerges with a friend, or when healing is needed, such as in psychotherapy. Once the high biological and psychological energy cost of empathy is accepted, we can understand the value of a group, community or society at large adopting normative patterns of behavior (rules) to represent a consensual view. The advantage of consensual reality and its expectations is the reduced exhaustion from not constantly needing to be empathic in all interactions. This non-empathic, consensual system works reasonably well in a homogeneous group or society until something goes wrong. With a relatively heterogenous group or society, however, empathy is likely to be needed in interactions between persons whose backgrounds are divergent subcultures, whether majority or minority. The greater the divergence between the beliefs and practices of subcultures, the greater the need for empathy in intercultural interactions. And in multicultural countries, as the old, formerly consensually validated patterns break down, the need for the empathic way of knowing increases, because as Gadamer indicated, empathic understanding involves formulating the prejudices that each person, group, organization, religion, or culture brings to a relationship.

The empathic method in psychotherapy is open to misuse and abuse. One such misuse, mentioned earlier, are actions arising from a psychotherapist who believes in intuitive empathy. Kohut countered such grandiosity by defining empathy as the experience of the patient. However, this new emphasis created the potential for a different type of abuse, a reinforcement of a patient's arrogant grandiosity that is difficult for a psychotherapist to manage, especially if it is extreme. One disadvantage of the privileging of the patient's point of view is that the psychotherapist is then more vulnerable to manipulation by a patient. A patient may ask the psychotherapist to do all kinds of things, generally linked to a reenactment of some sort, and expect to be obeyed. One example is the well-known Ferenczi case of RN, whose behavior with Ferenczi eventually led to a deteriorating relationship where she tenaciously bullied him into her way of doing mutual psychotherapy (as elaborated in chapter 7). This was a misuse of the material that she had "empathically" gained from Ferenczi during her analysis.

Cooperating or not cooperating with a patient's demands depends on understanding the meaning of this behavior for the patient—the empathic component of the interaction. The psychotherapist is confronted with the situation where the patient equates empathy with obedience of any request he/she may make, and experiences a psychotherapist's refusal as unempathic at the time, even though such a refusal may be necessary. Indeed, the refusal may turn out to be one of the most important experiences in the patient's life. Such extreme situations, however, point to the need for auxiliary hypotheses in addition to the concept of empathy in order to conduct psychotherapy for a good outcome.

Summary

Although an epistemologically updated, intersubjective, constructionist view of Kohut's concept of empathy is the key postulate of a self psychology theory, empathic understanding was never intended to theoretically explain everything that happens in psychotherapy. This is clearly illustrated by the second postulate, the selfobject experience, a Kohutian construct used to explain the needs of narcissistic patients as a way of understanding them empathically. To this we turn as the subject of the next chapter.

CHAPTER THREE

Selfobject Experiences

In the early 1960s Miss F sought psychoanalysis from Heinz Kohut because of "diffuse dissatisfactions" (Kohut, 1968, pp. 503–8; 1971, pp. 283–93). Twenty-five years old, active in her profession, she had been unable to sustain a satisfying experience of emotional intimacy with anyone despite numerous social and love relationships. And although Miss F had a well-functioning peripheral self, her nuclear self was weak and isolated and made her feel a sham. Miss F had severe mood swings associated with a pervasive uncertainty about her feelings and thoughts, a secret sense of preciousness and superiority to anyone else, and states of emotional depletion and enfeeblement.

Miss F's mother and brother were a significant part of her personal history. During Miss F's childhood, her mother's depressive episodes meant that when Miss F tried to talk about herself, her mother deflected the topic to her own depressive self-preoccupations. Miss F's emotional needs were also rejected by her older brother, who bullied her and thrust himself into the limelight on every possible family occasion, deflecting parental attention away from anything that Miss F said or did.

The analytic sessions developed into a pattern. Miss F "would arrive in a friendly mood, would settle down quietly, and begin to communicate her thoughts and feelings about a variety of subjects: interactions at work, with her family, or with the man with whom she was currently on friendly terms. [She would also present] dreams and relevant associations, including tentative but genuine references to the transference. . . . In brief, the process of therapy had the appearance of a well-moving self-analysis" (Kohut, 1971, pp. 284–85)—at first.

Although the analysis seemed to be "on track" (Strozier, 2001, p. 208), as the period of Miss F's self-analysis became more protracted than usual, Kohut became increasingly bored. He says, "My attention would often lag, my thoughts began to drift, and a deliberate effort was required to keep my attention focused on the patient's communications" (Kohut, 1971, p. 285). At other times he wanted to argue with the patient after she rejected one of his interpretations. If he kept silent, about half way through the session Miss F would suddenly get violently angry with him for not supporting her. Kohut then learned to calm Miss F by summarizing what she said, but if he went beyond a summary and added an interpretation, Miss F would fly into a rage and "furiously accuse" Kohut of "wrecking the analysis." Eventually, after "a prolonged period of ignorance and misunderstanding" during which Kohut found she had no need for him as an instinctual object for a libidinal or aggressive "transference" [a target for love or hate feelings], he recognized that she "demanded a specific response to her communications, and that she completely rejected any other" (p. 285).

Kohut's response to Miss F, which he later termed "mirror," was an important experience for Kohut as well as Miss F. Kohut recognized she needed this special response, "an impersonal function" (Ornstein, 1978, p. 53) in which she made him her psychological "extension," and from which he was not allowed to deviate. Earlier in his life he had noted the possible influence of a mirror function from observing Aichhorn's skill at offering "himself as a mirror image of the delinquent's grandiose self" (Kohut, 1971, p. 163). Now, in experiencing the importance of this mirror function for Miss F, he realized the applicability of Aichhorn's approach to narcissistic patients and not just the adolescents that Aichhorn had treated. He, of course, had recognized that her need for this special response was connected to experiences of her mother and brother. He wrote,

> Whenever I did more (or less) than provide simple approval or confirmation in response to the patient's reports of her own discoveries, I became for her the depressive mother who . . . deflected the narcissistic cathexes from the child upon herself, or who did not provide the needed narcissistic echo. Or, I became the brother who, as she felt, twisted her thoughts and put himself in the limelight [1971, p. 288].

Significantly, Kohut had grasped that Miss F's motivation was not primarily a repetitive transference to him as a rejecting mother or brother, but a hungry seeking of approval and confirmation. And in having Kohut function as a mirror, Miss F formed a belief that if the mirror response could be consistently sustained, it would facilitate development of something that was missing in her nuclear self. Kohut had respected her need, responded to it, named it, and then experienced changes in himself and Miss F as a consequence.

In formulating this discovery, Kohut's theoretical understanding of psychoanalytic psychotherapy grew in two ways. He recognized the specific "mirror" function Miss F sought and then abstracted from his functional status as Miss F's psychological extension, which he labeled a "selfobject" function. Combining these two constructs of "mirror" and "selfobject," Kohut described his function for Miss F as a "mirror selfobject." This new, theoretical idea emerged because Kohut had persisted in seeking to understand Miss F from her point of view, consistent with his theory of empathy.

Before the case of Miss F, Kohut seems to have been influenced by Anna Freud (1968, 1970, 1976) and Greenacre (1971) who distinguished between the central pathology of the infantile neurosis—conflicts between id, ego, and superego structures—and central pathology of self-formation—in the pathology of self-deficits. This difference is crucial for successful results in psychotherapy, where the transferences of the neurotic conflicts make the therapist a target object for the dual drives of sex and aggression, and selfobject transferences which are sought to facilitate the formation of compensatory self-structures, thus enabling more self-cohesion and adaptability (M. Tolpin, 1978). In the context of a differentiation from the object of classical transference, the term selfobject makes sense. But now that the influence of classical analysis has waned, the need for a less technical way of depicting a selfobject function exists, although nothing has been accepted by self psychologists as a suitable substitute, as yet.

We shall now explore the extension of empathy into the idea of being a selfobject for narcissistic patients in three sections. Section A explains further Kohut's concept of a selfobject experience; section B covers specific narcissistic selfobject experiences; and section C explores the complementary nature of attachment and selfobject theories.

A. Kohut's Selfobject Experience

Michael Basch, a colleague of Kohut, highly valued Kohut's selfobject concept. After thirty years of psychoanalytic practice and fourteen years after the death of Kohut, Basch (1995) expressed the opinion that "Kohut's discovery and formulation of the selfobject is the most significant and first truly original extension of Freud's work" (p. 370). Many of Basch's Chicago colleagues agreed with him. Meares (1988) made a similar assessment (p. 237). Stated formally, Kohut's oft-quoted definition of a selfobject is that selfobjects are objects we experience as part of our self, and the expected control over them is, therefore,

> closer to the concepts of the control which a grownup expects to have over his own body and mind than to the concept of control which he expects to have over others and of his control of them [Kohut, 1971, p. 33].

Psychotherapists from competing theoretical positions, in attempting to diffuse the significance of Kohut's formulation of the selfobject concept, pointed to its antecedents, indirectly acknowledging its importance. Grotstein (1983), for example, claimed "the subject of selfobjects has a long history," and illustrated this with Freud's concept of "secondary identification" and the similar ideas of Klein and Fairbairn. Winnicott's concept of "transitional object" was also cited. Boyer and Giovacchini (1967), it was claimed, came close to Kohut's idea with their terms "adjunctive ego" and "alter ego." In response to attempts to minimalize the significance of the selfobject construct, Kohut and his colleagues, readily agreed that there were many selfobject antecedents but claimed the idea had achieved originality by being embedded in a new theory of narcissism. The self psychologist Terman (1980), for example, points to the great similarity between Balint's primary love and Kohut's concept of selfobject experience. But Balint's term did not take root in the soil of a Freudian theory of narcissism.

By making the selfobject concept an extension of the empathy postulate, Kohut enabled self psychology theory to grow into a new research program. As Kuhn (1962) points out, ideas may float around the periphery of an old paradigm (research program), but if these new ideas do not vigorously challenge the emotional attachment to old central postulates—in this situation beliefs used in psychotherapeutic practice—there is no change in the research program. Changes in research programs occur because of the acceptance of a new nuclear postulate that reorganizes the older beliefs, as occurred with Kohut's revised ideas of empathy and narcissism, and particularly his concept of a selfobject.

Kohut's discovery of the importance of the selfobject construct in the psychotherapy of Miss F and with narcissistic patients came about because Kohut accepted her as a "lehrmeisteren" ("teacher"). Portraying Miss F as teacher and Kohut as learner, presents Kohut as a twin to Freud's experience with his "lehrmeisteren." Freud's famous patient was Baroness Anna Von Lieben (Cacilie M.), a member of a large clan of eminent Austrian Jewish families, very rich, intelligent, sensitive, and literary (Swales, 1986). Von Lieben had been plagued for years with hallucinations, spasms, and the strange habit of converting insults or criticisms into severe facial neuralgias, virtual "slaps in the face." Freud said of von Lieben, "I have had the most tangled threads to unravel, especially in the case of Cacilie M (Freud 1905D, SE 2, 1905, p. 175). Freud's treatment of Anna von Lieben took place daily for some three years (Swales, 1986, p. 45).

Breuer, the devoted physician of Anna von Lieben's extended family, overloaded by the demands of his general practice and the treatment of Bertha Pappenheim (Anna O), arranged for Freud to treat Anna under his supervision (Swales, 1986, p. 26). The purpose was to have Freud ameliorate Anna von Lieben's symptoms using the cathartic method, as Breuer had successfully done with Bertha Pappenheim. With this method, Freud induced Anna to recount traumatic memories under hypnosis, with the expectation that her symptoms would diminish. Swales (1986) says, "For nearly three years, she relived, under [Freud's] guidance, all of the many traumas of her past life—all of them involving long-forgotten but now vividly reawakened and re-experienced with the most intense suffering" (p. 7). Sometimes Freud was successful in easing the symptoms, but even then, the relief would be short-lived.

In seeking a more permanent alleviation of her symptoms, Freud eventually sent Anna to Charcot, and then, during a study visit to Nancy (France), took her to see the hypnotist Bernheim. Both these famous healers were also unable to produce any significant changes. For Freud, his difficult-to-treat patient had become an interesting enigma. For example, he had the following to say about Anna von Lieben's facial neuralgia:

> Frau Cacilie suffered among other things from an extremely violent facial neuralgia which appeared suddenly two or three times a year, lasted from five to ten days, resisted any kind of treatment and these ceased abruptly. . . .Earlier in her life—the neuralgia was fifteen years old—her teeth were accused of being responsible for it. They were condemned to extraction, and one fine day, under narcosis, the sentence was carried out on the seven criminals. . . . Even at the time of my treatment, at each attack of neuralgia the dentist was called in. On each occasion he diagnosed the presence of diseased roots and began to get to work on them; but as a rule he was soon interrupted. For the neuralgia would suddenly cease, and at the same time the demand for the dentist's services. During the interval her teeth did not ache at all. One day, when an attack was raging once more, the patient got me to give her hypnotic treatment. I laid a very energetic prohibition on her pains, and from that moment they ceased. I began to harbor doubts of the genuineness of the neuralgia. [Freud, 1905D, pp. 176–77].

Associated with Anna von Lieben's distress was a severe, chronic insomnia, for which she had a chess player available outside her room each night. At times, unable to sleep, she would also summon her children in the middle of the night for companionship. When the chess, the children, or anything else did not comfort her, she would spend the night crying, screaming, and raving in a crisis that involved the whole household. Against this distressing background, Freud achieved an extraordinary rapport with her. Freud told Ferenczi, once, that after she became distressed and flung herself on the floor, if he lay on the floor with her it eased her distress. This kind of response by Freud probably provided what Kohut would later call a "twinship" selfobject experience (discussed later in this chapter).

With Anna von Lieben, Freud was in uncharted territory. At times, when Anna tired of exploring the past and refused to be hypnotized, Freud encouraged her to report whatever came into her mind. This is the method she came to prefer. And as this preference for freely associating relieved her distress as much as hypnosis or the carthartic method, Freud eventually made the procedure the major mode of treatment. Free association and psychoanalysis had been born! This did not mean that the analysis was successful. There are now doubts about how much Anna von Lieben gained from Freud's treatment. From Swales' investigation (1986) we learn that as treatment continued, "members of the family became ever more skeptical and had no confidence at all in what Freud was doing" (p. 54), so they "probably with Breuer's agreement, brought it to a halt" (p. 56).

With the benefit of a hundred years of clinical practice, we can see that Freud's treatment did not focus on the needs of Anna's nuclear self. We know, for example, that Freud had not yet discovered the importance of transference. Even if he had understood this phenomenon, he does not seem to have understood the extent to which Anna's "pathologic milieu *par excellence*" (Swales, 1986, p. 16) had burdened her and therefore, did not consider it as a major underlying source of distress. Perhaps of greater significance is Breuer's prescribing of morphine to relieve Anna's distress. So, what Freud reports as "acute hysteria, may have been associated with morphine withdrawal" (Swales, 1986, p. 46), and his giving her cocaine seems to have been an attempt at weaning her from the morphine. In view of these facts, which took several generations to become widely known, a convincing diagnosis is difficult. It is conjectured, for example, that Anna von Lieben, who died aged fifty-three from "myocardial degeneration," may have had a serious medical condition, such as chronic fatigue syndrome. It is also possible that Anna von Lieben suffered from a severe narcissistic disorder. If so, Freud, with his experimental efforts at twinship may have created a way to proceed with such patients, but as the technique was not theoretically undergirded with the concept of selfobject, it remained undeveloped until Kohut proposed his theory of narcissism.

Kohut's selfobject construct fits Lakatos's (1970) ideas about theory. If empathic understanding is the core Kohutian postulate involving major assumptions about knowing subjectively, the selfobject construct is an auxiliary postulate derived from it. It was created from clinical experiences with Miss F and other narcissistic patients. The selfobject construct functions as a guide for the psychotherapist to understand the behavior of narcissistic patients who experience the therapist as being empathic. So, after taking the view that empathic understanding is primarily the experience of the patient, not a quality of the psychotherapist, Kohut took the next crucial step of including the same subjective emphasis in understanding the selfobject function. The selfobject function of the psychotherapist, too, ultimately refers to the experience of the patient.

Functioning as a selfobject, although partially determined by the psychotherapist's personality and theoretical assumptions, is mostly the experience of the patient. This privileging of the patient's position in the initial stages of the psychotherapy also means that a patient's selfobject experience is greatly influenced by the patient's personality, including assumptions both formed and unformed. And although narcissistic patients may experience a psychotherapist as understanding them when functioning as a selfobject, other narcissistic patients may find a psychotherapist's selfobject attempts, sometimes due to poor timing, not only ineffective, but very non-empathic or even disturbing.

Kohut's selfobject construct has implications for the diagnosis of narcissistic disorders. The DSM IV-TR (Diagnostic and Statistical Manual of the American Psychiatric Association, Text Revision, 2000) diagnosis of narcissistic personality disorder is based on symptoms such as grandiosity, exhibitionism, indifference, rage, humiliation, emptiness, entitlement, interpersonal exploitiveness, or an inability to be empathic. By way of contrast, Kohut's discovery of the selfobject experience gave psychotherapists the opportunity to diagnose narcissism from the nature of the relationship a patient establishes with the psychotherapist. A hunger for mirroring—referred to as a narcissistic transference—that emerged as a result of Kohut's therapeutic relationship with Miss F, became evidence of the diagnosis of a narcissistic patient whether or not traditional symptoms were present. As other narcissistic transferences such as idealization and twinship, also may emerge during a therapeutic relationship, these too are considered as evidence of a narcissistic personality.

Diagnosis based on the nature of the therapeutic relationship (transference) is at variance with the model of diagnosing from symptoms, which are described in the DSM. As happened with other concepts, Kohut's diagnosing from the transference was not a new idea. It was used in classical psychoanalysis to diagnose neurotic disorders, based on a patient's need for the psychotherapist to be a target for libidinal or aggressive drives. Kohut simply expanded the concept of a transference-based diagnosis, just as he had expanded the Freudian idea of transference to include the narcissistic transferences. And Kohut's expansion invites ongoing expansion with regards to other clinical syndromes. As new kinds of psychotherapist/patient relationships are identified, understood, and responded to, patients presenting with other forms of psychopathology besides neurotic or narcissistic disorders, have the potential to stimulate the development of new theoretical constructs that will help guide a psychotherapist to be more empathic, as experienced by a patient.

One example of a seemingly failed attempt to expand the diagnosis by attending to transference was the project of Cohen and her colleagues (1954), who intensively studied twelve "manic depressive" patients. They sought to empathically understand the early "experiences with significant people that made it necessary for the prospective manic-depressive to develop the particular patterns of interaction, which comprise his character and his illness" (p. 104). We can only speculate why their work did not lead to fresh theoretical constructs. Perhaps it was because the constructionist and new hermeneutic ideas of such a philosopher as Gadamer had not yet taken hold in psychotherapy circles? It may have been that these psychotherapy researchers were still operating from a one-person model. Whatever the reason, syndromes where transferences are, as yet, dimly understood, means the possibility of fresh postulates eventually taking their place alongside the selfobject experience.

The postmodern analysts have labeled Kohut's self psychology a "one-person model" of psychoanalysis—mistakenly in our view. Classical analysis, for example, is a one-person model primarily focused on a patient's intrapsychic experience. A one-person model sees the patient's patterning of past experiences (transference) as the major shaping force of the psychotherapy. In contrast, psychotherapy with an emphasis on the intersubjective "here and now" experiences of psychotherapist and patient, is primarily a two person model, an idea proposed by Balint (1950) after being influenced by ideas expressed by Rickman (p. 123).

Aron (1996) takes the position that modern psychoanalytic psychotherapy is better understood as a relational theory that includes both one person and two-person perspectives. Aron's views are similar to Benjamin (1988). Where does self psychology theory fit into this framework? Aron (1996) views "self-psychology as an example of a contemporary 'relational' psychology that began as a one-person psychology" and remains that way for its "conservative practitioners" (p. 53). This coincides with the opinions of Shane, Shane, and Gales (1997) who stated that "Kohut's self-psychology [is] essentially a one-person psychology" (p. 28). They claim that Kohut's early concepts emphasized the intrapsychic more than other relational and self-psychology theorists, including the intersubjectivist Stolorow and possibly, the later Kohut.

Kohut's concept of a selfobject experience can be presented as a relationship that privileges the patient's point of view and where the psychotherapist's subjectivity is temporarily suspended when he or she becomes an extension of the patient. The postmodern analysts criticize this suspending of the psychotherapist's subjectivity (Teicholtz, 1999, p. 66). Teicholtz thinks that Kohut's selfobject function does not limit the psychotherapist's subjectivity, but rather presents an opportunity "in which the analyst selectively uses her subjectivity in the service of her affective resonance with an understanding of the patient" (p. 66). For a postmodern, the selfobject lens creates too narrow a view of a therapeutic relationship. But if privileging the patient's point of view is all that happens in a self-selfobject therapeutic relationship, then a one-person, intrapsychic model would be appropriate for self psychology. But, obviously Kohut's theory is more than the privileging the patient's subjectivity because, "at the heart of self-psychology, there is always an essential concern with the experience of relationship" (Teicholtz, 1999, p. 62).

According to Teicholtz (1999), the postmodern criticism of Kohut's selfobject theory (Aron, 1996), is that in it, the uniqueness of the analyst's character is irrelevant to the analytic process (p. 53). Benjamin (1990) who acknowledges Kohut's selfobject concept as relational thinks Kohut does not go far enough. So, there is a critical difference between Kohut and the postmoderns: for Kohut, parental affirmation of a child's feelings enables the child to accept the feelings of others; for postmoderns, the child recognizes a parent's subjectivity by virtue of the parent's insistence. Teicholtz (1999) thinks the postmodern "preoccupation with the analyst's subjectivity and self-disclosure is based on the conviction that development is generally facilitated by the encounter with the separate and different other" (p. 68), not a selfobject.

It seems that postmodern theorists are uncomfortable with Kohut's ideas because these presuppose a psychotherapist knows in advance what the patient will need (Teicholtz, 1999). They see the psychotherapist entering a therapeutic encounter with the expectation to provide preformed experiences ("techniques") such as mirroring, idealizing, or twinship and they complain that the number of selfobject concepts has been limited to these. But such a rigid interpretation of the selfobject concept does not do justice to Kohut's extensive discussions and illustrations from case material. From his material it is clear that his specific selfobject concepts overlapped and that the general concept of using the psychotherapist as a self-extension allows for many creative descriptions of selfobject functioning to emerge in response to a patient's need. In attacking Kohut's selfobject construct, postmoderns seem to have lost sight of the empathic attunement that these functions expressed.

Postmodern theorists also overlook Kohut's "archaic selfobject experience [as] optimally evolv[ing] through its own 'line of development' into a mature selfobject experience, which involves the recognition of the other's subjectivity through mutual empathy" (Teicholtz, 1999, p. 69). Once the patient experiences the psychotherapist as a mature selfobject, Kohut agrees that a patient's newly energized self-development will thrive from a non-shaming exposure to differences with the psychotherapist. In treatment where a patient seeks an archaic selfobject experience, the psychotherapist temporarily gives up his/her personal subjectivity for the needs of the patient. For a patient seeking an archaic selfobject experience, the postmodern recommendation of exposing him or her to the psychotherapist's subjectivity, will typically be experienced as traumatic and disruptive and may even increase a patient's paranoia. Not only do a patient's selfobject needs change with development, they vary from session to session, or even within a session where the need may take place only about a third of the time (see the 1989 Tronick and Cohn study detailed a little later).

A major difference between self psychology as a relational theory and other relational theories, particularly the interpersonal theory, lies with the different images of "self" of each model. Interpersonal relational theorists view interactions taking place between two differentiated selves (depicted by two closed, separate circles in Figure 3.1). This is a model of a healthy, symmetrical, adult-to-adult social relationship. In the self-selfobject relationship of self psychology, the therapeutic relationship is between a differentiated self, which functions as a selfobject depicted by a circle, and a non-differentiated self, depicted by a circle that overlaps the other circle (Figure 3.2). These overlapping circles are meant to depict a self-selfobject relationship. In a self-selfobject therapeutic relationship, the differentiated self helps the undifferentiated one to develop more differentiation by first using the differentiated one as a self-extension, and then by the psychotherapist accepting the steps the undifferentiated patient takes toward differentiation.

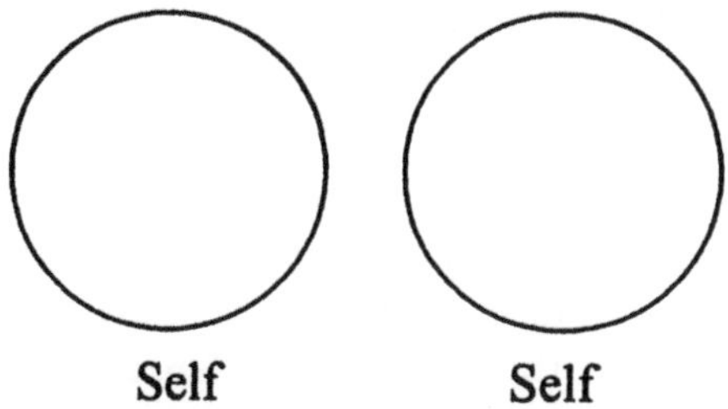

Figure 3.1. Interpersonal Relationship

The issue of whether self psychology is a one-person or two-person model spilled onto the floor of the twenty-ninth International Conference on the Psychology of the Self (Chicago, 2006). The panel speaker, heavily influenced by the interpersonal model of psychotherapy, claimed that self psychology was a one-person model. We believe this speaker demonstrated Chodorow's (1999) claim that the "criticisms of one-person psychologies may have been overdone" (p. 128). When the session opened for audience comments Marian Tolpin, a colleague and collaborator of Kohut, told the speaker bluntly that he "had plain gotten it wrong" because Kohut's self psychology was not a one-person but a two-person theory of psychotherapy that included essential elements of one-person theory. This essential element was the need, based on intrapsychic factors and not just the "here and now" interaction, to make the psychotherapist an extension of the patient's self, as a means of modifying the transference. As Tolpin spoke, other theorists lined up in support. By the time they finished the heart and soul of self psychology had convergently committed to a selfobject construct that helped form a special kind of two-person model.

In the selfobject construct, self psychology shifted the question from a "one- or two-person model," to "which two-person model is best conducive

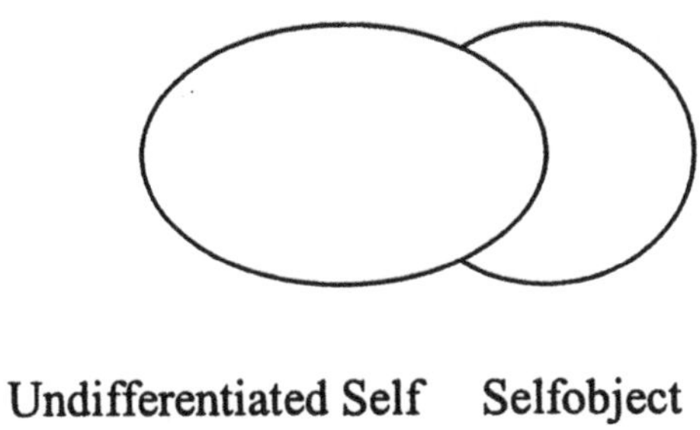

Figure 3.2. Self-selfobject Relationship

to psychotherapy." The self-selfobject relationship is a special dyad that emerges in a psychotherapeutic experience, and becomes a mutual self-object functioning (R. Lee, 1999) as the patient develops new self-structure. Goethe (1990) recognized such mutuality when he said, "All weaves itself into the whole, Each living in the other's soul" (p. 99). So, although a therapeutic relationship may commence as a one-person model out of a patient's archaic need, as the patient experiences a psychotherapist as a selfobject, he or she invariably eventually responds as a selfobject for the psychotherapist, albeit initially as a minor component of the dyad, to create a sense of mutuality. If a shift to mutuality does not occur, the patient may not be having a selfobject experience, or if the patient is, it may be fixated in an archaic form.

Beebe and Lachmann (2002) depict a turn-taking structure in healthy mother-infant relationships, which is illustrated by various coordination studies. Tronick and Cohn (1989), in an extremely important study of fifty-four mother-infant pairs, report that on the coordination of their behavior, "70 percent of the time of these interactions was spent in mismatch/dissynchronous states" (p. 90). Other studies summarized by Tronick and Cohn are "movements by [mother and infant] (Condon and Sander, 1974; Dowd and Tronick, 1986), gaze patterns (Perry and Stern, 1976; Daniel Stern, 1974), clusters of behaviors (Bakemann and Brown, 1977; Cohn and Tronick, 1987; Fafouti-Milenkovic and Uzgiris, 1979; Fogel 1977; Kaye and Fogel, 1980; Uzgiris, Benson, and Vasek, 1983), levels of engagement (Beebs and Gerstman, 1980; Lester, Hoffman, and Brazelton, 1985; Tronick, Als, and Brazelton, 1985)" (Tronick and Cohn, 1989, pp. 85– 86). All these point to levels of coordination between 30 percent and 40 percent and suggest that a healthy mother-infant dyad comes *not from a mother's continuous high level of attunement with the infant* (and psychotherapist with patient), but from a moderate level of engagement that fluctuates enormously, with lots of turn-taking and mutuality that enables both the patient and psychotherapist to have selfobject experiences. As Beebe and Lachmann (2002) indicate, "midrange scores of bidirectional coordination were optimal" (p. 102). So, in a therapeutic relationship in general and in sessions in particular, both psychotherapist and patient function as differentiated, and at other times, undifferentiated from each other.

Although Kohut discovered the selfobject construct in his treatment of patients, he soon resorted to an infant-mother model to explain it. In "The Two Analyses of Mr. Z" (1979), Kohut depicts a good early relationship in which his mother gave him "good-enough" selfobject experiences. As Strozier [2001] says,

> at twenty-two she [Else, Kohut's mother] was young and full of vitality when Heinz was born. She had an "intense relationship" with her little boy. As long as he remained a baby, the "interweaving of her with him" seemed to bring out her "healthiest attitudes." He was the "apple of her eye." This is quite clear from photographs of the period, as Kohut says in "Mr. Z." When in her arms, the "facial expression and general demeanor" of the boy is that of a healthy and happy baby [p. 12].

Kohut's description of his early experience of his mother is very similar to Daniel Stern's (1985) model of a mother and infant attuned to each other, during which there is some form of direct perception in both mother and infant, especially through the infant's ability to imitate the mother's face. Beebe and Lachmann (2002) make a strong case for an infant developing the capacity for pre-symbolic representations based on perceptions of the mother's gaze. Infants need this direct perception before the prefrontal areas, needed for inferential thinking, are developed, because their neural dendrites remain unmyelinated until approximately fifteen (right orbitofrontal lobe) to eighteen months (left orbitofrontal lobe). So to match the infant's perceptual state in the initial postnatal period, the mother must regress into a self-state that directly perceives the infant's state.

Investigators of the early mother-infant behavior have described in detail the chains and sequences of such attuned reciprocal behaviors as sucking, gazing, relief of distress such as teething, all of which become the medium for "dialogues" during an infant's first twelve months of life (see also M. Tolpin, 1997). During these "dialogues," the mother constantly imitates the infant's behavior with slight modifications, in a manner similar to a piece of classical music that repeats a theme with countless variations. So, in a mother-infant interaction both have experiences of patterns of invariance interspersed with experiences that are novel.

As an example of the early self-selfobject relationship, Daniel Stern (1974) studied the mutual gaze interactions between mothers and their four-month-old infants when they were attuned and responsive to each other. He found that an infant's initiation of gaze increases the likelihood that the mother will continue gazing, and that when mutual gazing occurs, it is more likely that the infant will be the first to gaze away. These observations suggest that *the needs of the infant* primarily determine mutual gazing patterns, and therefore, that the gazing is primarily—but not exclusively—for the infant's sake and reinforces the infant's experience of self-agency. Such a conclusion suggests that in successful psychotherapy, the relationship between the therapist and patient permits an evolving experience of mutuality while simultaneously privileging the selfobject needs of the patient.

A similar conclusion is reached about attunement and mutual influence in the sleep-awake studies of Chappell and Sander (1979). In these studies they demonstrate that in the first few weeks of infancy, the infant's pattern of sleeping, eating and wakefulness are very much affected by the mutual attunement between mother and infant. As Chappell and Sander describe it,

> The infant's wakefulness determines the activities of the mother, the activities of the mother determine in some degree the course of the infant's state over the interaction period, and the modifiability of the infant state by maternal manipulation determines the mother's further activities [p. 106].

In another mutual selfobject experiencing experiment, Beebe and Lachmann (1988) use split screen videotaping of the mother and infant to demonstrate the interactive pattern of "affective engagement." The results showed that mother and infant tended to match each other's engagement but not the actual level of engagement. They observe that both "match the direction of the engagement change, both increasing and decreasing. That is, mother and infant match where the other is going, tracking the process of change as it is happening, moment by moment" (pp. 12–13).

Kohut's concept of a selfobject was partially foreshadowed in the philosophical ideas of Buber (1937). A feature of Buber's theorizing was its relational rather than static thinking, and particularly its emphasis on two different relational experiences: the sacred (the "Thou") and the non-sacred (the "It"). These two experiences are depicted as "I-Thou" and "I-It" relationships. As taught in one theological seminary, Buber's concepts were interpreted to mean that the "I-Thou" experience resulted from living in relationship with God, and an "I-It" experience from living without God. In such a theological view, the "I-Thou" God experience was assumed to be good and the "I-It" experience bad. But do these assumptions of moral value stand up to scrutiny? As significant as these ideas were, they needed to be tested in the refining furnace of a therapeutic relationship. When they are, new theoretical understandings emerge.

Kohut's introduction of the selfobject construct challenges such a theological view of the "I-Thou" and "I-It" relational constructs. When a psychotherapist is experienced as a selfobject by the patient, the patient can experience the psychotherapist as a "Thou." During such an experience, the infant/patient is enlivened by an increased sense of powerfulness as the parent/therapist—functioning as a selfobject—primarily privileges the infant's/patient's needs and gives the infant/patient an experience of being the center of initiative. The infant/patient, in being privileged as a Thou, increases his or her experience of "I-ness" (self-awareness).

While this privileging of the infant/patient is taking place, what is the experience of the parent/therapist? In functioning as a selfobject the parent/therapist temporarily surrenders his/her functioning as an independent center of initiative and willingly tolerates being treated by the infant/patient as an "It." The parent's/therapist's experience of "It-ness" is accompanied by a temporary suspension of a feeling of "I-ness." The eventual goal of psychotherapy is the development of an increased capacity for an "I"-"I" relationship, or in Kohut's terms, an adaptive relationship between two robust selves. The formation of an "I"-"I" relationship, according to Kohut's thinking, is through the experiences of "Thou" and "It" relationships. As evidence accumulates that infants/patients are better able to develop "I-ness" when they have the "Thou-It" experience about 35 percent of the time, the usefulness of periods of not experiencing a "Thou" highlights the "Thou" experience. So, we characterize the therapeutic relationship as one in which "Thou-It" experiences are accompanied by "It-Thou" experiences, where the infant/patient functions as a selfobject for the parent/therapist (R. Lee, 1999).

A key difference with this selfobject view of "Thou"-"It" relationships is not that as many "Thou" experiences and as few "It" experiences as possible are needed for the development of healthy self-functioning. Both foster growth and development of a healthy, mature "I-I" relationship. For the experience of "Thou-ness" and "It-ness" assist and complement each other as they develop hand in hand to create an "I" who is a healthy, adaptive center of initiative. It is the "It" experience that highlights the special "Thou" experience, but it is also the privileged "Thou" experience that highlights the wonderful relief of a non-burdened, playful, "It" experience.

Once the key components of a therapeutic relationship are recognized as an alternating "Thou-It" relationship that eventually develops into an "I-I" relationship, it is possible to see how excessive "Thou" or "It" experiences, or insufficient "Thou" or "It" experiences, are detrimental to the development of a healthy experience of functioning as an "I," that is, a self in "I-I" relationships. The deleterious effects of excessive "It" experiences may be reflected, for example, in a schizophrenic's "influencing machine" as reported by Tausk (1933). And the deleterious effects of excessive "Thou" experiences may be seen in severe grandiose narcissistic disorders. The depleted "Thou" or "It" experiences may be seen in cases of severe depression.

What is needed in healthy human development is a balance of both "Thou" and "It" experiences.

So, the "I" experience of feeling alive and human comes from "good enough" selfobject experiences that create moderate, optimal levels of both "Thou" and "It" experiences. Having both "Thou" and "It" experiences in the moderate range, more sharply defines and helps shape an adaptive, healthy self. Unlike what is depicted in idealistic theology, the perfect "Thou" experience is neither good nor sufficient, for it is in relation to both a "Thou" and an "It" that a healthy, robust "I" develops. Such an idea was suggested by Winnicott's (1960) "good enough mothering," which resonates with this "Thou-It" interpretation.

To reiterate using the language of a self-selfobject relationship, when the patient experiences the psychotherapist as a self-extension, the patient feels more whole, more cohesive, more a center of initiative, and less of a thing; and the patient does not experience the psychotherapist as a differentiated self. For a patient to have a selfobject experience, the psychotherapist has to accept being a temporary "emotional servant," just as second Isaiah (Old Testament) saw the nation of Israel as the suffering servant of "Yaweh" (God). The acceptance of this selfobject function involves a psychotherapist's "decentering" (Piaget and Inhelder, 1969) from his or her self-interests to make the needs of the patient primary. The process also reinforces the psychotherapist's experience of being a thing—without self-agency. So, in enabling a patient to have a selfobject experience, the psychotherapist temporarily experiences *being less of a self and more of a thing as the patient experiences being less of a thing and more of a self*. This is like a transfer of selfhood feelings that temporarily loosens the psychotherapist's self-organization, while strengthening the patient's. In order to facilitate this experience, the psychotherapist relaxes his or her self-differentiation, while the patient relaxes his or her differentiation as a thing.

If in Lakatos's terms the concept of a selfobject is a Kohutian auxiliary postulate, and a derivative of the primary postulate of empathic understanding, the specific, experience-near concept of functioning as a "mirror" can be viewed as a specific form of the selfobject postulate. To such a mirror selfobject hypothesis, Kohut added other selfobject concepts such as idealization and twinship. We shall now examine more fully Kohut's key selfobject experiences that developed out of his concept of narcissistic transferences that he used during a transitional period when he was trying to reconcile his clinical observations with libido theory. These specific selfobject experiences are (1) a mirror selfobject experience, (2) an idealizing selfobject experience, and (3) a twinship selfobject experience.

B. Kohut's selfobject experiences

(1) A mirror selfobject experience

As a result of his clinical experiences with Miss F and other narcissistic patients, Kohut (1977) defined the mirror selfobject experience as

> the therapeutic reinstatement of that normal phase of the development of the grandiose self in which the gleam in the mother's eye, which mirrors the child's exhibitionistic display, and other forms of maternal participation in and response to the child's exhibitionistic enjoyment confirm the child's self-esteem and, by gradually increasing selectivity of these responses, begin to channel it into realistic directions [p. 116].

In psychotherapy this mirror response is often appropriate when patients joyously share some achievement or news with the psychotherapist. Congratulating a patient for some achievement enables the psychotherapist to participate in the patient's joyousness, the "exhibitionistic display" that Kohut mentions in his definition. Mirroring is not a technique by a psychotherapist but a joyous, affirming, intersubjective, participation.

One reason for mirroring a patient's achievements is that without this a patient may remain in an over-stimulated state. A persisting overstimulated state not only heightens grandiose feelings and expectations, but may also lead to manic-like states, chaotic behavior, and self-destructive, shameful experiences. Repeated experiences of non-mirrored exhibitionism may result in significant feelings of boredom, deflation, and depression. This may have happened to Kohut's (1971) Mr. I who reports a dream: "[I am] on a dock fishing, caught a big fish still on a pole, carried it into the cottage to show it to Dad, and probably to Mom too. Expected him to say, 'Good fish.' He said, 'You clean it.' I didn't want to; just wanted to show it. The fish then shriveled up a bit as a result of the conversation." In associating to the dream, Mr. I indicated that he had brought some diaries in a previous session to the analyst, who had focused too much on their content, instead of saying, 'very interesting' and admiring (mirroring) them. Then Mr. I added, "No sense in bringing these in; you didn't admire them."

The purpose of appropriate mirroring is to transform a patient's narcissistic investment in his achievements into wholesome pride, which leads to sustained self-esteem and to internal structures that regulate affects and "discipline" behavior. There is much popular literature on self-discipline that implies it can be taught or enforced through the "setting of limits." Yet Kohut clearly understood that the basis of self-discipline is a successful mirroring experience that fosters wholesome pride and realistic ambitious goals.

Fonagy et al. (2002) in their empirical research supports Kohut's emphasis on the importance of a parent's mirroring of an infant because faulty mirroring can derail development and lead to insecure attachment behavior. Kohut sees faulty mirroring by parents or psychotherapists as producing addictive-like states. Criticism of Kohut's mirror construct is usually based on, or is at least supported by the classical Freudian theory of gratification, which holds that an unfettered libidinal drive gratification leads to addiction.

In answering these critics, Kohut stated that a mirror selfobject experience does not lead to addictive states but to new self-structuralizations that reorganize the self. This reorganizing eventually reduces the necessity for mirroring and hence the tendency toward addiction. Meares (2004) has warned "a literal understanding of Kohut's definition, [of a selfobject] . . . leads to the danger of addiction to certain responses of the other" (p. 56). Regarding such a danger, we accept that if "mirroring" is mistakenly thought of as a technique and not as the experience of the patient, it may well lead to an addictive need for further mirroring. But, to repeat, Kohut never understood selfobject functioning as a technique of the psychotherapist, but rather as a participatory response that the patient experiences as empathic.

A fear of gratifying a patient is a remnant of the Freudian theory of narcissism. Just as Freud thought that all narcissism was pathological, so Freudians have traditionally seen a patient's need for continuous, immediate gratification as pathological and hence as leading to addictive states. And just as Kohut saw narcissism as having both pathological and transforming dimensions, so he saw that narcissistic gratification could either become pathologically addictive or a move toward creative self-development. In taking the theoretical step of conceiving a "mirror transference," Kohut broadened the Freudian notion of gratification to include both addictive and growth-promoting potentials. Empathic responsiveness leads to a deeply satisfying gratification that is not addictive. Replying to the Freudian claim that gratification leads to malignant regression (M. Balint, 1968), Bacal (1985) points out that malignant regression and fragmentation come from persistent, catastrophic selfobject failures, not from gratifying the patient. To Kohut, a patient's archaic merger with the therapist is a desperate regressive defensive act to prevent a dangerous state of fragmentation, not a selfobject function.

The issue of gratification was central to Mr. O who presented for psychotherapy feeling defeated and depressed, after struggling for seven years to make his childless marriage work. His wife, who had found another man, was seeking a divorce. After he developed an idealizing transference, he began to feel better despite taking several years to reach a divorce settlement with his wife. He reported that during the last year prior to their breakup, both he and his wife had engaged in a lot of sex, apparently to keep themselves cohesive. He thought, however, that his addictive craving reflected his lack of deep gratification from sexual experiences. This belief was strengthened when he eventually dated another woman who was empathic and functioned as a selfobject for him. Fearing a new sexual addiction, he reluctantly became sexually involved, but soon discovered that sexual experiences with her were "deeply" satisfying and his addictive sexual craving diminished. His new partner's functioning as a selfobject had changed how he experienced sexual behavior with her.

Clinical experience with nonsexual issues has shown that what is mirrored by the therapist will aggravate or attenuate a patient's addictive behavior. For example, narcissistic patients with a hunger for mirroring will often present their hopes or general plans in the expectation of pleasing the psychotherapist, and of being congratulated or praised. In some of these patients a pattern will emerge where achievements, even minor ones, are never presented, and it becomes obvious that the patient is presenting future plans as a substitute for here-and-now achievement. Such a strategy reflects an addiction-like state of a patient, who as a child, developed a "mirror hunger" when parents were not attuned to his/her needs. In such a transferance, a psychotherapist's mirroring a stream of vague future plans fosters the patient's grandiosity rather than promoting real-world achievement. A "wait and see" response with such a patient's plans encourages some achievement, and then by affirming these small achievements rather than great plans, such patients are helped to grow. Mirroring grandiose plans discourages personal growth and eventually makes the patient more susceptible to intense shame. Kohut's mirror response also rejects the "technique" of flattery, which is not only inauthentic, but also stimulates grandiosity that discourages therapeutic change.

Even if accomplishments are mirrored, this narrowing may not lead to an increased sense of self-agency. Again, it is a matter of what is mirrored. As indicated previously (Lee and Martin, 1991), in one example a boy "was taken by his mother to swimming, skating, tennis and piano lessons each week. As small, significant progress was made in these areas, she praised and affirmed him for the increased skill." This was indeed an example of a child who experienced his mother as a selfobject when he conformed to her wishes. "When, however, using pillows, cushions and blankets, he [playfully] created his own cubby house [for a couple of hours] within the living room of his home and sought her praise, it was not forthcoming. He was, in fact, rejected for 'making a mess'" (p. 138). She would not affirm his self-agency or his creativity, only his need to please her. So, what is mirrored and not mirrored helps shape self-organization.

(2) An Idealizing Selfobject Experience

Just before the Orient Express left the Vienna railway station on June 3, 1938, the platform was empty, except for a few people saying goodbye to relatives or friends. In one small group, Sigmund Freud and his party were being fare-welled as they headed for London. The Viennese psychoanalytic community had not been told of Freud's departure to prevent a large station gathering and avoid attracting the attention of the Gestapo, who had agents there, watching. Heinz Kohut, accompanied by a friend, was there and, as the train began to move, "Kohut, who had held himself back up to that point, walked up to Freud's compartment, caught his eye, and tipped his hat. Freud graciously took off his traveling cap and waved back at Kohut" (Strozier, 2001, p. 58).

Although few knew of Freud's departure, his personal friend August Aichhorn did, and shared this with his analyst and Kohut, knowing as he did that Kohut idealized Freud. Kohut's experience of Freud's departure from Vienna made an enormous impression on him, and he never tired of telling the story. And the idealization of Freud, which faded with time but never completely disappeared, eventually helped motivate Kohut to master Freud's theory and to move into the leadership ranks of the U.S. psychoanalytic community. So Kohut had not only experienced and appreciated the value of idealization, but was supported by the knowledge that Freud too had needed an idealized relationship with persons throughout his life (Gay, 1988, p. 141): Brucke, Meynert, Fleischl-Marxow, Charcot, Breuer, and Fliess.

From a statement Kohut made upon Aichhorn's death, it is evident that Kohut had idealized Aichhorn too. Kohut (1949) says, "I can speak as one of those who have known him personally as psychotherapist and teacher, but above all as a warm, vigorously living human being" (p. 131). As valuable as Kohut's idealizations of Freud and Aichhorn seem to have been, the most significant aspect of his analysis with Aichhorn may have been Kohut's "twinning" Aichhorn's use of his adolescent patients' idealization of him to bring about therapeutic change. This suggests that Kohut began his psychoanalytic career with some possible reservations about the classical psychoanalytic understanding of idealization as a "reaction formation" to an underlying aggression before he developed the "mirror selfobject" concept while working with Miss F.

Once Kohut's idea of a "mirror selfobject" emerged during his case of Miss F, idealization became his second selfobject function. Kohut (1971) thought that the idealizing transference was an attempt to save "a part of the lost experience of global narcissistic perfection by assigning it to an archaic, rudimentary (transitional) selfobject, the idealized parental imago" (p. 37). Stated less technically, Kohut viewed idealization as a hunger to overcome arrested development from the lack of structuralization of positive experiences. His colleague Basch (1988) defined the idealizing therapeutic relationship (transference) as

> one's unrequited longing to be strengthened and protected when necessary by an alliance with an admired, powerful figure. . . . It is the need to be united with someone one looks up to, and who can lend one the inspiration, the strength, and whatever else it takes to maintain the stability of the self system when one is endangered, frustrated, or in search for meaning [p. 14].

The major characteristic of a patient's idealization of a psychotherapist is its silent quality, at least in the beginning of the psychotherapy. This silent idealization reflects the experience of a selfobject's availability and perfection being taken for granted. The idealizing experience is not verbalized by the psychotherapist because if it becomes explicit, thereby objectified, its vitalizing ability is diminished. Toward the end of a long psychotherapy, some realistic objectification of the idealization will have occurred; it assists in the internalization of the psychotherapeutic experience. But the most characteristic sign of a silent idealization is a patient's increased energy and vitality in everyday life soon after the psychotherapy gets underway. The patient's complaints of distress diminish; he or she reports feeling better.

Kohut's (1971) case of Mr. A, a young man in his mid-twenties, illustrates the hunger for an idealizing therapeutic relationship. Although Mr. A's presenting complaint was having a sexual attraction to men, Kohut soon realized that Mr. A's homosexuality "occupied a rather isolated position in his personality" (p. 57). He was suffering from depression, general lack of zest, a sensitivity to criticism, and low self-esteem, all signs of a "broad personality defect." Mr. A had a history of searching for an idealized person among those in authority over him and from whom he could obtain guidance and approval. If these idealized figures seemed disappointed by him, Mr. A became drained and depressed, then defensively cold and haughty and no longer productive.

Mr. A's overriding childhood experience was of disappointment in his powerless father. The family had been forced to flee Europe prior to World War II, when Mr. A was nine years of age. In the United States, as the father failed in one business venture after another, always selling the business out of panic, Mr. A had noted the difference between his father's high ambitions and his actual failed performances. There was no question in Kohut's mind that Mr. A was profoundly disappointed in his idealized father. "Whenever A. was disappointed in figures of authority in his life, or in Kohut himself in the transference, he became cold and haughty, adopted certain odd speech patterns, and combined a manifest sense of superiority with self consciousness, shame, and hypochondria" (Strozier 2001, p. 204)—manifestations of the grandiose self.

In the case of Mr. A we see not only a hunger to idealize, but also a hunger for Kohut to twin him and mirror him. Kohut (1971) says,

> in the transference manifestations of his specific structural defect, he seemed insatiable in two (tyrannically and sadistically asserted) demands that he directed toward the idealized analyst: (a) that the analyst share the patient's values, goals, and standards [twin him] (and thus imbue them with significance through their idealization); and (b) that the analyst confirm through the expression of a warm glow of pleasure and participation [mirror him] that the patient had lived up to his values [p. 62].

This paradigm case of idealization is a clear illustration that any combination of Kohut's three selfobject transferences can arise during psychotherapy. A careful reading of Kohut leads to the general concept of selfobject experiences where the psychotherapist is an extension of the patient that promotes structuralization. There is little to be gained, therefore, from attempting to determine precise differences among these three narcissistic transferences. They are generally combined in one way or another.

In emphasizing the potential value of an idealizing transference for facilitating psychotherapy, Kohut did not abandon the idea that idealization could be a defense against aggression. In some cases it was. But Kohut thought that in overgeneralizing idealization as reaction formation, classical Freudians failed to grasp the basic need of narcissistic patients to use idealization of authority figures as a source of vitalization. In self psychology theory, when the idea of an idealizing transference was proposed, the classical view of idealization as the reaction formation of aggression was retained and became incorporated in self psychology theory as defensive idealization (Kohut 1971, 75).

A common sign of defensive idealization is the patient's open admiration of the psychotherapist. One such patient, Mr X, told the psychotherapist how brilliant he was in the second session. He had come into the psychotherapy because of his provocative wife whom he claimed he loved dearly. Having used the MMPI (Minnesota Multiphasic Personality Inventory) (1975) to test patients over many years, the psychologist/psychotherapist envisaged this patient as scoring high on the over-controlled hostility (O-H) scale (Megargee, Cook, and Mendelsohn, 1967). This scale had been derived from testing model prisoners who had been jailed for killing someone they had seemingly idealized, but then killed after erupting with pent-up, murderous rage from a silently endured, long-standing intolerable situation. In prison, they were well-behaved and cooperative. Mr. X's avowed idealization of his wife, despite her intense provocations, suggested that his idealization was a defensive function that helped contain the expression of his anger that he was using to keep himself cohesive. The psychotherapist then realized the patient's idealization of him was a repetitive transference manifestation of his experiences with his wife and others. The defensive nature of the transference was eventually explored when it was appropriate, based on the patient's presenting material, and this set the stage for the patient to grow from the positive experiences of the therapeutic relationship.

The emergence of a genuine idealizing transference may also trigger a repetitive defensive idealization. Miss D came for psychotherapy because she wanted to increase her self-esteem. In the initial sessions it appeared that Miss D was bonding to the psychotherapist and developing a silent idealization. Before long, however, she began to report increasing feelings of inferiority, and a pattern emerged that the more she idealized the psychotherapist, the worse she felt. This was puzzling because it was not the vitalization that is expected from a Kohutian type of narcissistic transference.

Exploration with the patient soon revealed that the bond had triggered a repetitive transference of being humiliated by a defensively idealized parent. Her low self-esteem and intense feelings of inferiority were residues of those early childhood experiences. This case also illustrates the potential therapeutic potency of the twinship experience. After the patient's fear of repeated humiliation experiences was openly acknowledged, the psychotherapist was able to gradually share some of his own experiences of being humiliated in the past and, as a twinship relationship developed, the defensive idealization diminished.

Defensive idealization is an idea close to the Old Testament concern about idols and idolization. As depicted by Tillich (1953), idolization is the worship of something static or dead in comparison with the Hebrew concept of a living God who spontaneously reveals to humans and is not captured or controlled in a concrete form. Applied to a clinical case, a conceptual connection between idealization and idolization occurred when P, a female patient who had been severely rejected by her father whom she had not idealized, transformed her archaic narcissism as a result of psychotherapy and relationships outside the nuclear family. Through focusing on education, P entered university and successfully functioned as a professional, whereas her brother, who idealized the father and went through eight years of psychoanalytic stagnation, was unable to moderate his obsessive-compulsive symptoms. What, we ask, prevented this idealization from becoming a growth-producing, selfobject experience for her brother? Why was the idealization so static that it could be called idolization?

The patient P reported that although her father never affirmed or mirrored his children, she was not troubled by this because she sought mirroring from teachers and others. But her brother developed his obsessive-compulsive symptoms because although he idealized his father, his father never mirrored him. There was not a reciprocal interaction that involved an intersubjective relationship of idealization and mirroring. This suggests that a "technique" of mirroring without idealization, or idealization without mirroring belong to the limitations of a one-way communication of a one-person system. Idealizing and mirroring experiences become more enlivening and growth-enhancing when they are experienced as elements of a unique, interactive two-person system of complementary selfobject functions. As the philosopher Macmurray (1957 [1991]) affirms, personal growth occurs through relationships of deep relational communication. A similar intersubjective view can be taken of the twinship selfobject experience, as discussed in the next subsection.

An idealizing transference can trigger countertransference problems. If a patient develops an idealizing selfobject transference that leads to increased structuralization, when the need for it recedes, a psychotherapist may resent feeling abandoned by the patient, or even feel belittled for no longer being valued. The basis of such resentment may be the tendency to believe that the idealization was a realistic response to him/her as a person. An idealizing transference can overstimulate and inflate a psychotherapist's grandiosity. In another case, when the patient began talking about termination, the psychotherapist became hurt, angrily rejected the patient, and negated many of the therapeutic gains. Exploration of the psychotherapist's feelings in supervision led to the conclusion that she was reenacting the mother's envious attack on her for idealizing the father and emotionally abandoning her, the mother.

Kohut advocated neither encouraging nor preventing idealization. He saw encouraging a patient's idealization as a reflection of the psychotherapist's need for being idealized, not the patient's need, hence a form of manipulation. He also thought that explaining to the patient that idealization was "resistance," in the traditional Freudian manner, not only reflected a misunderstanding of the idealizing transference but tended to discourage and squash it. He thought too that a psychotherapist's sense of shame, if too excessive, could discourage an idealizing transference. He (Kohut and Wolf, 1978) gave the example of the little boy, eager to idealize his father, and wanting to hear of his life, the battles won or lost, and whenever the boy asks, is reacted to with embarrassment. Clearly, patients seeking an idealizing transference reveal a need for psychotherapists to work within the framework of Kohut's psychology of the self.

(3) A Twinship Selfobject Experience

Among the first 1,000 children from German concentration camps admitted into Great Britain at the end of WWII, were six very young orphans from Thieresienstadt, Moravia. As these orphans were bonded to each other, they were given a year's transitional experience in a peaceful Sussex country home next to Bulldogs Bank woodland, under the care of Anna Freud and two experienced child nurses, Sophie and Gertrude Dann. As the gas chambers took the lives of their parents—and subsequently their overworked, undernourished substitute parents—these children were, at first, understandably distrustful of their caretakers. Yet as Anna Freud observes, "It was evident that they cared greatly for each other and not at all for anybody or anything else" (A. Freud and Dann, 1951, p. 131). As an example of their sibling-like caring, when John kicked and screamed and refused to get up one morning, Ruth, another child, brought his clothes while Miriam offered him her doll in a soothing gesture and with a sweet smile. After this John calmed down. Such observed interactions suggest that when parents or parent substitutes are absent, toddlers are able to use peers as selfobjects (R. Lee, 1988, p. 417). Inadvertently, Nazi totalitarianism had created an experimental sibling group without parental continuity amid a traumatic milieu (Young-Bruehl, 1988). Bettleheim reports similar peer group bonding—hence selfobject experiences—among children of Israeli kibbutzim (Bettleheim, 1969).

Young-Bruehl, Anna Freud's biographer, thinks that observations of the children at Bulldogs Bank challenged theoretical beliefs about trauma. She (1988) reminds us that "according to the assumptions of Melanie Klein's prewar work and to those of John Bowlby, who had . . . written about 'separation anxiety' and children's responses to a 'rejecting mother,' the kind of deprivations the Thereisenstadt children had endured should have been massively pathogenic" (p. 321). Yet to the observant Anna Freud (Freud and Dann, 1951), these children were not. Anna indicates that although they were "hypersensitive, restless, aggressive, difficult to handle" and "showed heightened autoeroticism. . . . they were neither deficient, delinquent nor psychotic." She then adds "that they were able to acquire a new language [English] in the midst of their upheavals, bear witness to a basically unharmed contact with their environment" (p. 168). Why, then, were these children, raised in the most horrible of circumstances, so open to learn, despite their distrust of adults? The evidence points to learning to trust each other and use each other in what Kohut describes as a "twinship selfobject experience."

What is a twinship selfobject experience? Kohut says this is "where the patient assumes that the analyst is like him or that the analyst's psychological makeup is similar to his" (Kohut, 1968, p. 489). Winnicott (1945) may have been close to this idea when he referred to a mother and child unit who "live an experience together" (p. 152). Detrick (1985) calls twinship an experience of sameness, a view confirmed by a letter from Kohut that mentions the "alikeness" selfobject experience (p. 241). We think the major component of twinship consists of sharing subjective experiences, especially affect states. Adorno (1973) had a similar idea that he called "mimesis," which was identifying with the other person by becoming like them in their imagination. It is also close to the Japanese idea of "amae" (Doi, 1971) where a person has a feeling of being emotionally close to another who has a similar reciprocal feeling. When twinship transference emerges in psychotherapy, the patient wants to be like the psychotherapist, in the sense of feeling what the psychotherapist is feeling, or wants the psychotherapist to experience what the patient is feeling. The patient seeks a twinship in order to feel connected to another through shared feelings, to be less lonely, and to have an increased sense of a cohesive nuclear self-organization.

A twinship experience can result from shared thinking, doing, and feeling. On the matter of doing, one can read Kohut's (1984) account of a patient who, as a little girl of four years of age, silently kneaded dough on a little table alongside of a big table on which her grandmother was kneading dough (p. 197). Yet what commenced as a "sameness of doing" with the grandmother, turned into a feeling experience. For when her nuclear family moved away from this grandmother, the intensely lonely girl developed the image of a genie in a bottle. She claimed that this captive in the bottle was a twin, just like herself, a silent presence, "who would keep her company and made it possible for her to survive the hours of loneliness." As Kohut reports, "Just being together with the twin in silent communion was often the most satisfactory state" (p. 196). And one can read Kohut's other example where a little boy "shaves" alongside his daddy or is sustained by working next to his daddy with his daddy's tools. These examples indicate that Kohut's concept of twinship was close to the Freudian concept of identification, an idea akin to cloning. It is more than just imitating another person in the peripheral self, however, because imitating can be a conforming acquiescence that does not lead to experiences of sameness in the nuclear self. So twinship experiences do require an experience of idealization.

For Kohut, the major consequence of an idealization and mirroring reciprocal process is vitalization, stronger cohesion, and increased adaptability of the idealizer. It is a distinctive feature of Kohut's thinking that idealization could vitalize without identification taking place. He recognized that for some patients, viewing someone else as being "wonderful" motivates them to develop their own center of initiative, a view in line with Freud's (1919) comment that mentoring "must always be done with great caution, and the patient should be educated to liberate and fulfill his own nature, *not to resemble ourselves* [italics added] (p. 165)." Even so, for others, idealization includes an element of twinship, where persons seek to be like someone else, and this combination of both idealization and twinship seems to cover much of what has been conceptualized in the past as identification. The key element in wanting to be like someone is twinship, however, not idealization. Twinship is an experience of sameness.

Is the experience of sameness a selfobject experience? By sameness we mean that a patient experiences the psychotherapist sharing in what he or she is experiencing. This sameness may be experienced as sharing similar feelings, thinking similar thoughts, or holding similar nuclear values. After all, this experience of emotional sameness was what Miss F sought from Kohut in the paradigmatic case of mirroring, and what Mr. A in the paradigmatic case of idealization also needed. It is what Freud found worked with Von Lieben when nothing else would. Furthermore, Kohut (1987) gives Greenson's example of a patient sigh. "The patient sits down, very depressed. And after a long silence he sighs deeply. The psychotherapist waits a while, and then he too sighs deeply" (pp. 67–68). Based on the patient's need for the psychotherapeutic experience of sameness, we argue that the twinship selfobject experience is developmentally the earliest developmentally of the Kohutian selfobject experiences, as does Michael Basch. Basch (1992) says,

> My clinical experience leads me to agree with Douglas Detrick (1986) that the most basic of these three is the alter ego or twinship experience. I prefer to call this the "kinship experience" because it asserts and strengthens the sense of being a member of a group—the acceptance of "being like" the other [p. 17].

There are examples in the literature of twinship experiences in psychotherapy before Kohut, but the experience was given increased recognition in the context of Kohut's theory of narcissism and selfobject functioning. Freud seemed to have created such a twinship experience when, as mentioned earlier, he lay on the floor in response to his patient, Von Lieben, flinging herself on the floor in distress. It had a calming effect. Another example was Lindner's (1955) patient, the atomic scientist Kirk Allen, in the "the jet propelled couch" case. In twinning Kirk, Lindner entered Kirk's delusional world of traveling through space to visit planets. Eventually Kirk told Lindner that he was worried about Lindner, as he believed Lindner was losing his mind. When Lindner asked Kirk what the signs were for Lindner's madness, Kirk said, "I think you are beginning to believe this rubbish about inter-planetary travel." Through twinning Kirk, Lindner had succeeded in inducing him to leave his delusions behind, because twinship experiences, as a special kind of social experience, and delusions are incompatible. But an even more extreme use of twinship is Jonathon Lear's description of animal trainer Vickie Hearne's treatment of Bandit, a mad pit bull terrier who incessantly dug holes in the back yard. Hearne got down on her hands and knees next to Bandit—and dug a hole. She dug longer than Bandit, and deeper, and just as often. Bandit, of course, got bored and let Ms. Hearne have the symptoms to herself (Lindner, 1955, 1982, p. xiv). In this example, it is possible that mirror neurons, mentioned in the previous chapter, enabled this communication to take place between an animal and a human. So, these examples suggest that the more broadly the concept of twinship is understood, the more creative the twinship experiences that will become a part of clinical literature.

Not all twinship experiences are selfobject experiences. Just as with mirror or idealizing experiences, a patient's twinship experience can shift from defensively attempting to ward off the threat of self-fragmentation, into a dangerous attempt at psychologically merging with the psychotherapist. So, if a defensive form of mirroring tends to be addictive, and a defensive mode of idealization attempts to mask hostility, *an archaic defensive manifestation of twinship seeks to be exactly like the psychotherapist in every sector of the psychotherapist's self*, in effect, to become the psychotherapist, so as to avoid the dangers of extreme fragmentation. With a patient's need for merger and absolute control, Kohut thinks twinship can turn into an archaic merger experience as a last line of defense against a psychotic break. It is a defense against Balint's (1968) "malignant regression," and against Menninger's (1963) "ego [self] rupture" (p. 222). Such malignancy is signaled by a patient's desperate dependence on the psychotherapist in an extreme hunger for a merger experience, twenty-four hours a day, seven days a week. Of such behavior Kohut (1987) says, "If one expects to be taken in totally by the other person, then it can only lead to tyrannical demands without any regard to the reality of the situation or to the other person's readiness or capacity to respond" (p. 85).

One example of a person regressing into such a malignant merger state was the desperate, unfortunate woman in the movie "Fatal Attraction." Treatment of such patients makes "limits" a major therapeutic focus. The therapeutic art is to negotiate arrangements so that the negotiating process eventually produces constructive growth (R. Lee, 2004). A key to treating these patients lies in turning the hunger for twinship, in these extreme cases of defense against fragmentation, into a therapeutic advantage. In a primitive regressed state, a patient's need for twinship results in unconsciously imitating a psychotherapist's behavior, so that whatever the psychotherapist feels and does, the patient matches. In a primitive regressed state, this imitating twinship can be used to develop interpersonal boundaries. This, however, is easier said than done.

Limiting a patient's access to the psychotherapist with the interpretation that "Its for your good"—which the patient experiences as control—results in the "borderline" patient trying to control the psychotherapist even more, because the patient in such a regressed state will imitate a psychotherapist's behavior. Seen from the outside, such patient behavior is generally considered resistance. Understanding that such patients are defensively merging with the psychotherapist rather than resisting, presents an opportunity for inducing change in the patient. In these critical merger moments, the psychotherapist's forbearance in gently but firmly insisting on limits to *preserve himself or herself* (not the patient), demonstrates the psychotherapist's capacity to do so for his/her own benefit. The psychotherapist's behavior eventually encourages a regressed patient to do likewise and limit himself/herself, despite lots of complaining in succeeding sessions. One of the major signs of an increasing imitating of the psychotherapist is when the patient begins setting limits on intrusive friends.

Although Kohut conceived of the twinship selfobject experience during the 1960s, it was not until his posthumously published book *How Does Analysis Cure* (1984) that the twinship selfobject experience was given a more prominent role in his theory. It has become particularly useful in the treatment of the more severely disturbed self-disorders, such as borderline states. Patients with severe self-disorders often present for psychotherapy wanting the psychotherapist to have a twinship experience of them. If, for example, the patient's experienced heavy and constant criticism growing up, the patient often criticizes the psychotherapist. It's a way of cocreating a relationship with the psychotherapist that the patient had experienced with a parent, only this time the parental role is played by the patient, and the psychotherapist is cast in the patient's role as a child. In effect, the patient creates his or her feelings of growing up in the psychotherapist, rather than telling the psychotherapist about it. This is called a "reverse twinship experience" (R. Lee, 1988, 1999), an idea we will return to in the last chapter.

Just as with the reciprocal process of idealizing and mirroring in an intersubjective relationship, so twinship and reverse twinship experiences also become involved in transactions that enables a patient's growth and self development as a forward momentum takes place in the therapeutic relationship. Twinship can be understood as a two-way relationship in a special two-person system that selfobject experiences create.

That a twinship experience can be a powerful therapeutic tool is suggested by an incident at the 1992 Olympic Games (*USA Today*, 2 August 1996). British runner Derek Edmond's 400 meter semi-final race is officially recoded as "race abandoned." Halfway through the race he fell with a ripped hamstring muscle, but then got up, his face contorted with pain, and defiantly hobbled along the track as the race ended. The stadium became deathly quiet. Minutes passed. With one hundred yards to go, his father Jim bolted from the stands and put his arm around his son, and said, "You don't have to do this. You don't have anything to prove." Tears streaming down his face, Derek stubbornly said, "Dad, I'm going to finish. I have to finish the race." So Jim said, "Well, we've started everything together. We'll finish this together. So with the father supporting his son—a "human crutch"—the two slowly walked to the finishing line, while the whole sporting world felt a lump in its throat. What a powerful story! In his twinship selfobject experience, it is no wonder that Kohut discovered a power to heal.

C. The Complementarity of Selfobject and Attachment Theories

Based on the early studies of Burlingham and Anna Freud (1942, 1944) and Spitz (1945, 1946), modern attachment theory, as developed by Bowlby (1969, 1973, 1980), Ainsworth and colleagues (1978) and Main (1996), can creatively engage and complement selfobject theory. This is because, as Orange (1995) points out, "self psychologists and attachment researchers share a common central belief in the overriding importance of the tendency of human beings to form strong emotional bonds to individual others" (p. 172) very early in development. Like the attachment theorists, Kohut believed an attachment bond was "critical in infancy, when young children are helpless and totally dependent on caregivers for maintaining and reinforcing what he called healthy narcissism . . . [when] the child's self is immature, and he or she relies totally on caregivers as external sources of self-cohesion" (Banai, Mikulincer, and Shaver, 2005, p. 226). Bacal and Newman (1990) point out that both selfobject and attachment theories portray healthy human development throughout the life cycle, needing responsive persons, not just in the first few months of life. As with selfobject theory, attachment theory needs to be understood as an intersubjective process.

We very briefly outline attachment theory that has developed through three phases (Main, 1996) to illustrate the basic complementarity of selfobject and attachment theories. In the first phase, the English psychiatrist Bowlby (1969) drew upon evolutionary theory and nonhuman primate observations to undergird the importance of the mother-infant attachment in regulating an infant's safety and survival. Then the Canadian psychologist Ainsworth (1978) instigated an experimental investigation of attachment theory when she developed the Strange Situation procedure for twelve-month-old infants. Her test consists of eight one-way mirror observations, twenty-minute episodes of a mother with her infant, "to see how readily [the infant moved] away from her to explore a novel assembly of toys. While the mother was still present, a stranger entered and made a gradual approach to the [infant]. Only after this did the mother leave, because it was anticipated that separation from her would constitute a greater stress than the presence of a stranger and/or of an unfamiliar environment per se. After a few minutes the mother returned and the stranger slipped out" (Ainsworth et al., 1978, p. 33).

Observations during this procedure confirmed two major infant-mother attachment categories: "securely attached" and "insecurely attached." The "securely attached" (group "B") infants showed distress upon separation from their mothers, but were quickly comforted upon reunion and then used their mothers as a secure base from which to explore the room. Ainsworth, however, was interested in the specific dyads that created them. The mothers of the secure infants were consistently available, sensitive, and responsive, so that reasonably secure mothers help create reasonably secure infants. Self psychology describes this securely attached dyad as an "attuned" self-selfobject relationship.

In comparison to these "securely attached" infants, Ainsworth found that the "insecurely attached" coped with the distress of separation in one of two different ways. "Insecurely attached-ambivalent" infants (group "C") had mothers who were inconsistent, unpredictable, and insensitive, and who discouraged autonomy, although they sometimes displayed warmth. These infants were preoccupied with their mothers when the mothers were present, and did very little exploration of the room. As their brief separation from their mother made them fearful, the reunion with their mother alternated from intense proximity seeking—often clinging—to displays of anger. This behavior has neurological correlates. Although neurological studies have not yet been conducted on insecurely attached-ambivalent infants, adult patients with insecurely attached-ambivalent patterns of behavior have expanded excitatory tegmental circuits and extensive pruning (parcellation) of the inhibitory lateral tegmental circuits (Schore, 1997, p. 619). Such neurological evidence supports the idea of attachment theorists that after twelve months of development infants in this group have a relatively permanent neuronal structuralization of overly anxious behavior patterns.

The other group of "insecurely attached-avoidant" infants (group "A") had mothers who had constantly rejected and rebuffed their bid for contact with them. These mothers tended to avoid physical contact and withdrew from their children when they showed distress. After brief separations from their mothers, these infants ignored them upon reunion and busied themselves with toys. Overt attachment behaviors were not only absent with them, they had been replaced by an active avoidance of the attachment figure and an engagement with objects in their environment. Physiological levels of arousal, however, indicated they were affected by the separation—and were still emotionally attached. By eighteen months insecurely attached-avoidant infants of depressed mothers, when separated from their mothers, exhibited greater right orbitofrontal electro encephalogram (EEG) activity (Dawson and Fischer, 1994) than other groups. Neurologically, this attachment style in an adult shows expansion of the inhibitory lateral tegmental circuits and excessive parcellation of the excitatory ventral tegmental circuits. Their brains, therefore, have low parasympathetic states of arousal, reduced overt emotionality, and inefficient ability to cope with high arousal states which they seek to avoid. In later life such persons are defensive and find it difficult to remember their negative experiences (Schore, 1997, p. 619). They maintain some sense of cohesion by distracting themselves from a "relational" world by attaching to things and other substitutes. If these attachment substitutes are taken away or destroyed, "insecurely attached-avoidant" infants became angry. The neurological evidence of this group suggests that behavior patterns are based on a relatively permanent character structure after twelve months.

One of the most fruitful observations about the difference between the securely attached and insecurely attached-avoidant infants came from an Ainsworth study (see Shane, Shane, and Gales, 1997). Ainsworth measured the amount of time infants were physically held by their caregiver, and surprisingly there was no significant difference in the holding time between the groups. Nor was there a noticeable difference in the quality of the holding.

> *What distinguished the two groups was that the securely attached infant was held more often in response to signals coming from the infant, a contingent responsiveness, whereas the insecure avoidant infant was held when the impulse to hold came from the caregiver herself, a non-contingent responsiveness* [italics added; pp. 29–30].

This means experiences that reinforce an infant's belief in self-agency are critical in shaping interactive patterns that lead to adaptive rather than more maladaptive personality styles. The study also points to the value of thinking about attachment intersubjectively.

The more obvious it became that attachment theory was interested in the nature of the mother-infant relationship and not just attachment per se, the more questions arose about the reliability of attachment research results. The answer: replication studies of the Strange Situation have shown that approximately 60 percent of adults will classify themselves as "securely attached." Campos, and colleagues (1983), for example, used figures from American studies to conclude that 62 percent are secure, 23 percent are insecure-avoidant, and 15 percent are insecure-ambivalent. Similar percentages have been found worldwide (Van Ijzendoorn, 1995). For example, the two insecure patterns were found in approximately 40 percent of those severely neglected institutionalized infants who were adopted from Romania (O'Connor et al., 1999). Similar styles also emerged in 728 adults whose romantic attachment patterns were studied (Hazan and Shaver, 1987), and where, in responding to a questionnaire, 56 percent classified themselves as secure, 25 percent as insecure-avoidant, and 19 percent as insecure-ambivalent. The consistency with which these attachment styles have emerged in both infant and adult studies suggests that avoidance and ambivalent clinging behaviors are major personality traits. This view has been supported by three major longitudinal studies (Hamilton, 1994; Main, 1997; Waters et al., 1995), which showed a 68–75 percent correspondence between the percentages in the attachment classifications in infancy and throughout the lifespan. Together with the neurological studies reported by Schore (1994), there is strong support for the idea that the insecure attachment results reflect relatively enduring personality styles and structuralization.

Self psychology's selfobject theory may be enhanced through including the results of attachment theory research. The "attuned" persons of self-psychology are "securely attached," and the "mis-attuned mother/infant dyad" of self psychology may be attachment theory's "insecurely attached." Such an approximate equation of the two theories leads to an inclusion into self psychology theory of an important discovery by attachment researchers, namely, avoidant, distancing mothers create avoidant infants, and anxious, ambivalent mothers create clinging, ambivalent infants. Simply put, mothers with attuned childhood experiences create attuned mother-infant dyads, while mothers with misattuned childhood experiences create misattuned mother-infant dyads. This provides evidence for a transgenerational transmission of personality configurations.

Fonagy and colleagues (1991) went so far as to demonstrate that the maternal representations of pregnant mothers predicted the type of attachment of their infant at one year of age. Similar ideas have existed in clinical circles, but the research of attachment theory points to a transmission of personality traits in which twinship experiences between mother and infant may play a key role. The transgenerational transmission of personality traits also suggests that for infants from the insecurely attached groups, the general concept of being "mis-attuned" by a mother, is not a completely adequate explanation. For example, infants with an insecure attachment may become *very attuned to the mother* in a "reverse selfobject experience" (R. Lee, 1988), and become self-organized similarly to the parent. Attachment theory suggests that the concept of "attunement" may not adequately describe the difference between a healthy and unhealthy self-selfobject relationship. Attachment studies also complement self psychology theories by presenting evidence that supports the importance of twinship experiences in growth and development. A mother's need for a twinship experience is revealed by her need to have her child experience the feelings she herself experienced as a child. By creating a child in her own image, she is less lonely, more cohesive, and more adaptive in her interactions with others.

In the third phase of the development of attachment theory, the American psychologist Main (Main and Solomon, 1986) reanalyzed the original data of the Strange Situation and recognized "insecurely attached-disorganized" infants, who gave a disorganized response to the Strange Situation experiment. This small group (5 percent of those studied) was significant as it consisted of children who "froze" during the experiment, collapsed on the floor, or looked vacantly at a wall when the mother returned. These children were called "insecurely attached-disorganized." Crittendon (1988) thinks that most of the infants who present this way had been abused or highly traumatized, as they are obviously more susceptible to fragmentation during stressful situations. Siegel (1999) says that mothers who are extremely fear-ridden, frightened, or disoriented, tend to have disorganized/disoriented-attached infants. Communications with these parents present the infant with unsolvable problems. Furthermore, the infant's bind is that the parent cannot soothe because she is the source of the disorientation. So, as these disorganized infants have neither the option to fight or flee, they just freeze into a trance-like state, which suggests the beginning of a dissociative process. Such disorganized infants in the presence of adults, generally develop aggressive behavior with their peers.

It is with insecurely attached-disorganized infants that we seem to have the clearest evidence of neurobiological damage. Schore (1997) and Daniel

Stern (1985) point out that attuned infant-caregiver interactions, where the infant's needs come first, produce secure attachments as a basis for healthy psychological development and growth. Anything less than such attunement creates some neural pathology. As Greenough and Black (1992) have shown, synaptogenesis, the development of a neuron's synaptic junctions, is experience-dependent. Schore (1997) takes the position that abuse, neglect, and chronic misattunement lead to an overpruning of synapses (or receptors) in the right orbitofrontal cortex, and an impaired ability to regulate emotions in response to stress (p. 618). Higher levels of cortisol are released by insecurely attached-disorganized infants than by insecurely ambivalent and insecurely avoidant infants (Spangler and Grossman, 1993; Hertsgaard and colleagues, 1995), and without the interactive repair of a "good enough" attuned selfobject relationship, corticosteroid levels remain chronically elevated, and glucocorticoid receptors, critical for the modulation of the stress response, are then destroyed.

Main also developed an Adult Attachment Interview (AAI) because the Strange Situation procedure is inapplicable for testing adults. In the AAI, an hour-long interview, "participants are asked for descriptions and evaluations of childhood attachment relationships, loss of attachment figures, separations from attachment figures, and the effects of these experiences on the participant's development and personality" (Main, 1996, p. 238). The participant is then asked to provide five adjectives describing the childhood relationship to each parent and then, later, for memories of specific incidents to illustrate each adjective. These incidents are taped, typed into verbatim transcripts, and then judged as to their "states of mind with respect to attachment."

"State of the mind" analyses are based on the ideas of the linguistic philosopher Grice (1975). Grice thought that a person's discourse gave clues to an inner sense of cohesion based on (a) quality ("truthful, and have evidence for what you say"); (b) quantity ("succinct, yet complete"); (c) relation ("relevant or perspicacious"); and (d) manner ("clear and orderly"). The linguistic analyst asks, to what extent does the transcript reflect adherence to or violation of these four maxims? Using linguistic analyses, Main (Main and Goldwyn, 1985–1994) discerned four states of mind that corresponded to the four behavior patterns that twelve-month-old infants presented in the Strange Situation. These states were "secure-autonomous" (securely attached), dismissing" (insecure avoidant), "preoccupied-entangled" (insecure ambivalent), and "unresolved-disorganized" (insecure disorganized). As could be expected, coherent-collaborative responses using the AAI (a secure-autonomous person) have been found in the majority of adult population samples, but are "rare in clinically distressed populations, among psychiatrically distressed criminals, among individuals who abuse others, among German right-wing activist youths (Hopf, 1993), and from mothers of most clinically distressed children (Van Ijzendoorn and Bakermans-Kranenburg, 1996)" (Main, 1996, p. 240).

Studies show that the four attachment patterns found with toddlers when twelve months of age using the Strange Situation procedure occur through the lifecycle, using adults tested by the AAI. Not only do the percentages hold up for each group category, but longitudinal studies, mentioned earlier, confirm the relative permanence of these trait-like personality strategies. Even so, the 68–75 percent correspondence found in these studies between the test in infancy and retest as an adult, suggests that these traits are only relatively permanent, as changes may take place during development. Some insecurely attached at twelve months become more securely attached in adulthood. For example, clinical experience has shown that when patients can develop a self-selfobject therapeutic relationship, the archaic nature of their selfobject experience is modified and they develop subjective experiences of feeling securely attached. Others who were securely attached at twelve months go through the reverse process during childhood because of later experiences of trauma and become insecurely attached. If we accept Kohut's own account as mentioned in the case of Mr. Z, he was securely attached to his mother for the first twelve months of his life, but then had problems when he needed his mother to mirror his assertiveness as an independent center of initiative. As Siegel (1999) says, "Some deviations from these predictions seem to be related to adverse events, such as trauma and loss during the later years of childhood and adolescence" (p. 81).

Attachment theory complements the self psychological theory of selfobjects, especially through research into the insecurely attached-disorganized pattern. We are able to ask how do persons with a history of insecure attachment-disorganization and trauma experience empathic understanding in psychotherapy? With patients with an "insecurely attached-disorganized" history, it is unreasonable for a psychotherapist to expect them to develop trust as a precondition for the therapy. Main and Hesse (1990), in their research into "insecurely attached-disorganized" infants, have seen that although fear from the external environment leads to infant proximity behavior with a caregiver, if the caregiver's behavior has frightened the infant, it places that infant in an irresolvable paradox in which the infant cannot approach the caregiver, flee, or shift attention to the environment. "Insecurely attached-disorganized" infants don't have the structural, self-organizing facilities to trust. They are inclined to relapse into dissociated or trance-like states as suggested by Liotti (1992).

Main and Hesse noted that frightened caregivers with unresolved experiences of trauma and loss are more likely to create a disorganized state in their children. Such research provides a basis for understanding why psychotherapy with traumatized patients may be dominated by their experiences of intrusiveness. For example, after two years of psychotherapy with one of the authors, a patient shared that during the first two months of treatment she had experienced images of something smashing through the consulting room door—intruding into the psychotherapy. Her experiences of flashbacks, and the emergence of "altars" in a session, reflected the patient's experience of the therapeutic interaction and occurred every time the psychotherapist's response was experienced as too intrusive.

Treating traumatized disorders is more than just avoiding being intrusive. If a psychotherapist becomes extremely passive to avoid being experienced as intrusive, the patient's boredom and resulting acting out can dominate the therapeutic landscape. Is this intrusive-boredom transference a call for understanding a new selfobject function, or does psychotherapy with such patients need a new theoretical concept in addition to the selfobject function to help psychotherapists become experienced as being empathic with them? Certainly, such patients find it very difficult to feel understood by a psychotherapist, because even a psychotherapist's attempts at being a soothing selfobject (Tolpin, 1971) may be experienced as intrusive.

Although Kohut thought infants needed to bond to mothers (and patients to psychotherapists) self psychology looks more specifically into the nature of the needed psychotherapeutic bond. Kohut's selfobject experiences can be understood as reflecting different kinds of bonding, hence, different forms of self-organization. Attachment theory, meant to be dyadic and interactive, has also arrived at its four different types of bonding through experimentation. So, in moving to understand the reason for a bond, self psychology viewed it as a means to maintaining self-cohesion, not just for security purposes, even though security contributes to self-cohesion. Thus, out of his wrestling with the idea of a bond (attachment), Kohut made the broader concept of self-cohesion, not attachment, his central self-organizing idea. To Kohut the need for bonding is secondary to, and is a means of fostering, cohesion.

Although bonding is attachment theory's significant contribution to psychotherapy, its focus on the mother-infant relationship does not sufficiently take into account the contribution of sibling attachment to a person's adaptive, adult functioning. For example, supporting the earlier findings of Jenkins and Smith (1990), a Gass, Jenkins, and Dunn (2007) study concluded "that positive and warm sibling relationships moderated the relationship between marital discord and child symptomatology" (p. 172). These findings half a century later confirm the A. Freud and Dann (1951) results, mentioned earlier in this chapter, of studying six orphan survivors from the concentration camp at Thieresienstadt. Their sibling attachments prophylactic effect against severe trauma suggest that Kohut's concept of a twinship transference in psychotherapy, could be a useful complement to attachment theory.

Understanding the potential for a sibling/twinship attachment is useful when patients present for psychotherapy but are extremely resistant to bonding to the psychotherapist. They are often not prepared to trust the psychotherapist until the psychotherapist has "tasted" an experience similar to the patient's life pattern. For example, the patient who experienced chaos during development may create a chaotic type of transference as a means of the psychotherapist twinning the patient. When this "reverse twinship" relationship is understood and accepted, the patient begins to trust and form a sibling bond to the psychotherapist—meeting a deep-seated need to be "connected." This need to be "bonded" is presupposed in self psychology.

In presupposing the need for a sibling/twinship bond, Kohut clearly broadened the British analytic tradition of the mother-infant bond and, therefore, on the importance of psychotherapist/patient bond in psychotherapy. It clearly builds on the well-known position of Fairbairn and Guntrip, that the primary motivation for humans is not the libido, but the hunger for an "object." More accurately stated, the hunger for the "object" (person) is a hunger to be bonded to the "object." Kohut was intensely interested in the nature of that attachment through clinical experience. To Kohut, the hunger is not for a differentiated "object," but a special kind of "object" that he first called a "selfobject," then "selfobject function," and eventually "selfobject experience." With such a selfobject bond a person is not just attached to another but uses that person as a self-extension in order to grow and become differentiated.

Although selfobject and attachment theories acknowledge the importance of the mother-infant bond, each theory uses different methods. The complementarity of attachment theory and self psychology derives from their different methodologies. Attachment theory relies on ethology, experimental research in infant behavior, and linguistic analysis. These methodologies converge in findings that overlap with selfobject theory and tend to affirm the importance of the selfobject construct. Divergent methods that arrive at a similar conclusion, however, help underline the importance ("validity") of the attachment/selfobject experience. As Campbell and Fisk (1959) indicate in their multitrait-multimethod matrix, discriminant and convergent validity of concepts are increased where different methods show similar results.

Self psychology, which demonstrates what works clinically as a result of empathic understanding and utilizing selfobject transferences, not only adds another method to the matrix but provides clinical findings that bolster the validity of attachment research. In return, self psychology obtains new insights with which to explore the transferences with insecurely attached patients, especially those that are disorganized and dissociating. Making use of the AAI, it also has the opportunity to provide outcome studies of its empathic approach with self-disorders. Those experienced in conducting psychotherapy using a self psychology approach know that the approach gets results. It is time to demonstrate this to the broader community through outcome studies such as the one conducted (Meares et al., 1999) on borderline patients.

Summary

Although Kohut discovered the importance of selfobject experiences in the treatment of narcissistic disorders, he also recognized that a hunger for these experiences was only one way that patients presented. Frequently they begin treatment or a session by expressing subjective self-states of which they were aware. These subjective states raise questions of self-organizing, the third Kohutian postulate, which is the subject of the next chapter.

CHAPTER FOUR

Self Agency, the Organizing Self, and Self-Organization

In seeking to empathically understand a patient, self-psychologically-oriented psychotherapists face the questions, "How does this person express a sense of self-agency?" and "How does this patient self-organize?" These questions raise the question of what it means to be a person. They reflect whether a person is viewed as a snapshot in time, or a movie's unfolding story of "doing" that involves continuous self-organizing. In this chapter "self-organization" refers to a person's slowly changing structural residue as a result of continuously self-organizing. Yet, as a person's self-organization takes place in context, a Kohutian theory of empathy inevitably leads to a postulate of self-organizing as a constant creative activity resulting from dynamic interactions with context, and especially a selfobject milieu. By understanding a patient's expression of self-agency, self-organizing, and resulting self-organization, psychotherapists seek to optimize a person's ability to adapt to a context and, when appropriate, make these new adaptations relatively permanent. Included in an understanding of such a sense of self-agency and self-organization are a patient's ambitions, ideals, and skills.

A self-organizing theory of an empathy-based, long-term psychoanalytic psychotherapy uses assumptions that philosophers of the mind have debated for the last 400 years, since Descartes sought to resolve the "mind/body" problem with a dualistic solution. He claimed that just as the body was composed of physical substances, so the mind was composed of "immaterial souls" or mental substances that survived the destruction of the body and lived on immortally as spiritual entities. Taking a position opposite to Descartes, twentieth century "materialists" reject the existence of irreducible mental phenomena and such properties as consciousness. For example, the psychologist John Watson (1925) "solved" the problem of Descartes' dualism by denying the existence of the mind, and adopted a research strategy that measured behavior. For Watson the "science of psychology consisted of correlations between stimulus inputs and behavioral outputs" (Searle, 1999, p. 33). Skinner (1953) held a similar view, arguing that in a functional analysis of behavior it was heuristically bankrupt to invoke inner causes, such as a mind, as explanatory constructs (p. 33).

An empathy-based psychotherapy theory of self-organizing adopts a position different from either Descartes' mental substances/spiritual entities or the monistic ideas of a static materialism. The latter view has become increasingly difficult to hold because a modern theory of subatomic particles envisions "matter" as movement. Furthermore, empathy-based long-term psychoanalytic psychotherapy's concept of self-organizing is broader than just a conscious mind; it involves the body. It accepts MacMurray's (1957) pervasive argument that the Cartesian dualism of mind and body is overcome by the idea of "I do" (p. 78), reflected in the concept of self-agency.

This emphasis on action and self-organizing is supported by Searle (1999), who suggests that the problems of including both body and mind in the concept of self-organization have to do with definitions embedded in language. Specifically, definitions of body and mind assume a logical opposition between "materialism" and "immaterialism" (p. 14). Searle thinks this logical opposition comes about from arbitrary definitions reinforced by centuries of use. He says,

> We are supposed to believe that if something is mental, it cannot be physical; that if it is a matter of spirit, it cannot be a matter of matter; if it is immaterial, it cannot be material [p. 14].

Although such logical opposites were a characteristic of ancient Greek thought, they were not so in ancient Hebrew. For the Hebrews it was illogical to think of spiritual and material as opposites; they thought material was an expression of the spiritual. Humans of the flesh (Isaiah, 31.3) also had a living spirit (Genesis, 2.7) (Richardson, 1950). Searle holds a similar view when he argues that the concepts of material and spiritual, cannot be logical opposites in a modern view of neurobiology. He (1999) says,

> The brain causes certain "mental" phenomena, such as conscious mental states, and these conscious states are simply higher-level features of the brain.

> Consciousness is a higher level or emergent property of the brain in the utterly harmless sense of "higher-level" or "emergent" in which solidarity is a higher level emergent property of H_2O molecules when they are in a lattice structure (ice), and liquidity is similarly a higher-level emergent property of H_2O molecules when they are, roughly speaking, rolling around on each other (water). Consciousness is a mental, and therefore, physical, property of the brain in the sense in which liquidity is a property of systems of molecules [p. 14].

In a modern view of self-organization, body and mind processes are involved in complex self-organizing interactions; the mind is biologically based, and has a capacity to hold beliefs as an emergent property of the total self.

We now explore further the idea of self-agency and self-organizing in two sections. Section A covers ideas from fields outside of psychotherapy, pertinent to a theory of self-organizing and self-organization for psychotherapy. Section B then adumbrates Kohut's clinically formed theory of self-organization in comparison with these organizing ideas of the first section that have emerged from fields other than psychotherapy, especially from the neurosciences.

Section A: Self-Agency, Self-Organizing, and the Sciences

The rising sun greeted the middle-aged woman as she drove a van along a familiar rough paved road in the valley between the Chiricahua and Peloncillo mountains of the southeastern corner of Arizona. She pulled to the side and stopped the engine. Stretching before her was a twenty-five-acre site she had studied for the past seventeen summers. It was desert country, a small section of a working ranch that stocked 7,000 cattle. After Deborah Gordon (1999) got out, she pulled her heavy socks over her pants' cuffs. She could hear the songs of desert larks as she walked onto the site with relief and exhilaration. A coyote called as she passed a nest of harvester ants. There were 300 such ant colonies on the site she studied. She had long discovered that a colony grew to a population of about 10,000 after five years, and then stabilized at this size for the next fifteen to twenty years until both queen and colony died. Her field work sought to answer the question, "How do they organize as a colony when there is no central authority in an ant nest?"

Gordon observed that worker ants consisted of "nurturers" in the deeper parts of the nest (attending the queen, nursing the brood, and storing food), and "outside workers" (patrollers, foragers, midden workers, and nest maintenance workers), who moved between the nest entrance chambers and the world outside. She marked outside workers with a drop of paint and confirmed that they were never found in the deep chambers of a dug-up nest; Gordon realized that inside workers and outside workers were functionally separate. Gordon next observed the outside workers.

In the morning, the nest maintenance workers emerged first, to remove any blockage at the nest entrance and carry out dirt from new tunneling or from blown-in particles. The patrollers followed, scouting for food and challenging intrusions from ants of other colonies into the nest's foraging areas and trails. When patrolling activity reached its peak, foragers emerged to follow the trails of the patrollers. Then midden workers appeared with nest refuse, mainly husks from consumed food. In the process of placing the refuse on middens (mounds), the workers marked these with identification scents from their glands. Gordon, for example, found that after removing middens around a colony, ants from other species began to intrude into the nest area significantly more than when the middens were left intact.

Gordon discovered too that the foragers did not haphazardly search for food; they only carried back what the patrollers had found. This foraging pattern was confirmed when Gordon placed birdseed for the patrollers to find and noted the foragers rapidly whisked the seed to the nest. When, however, the same kinds of seeds were placed after the patrollers had left an area, the foragers ignored them, in fact, walked over them. So, if the patrollers "told" the foragers where to forage, Gordon asked, "How did the patrollers communicate this?" She noted that patrollers stayed around where they found food, and that foragers searched for food where they met the patrollers. Subsequent foragers followed the paths of the early foragers. Gordon concluded that food gathering is organized in a colony from two simple rules: one, that patrollers stay longer where they find food, and two, that foragers follow trails with larger than threshold numbers of patrollers. Such simple rules dispense with the need for a centralized command system.

Another feature of ant organization is the ability of worker ants to switch tasks. In one experiment, Gordon marked ants with paint according to their task that day. When she piled seeds for patrolling ants to find, ants from nest maintenance or midden tasks switched to foraging. In another experiment, when Gordon created the need for more patrolling (policing) by placing foreign ants near a nest, midden workers stopped their work and began to patrol. And when Gordon placed toothpicks near a nest to create a need for more nest maintenance workers, these extra workers came from unmarked insiders. All these results demonstrated to Gordon that "individuals, following simple, local rules, generate the achievements of colonies" (Gordon, 1999, p. 143).

Gordon noted that for ants to make simple decisions from interaction with other ants, they needed the capacity to count and to distinguish the task being performed from the ants they met. An ant's ability to distinguish between ants comes from its fourteen odor glands and its sensitivity to odor. Because of this odor-changing capacity, ants can tell the task of the ants they meet based on their odor; and their ability to generate and respond to odors highlights the importance of an ant's local decisions based on interaction rates with ants from the same nest. The key to communication between two ants is the pattern of contacts. If, for example, ants meet a threshold number of foraging ants with seed, they switched to foraging. So Gordon (1999) affirms that "ants show how simple parts make complex living systems" (p. 170).

Gordon's study of harvester ants offers a simple, clear example of self-organizing in the absence of a central authority. As it raises the important question about how self-organizing occurs in the development of human organisms, we shall now cover the following examples: (1) Llinas and phylogenetic neural development, (2) Mesulam's "channel" and "state" functions of brain neurology, (3) Thelen and Smith's study of movement systems, (4) developmental psychotherapy theory, (5) Jackson's theory of evolutionary development, (6) Fodor's modular view of the self, (7) Edelman's theory of neuronal group selection, and (8) Fast's theory of selving.

These specific theories cover a wide range; but a brief reconnaissance of them converges on the idea of human self-organizing from many different points of view. There has been no attempt to integrate these diverse theories within a self psychology theory of psychotherapy, although collectively they give the image of a human organism constantly changing in order to enhance actions that increase its chance of survival, an idea that Spinoza suggested with his concept of "conatas." Because these self-organizing theories are "experience-distant," they only have an indirect influence on clinical practice. But they present a nonlinear, dynamic form of development that holds promise of new experience-near theorizing that will enhance therapeutic effectiveness.

A nonlinear, dynamic view of self-organizing self-systems should eventually produce modifications to a psychotherapy theory whose clinical viability has been tested in practice. Admittedly, as Tolpin indicated (discussion group, the 2006 International Self Psychology Conference), it takes approximately fifteen years for new ideas to be tested out in psychotherapy, in a Darwinian-like selection process. We take the view that these self-organizing ideas may be included as a Kohutian postulate within a Lakatosian-like research program, as long as these new theories increase patients' experience of empathy, the central postulate of the research program.

(1) Llinas and Phylogenetic Neural Development

Just when does the need for self-organizing arise phylogenetically? Llinas (2001) takes the view that such a need began with the evolutionary divergence of plants from animals. Both species survived, but did so by evolving different strategies. Plants became sessile, remaining relatively fixed in one place, whereas animals survived by developing a strategy of movement, a "motoricity" that required a nervous system. Llinas thinks that as plants "have well-organized circulatory systems but no hearts, [they] appeared slightly later in evolution than did most primitive animals; it is as if sessile organisms had, in effect, chosen not to have a nervous system" (p. 15). Animals, in being selected for movement needed a nervous system to enable the organism to take action to ensure its continuing existence. Once this motoric evolutionary path had formed, it made activity, not feeling nor thinking, the key organizing self quality and led to the eventual emergence of a critical sense of self-agency as a consequence. There was no longer a question of "if" self-organizing would occur, but only matters of the timing, shaping, and the complexity of the emerging organizing self as a result of this evolutionary selection of movement.

Llinas supports the idea that a nervous system developed in conjunction with an organism's capacity to move by pointing to the primitive "Ascidiacea" (sea squirt). This organism goes through two forms: larval and adult. A larva, freely swimming for approximately a day, is equipped for this brief period with a tail and a neural ganglia notochord (primitive spine) of 300 cells that senses its surrounding environment using its organ of balance and a light-sensitive patch of skin. After a larva finds and attaches to a suitable location, it then adopts a sessile strategy. As it then survives by taking in food through filtering, it proceeds to absorb most of its brain and tail. Llinas (2001) thinks the Ascidiacea gives a clear message: "Evolutionary development of a nervous system is an exclusive property of actively moving creatures" (p. 17).

During its one day as a larva, the sea squirt has temporary, primitive input (sensing) and output (action) neurons, sufficient to achieve its immediate goal of finding a stable platform with a rich nutriment flow in order to survive. After the sea squirt, the sea sponge is the next step along the motile branch of the evolutionary tree; it is a very primitive multicellular organism with permanent "motile" cells that contract when touched. Senitive to touch, the sea sponge's neurons double as both input (sensory) and output (contractile) neural systems because "the size of the response is basically proportional to the size of the stimulus" (p. 80). The sea anemone, a further step in motile development, has neurons that have specialized into sensory cells and contractile cells. Then, in later evolutionary development, motor neurons develop to form a pathway between these sensory and contractile cells.

Llinas claims evolution selects organisms that best anticipate action needed for survival. An organism's ability to predict meant evolution eventually selected those organisms that could best understand the behavioral patterns of its food sources and those who would make them their food source. Such a predictive ability suggests a primitive version of what became known later in humans as a capacity for empathy. Much predictive knowledge tended to be specific, but as Fodor indicates later in this section, it also involved abstracting, which is what perception entails. Once predicting abstractions gave an evolutionary advantage to an organism, the organism developed more complex abilities to predict and anticipate. This evolving predictive ability meant that organisms with the capacity to "remember," even briefly, gained an advantage in anticipating what would happen next. Much of the simple, brief remembering and responding in early animal species was reflexive, using genetically derived fixed action patterns (FAPs).

Eventually, more extensive memory came with the development of learned FAPs that automatically unfolded after being perceptually triggered (see subsection 6). Here we make note that an organism's practice of perceptual abstracting and predicting eventually developed into mental modeling that recognized long-term trends and greater levels of abstraction. And with the development of long-term modelling, there was an increased responsive flexibility (greater "degrees of freedom") that enabled behavior to become less dominated by automatic, reflexive action. As Bergson (1988) conceived it, a self-organization utilizes both involuntary and voluntary processes, the latter (voluntary) having emerged out of the former (involuntary).

Llinas describes how, in conjunction with increasing evolutionary selective pressure on prediction and modeling, an "interneuron" interfacing with the sensory and motor neurons, developed. "In the strict sense" says Llinas (2001), "the interneuron [is] any nerve cell that does not communicate directly with the world outside the nervous system. Interneurons send and receive signals by means of synaptic contacts to and from other neurons exclusively, and serve to reroute and distribute sensory input to different components of the motor system" (p. 80). From these interneurons a conscious awareness of self eventually emerges. And thinking isotropically (by analogy), we can't help noticing a similarity between the human brain's specialized input/output neurons and interneurons and the behavior of Gordon's ant colonies where a quarter of a colony's ants specialize in interfacing with the outside environment. Similar to the brain's interneurons, the other three quarters manage the internal environment of the nest and only interact with the "outside" ants in the entrance chambers. The interfacing of the inside and outside ants, symbolize the beginnings of a primitive self-organizing entity.

In the human spinal cord, the neural system demonstrates an early phylogenetic development of interneurons. These spinal cord neurons are wide branching, reflecting the multichanneling (Edelman's "degeneracy"—see subsection 7) that enables many muscles to move simultaneously. The majority of the brain's neurons are interneurons. These interneurons form two major types: those whose axons never go outside their brain region, "local circuit neurons," and those with axons contacting other brain regions, "projection neurons." Because of these interneurons, Llinas (2001) claims that most of the brain, most of the time, functions as a closed system. Information is fed into the central interneuron system "from the external world, and the results of the operation are put back out into the external world as active, purposeful movement that is necessary for survival" (p. 81). As a result of interneuron brain development, especially in the cerebral cortex, an increasingly better predictive organism takes more efficient and effective actions to increase the chances of survival and a more creative life.

Llinas's account of neural development shifts away from the enlightenment idea of the supremacy of "reason" in a self-organization, toward the kinds of long-range planning that enhances an organism's self-survival strategies and behavior that lead to the development of a sense of self-agency. Long-range strategizing is not necessarily superior to the need for immediate perception and action, for both immediate responding and long-range planning serve self-survival in different ways. Yet phylogenetically, the development of abstracting and modeling processes in the central nervous system significantly enhanced an organism's activities that further the prospect of survival. This means that whether the prediction is short-term or long-term, both these predictive systems enhance the effectiveness of action, especially where the action gathers food or avoids being food for someone else. As Llinas (2001) says, "the organization and function of our brains are based on the embedding of motoricity over evolution" (p. 59).

Llinas has given us a brief overview of the development of human self-organization from the point of view of neurons. The beginnings of self-organizing at this neural level, simplified and succinctly portrayed by Llinas, is really very complex. And although these beginnings are less complex than the human self-organizing that is the focus of psychotherapy, Llinas's description of neuron development makes it clear that action that enhances an organism's survival is one of the most basic strategies of self-organization. Such early phylogenetic action is not the concept of self-agency as understood in later human development, but can be considered a simple beginning from which self-agency eventually emerges in human development.

(2) Mesulam's Channel and State Functions of Brain Neurology

As Llinas's description of neural specialization depicts, human development is initially genetically driven, and then increasingly develops a capacity for long-range planning based on increased learning. For Solms and Turnbull (2002), self-organizing responds to information from both the outer world and the inner world of the body. Information from the external environment, perceived by sense organs, stimulates the posterior circuits of the cerebral hemispheres. In these posterior circuits sensory information combines into information about the outside world and integrates with previous experience. This integration is transmitted to the frontal cortex as a component for potential action. In comparison to external information, internal information such as respiration, digestion, blood pressure, temperature control, and sexual reproduction are sensed by the peripheral nervous system and by the sensorimotor musculaoskelatal movements that are mapped in the tectum and dorsal tegmentum. Information about the body is constantly being registered, first by the hypothalamus and other limbic circuits, and then projected to the frontal cortex. In this way, the reactions of the frontal lobes take into account external and internal conditions and previous experiences as well. So, the brain is organized anatomically and physiologically to represent these outer and inner worlds—with the constructs "inner" and "outer" using the body as the reference point.

This idea of the brain having two major subsystems, one oriented to inner information and the other toward outer information, is proposed in a detailed technical paper by Mesulam (1998) that draws attention to the physiological differences between the brain's representations of these worlds. He describes these differences as "channel" and "state" functions. Information derived from the outside world is channel-dependent, processing information through distinctly specific neural pathways to reasonably defined regions of the posterior (caudal) brain; it is not widely distributed to the whole brain. It also uses neurons whose primary neurotransmitters are glutamate and aspartate ("excitatory"), and GABA ("inhibitory").

In contrast, information from the sensors representing the inner world of the body diffuses throughout the anterior (rostal) brain, with widespread neural effects. The neurons serving this inner "sensing" system reflect changes in the general state of the organism. These neurons use neurotransmitters from specific brainstem nuclei and projecting axons to influence neurons in the forebrain simultaneously. Although information from the visceral areas uses neurotransmitters of the channel system (glutamate, asparate, and GABA), they also employ such neuromodulators as dopamine, serotonin, acetylcholine, and norepinephrine. These are expressed in nuclei in the brain stem: acetylcholine in the tegmentum; serotonin from the raphe nuclei; norepinephrine from the locus coeruleus; and dopamine from the ventral tegmental and substantia nigra nuclei. These neuromodulators globally affect broad regions of the rostal brain, especially the frontal lobes.

To summarize, the self responds to information from outer and inner worlds. More accurately, Solms and Turnbull (2002) see the self as an integration of the representations of the outer world in the anterior cortex and those of the internal world of the visceral and sensorimotor body that are projected to the frontal cortex. Panksepp (1998) calls the results of this integration "the SELF." Solms and Turnbull (2002) agree: "What binds our external perceptions together is the fact that they are grounded in our internal perceptions" (p. 75). Although we don't disagree about the idea of integration, the use of the word "perception" for sensing internal information may be confusing.[1] Obviously, with the viscera and sensorimotor information, we don't perceive with sight, but sense our inner condition with feelings akin to touch. From these feelings we gain information about our inner world. So, as Solms and Turnbull (2002) claim, the early foundations for a sense of self are "ultimately generated by our inner awareness of living in a physical body" (p. 77).

Although a fully developed self-organizing human is much more than visceral bodily experiences and sensorimotor information, internal information is given motivational priority over other self-needs. For example, if stalked by a lion, a desperate dehydrated human will risk being attacked and drink at a stream rather than face the certainty of dying from thirst. But a person is also far more than visceral bodily experience, sensorimotor information, and mapping of the outside world, as the material on self-organizing and self-agency indicates in the subsections that follow.

(3) Thelen and Self-Organizing Movement Systems

In the last few decades, a theory of self-organizing in human development has replaced the concept of a "homunculus" in self-organization. Damasio (1999), for example, expresses the consensus in the neurosciences that the "homunculus solution" has failed. According to medieval embryology, the homunculus was "a minute, but complete, preformed man waiting in a man's semen to be delivered into a woman's uterus" (Erikson, 1950). In the modern version, a homunculus is the knowing part of the brain, thought necessary in order to interpret brain images. Self-evidently, the certainty of an all-knowing homunculus is very different from Llinas's idea of abstract modeling to aid increased probability in predicting behavior. As Damasio (1999) points out,

> The all-knowing little person [homunculus] would do all the knowing for each of us but would then face the difficulty with which we began in the first place. Who would do its knowing? Well, another little person, of course, but only smaller. In turn, the second little person would need a third little person inside to be its knower. The chain would be endless and this postponing of the difficulty [by what is] known as infinite regress, effectively disqualified the homunculus solution [p. 190].

Despite the inadequacy of the homunculus solution—with its logical problem of "infinite regression"—homunculus-like solutions covertly exist in psychotherapy theory where human development is portrayed as following a detailed innate cognitive set of blueprints with exact, predetermined goals (Thelen and Smith, 1998, p. 33). In criticism of the innate cognitive blueprint idea, Lehrman (1970) points out that although the idea is seductive, it doesn't help because it is merely functional shorthand for any unexplained development. He thinks that a blueprint view of development, presented as the unfolding of genetic instructions, is yet another version of an all-knowing homunculus.

Examples of developmental blueprints containing predetermined roles came from the work of Gesell (1939) and McGraw (1945). These theorists assumed that infants progressed through identifiable stages, driven by a process called maturation ("central control"). Building on blueprint assumptions, Gesell described twenty-three stages and twenty-eight substages of prone behavior; and McGraw sketched out "seven phases of erect locomotion." As Thelen and Smith (1998) explain,

> [for these theorists,] development was a linear, stage-like progression through a sequence of increasingly more functional behaviors, driven towards adult forms by a grand plan (and scheduled by a grand timekeeper). This is what ontogeny looked like when the magnification was low, when the details from the individual subjects were averaged, and a series of more-or-less finely sculptured categories were imposed upon them [p. 6].

Thelen and Smith argue that what began as a cataloging of behavior became reified when description became accepted as explanation. They (1998) say,

> It has been accepted as dogma in many developmental textbooks that the stage-like progression of motor development, leading to a species-typical outcome (all humans sit, walk, and climb), is evidence for "maturation," or a "biological" process uncontaminated by "experience." Here was a subtle shift from description to causality [p. 7].

Thelen and Smith (1998) claim that when neurophysiologists theorized about locomotion, they accepted a genetic variant of the homunculus idea. They conceived of "a central pattern generator" (CPG), a "network of neurons in the spinal cord that could autonomously generate the muscle-specific neural activation of natural locomotion" (p. 8). This CPG model, the idea of a neural encoded pattern of movement, sees locomotion as following an innate program within the organism. But this innate programming idea is unworkable because it fails to include the need for locomotion to continually adjust to the changing topography. Cats, for example, maintain an erect posture against gravity, and move limbs that have mass and muscles with varying elastic qualities. These mass and muscle components make it impossible for pre-set neural codes to function as adequate instructions for locomotion, especially without a feedback system to facilitate adjustments. Because of feedback, movement systems are continuously self-organizing as animals move limbs and constantly take into account terrain, gravity, and other factors.

Applying the idea of self-organizing movement to humans, Thelen conducted a study of infants and found their walking did not follow incremental learning during the first year of development, as predicted by stage-like, developmental theory. She noticed that infants were able to make coordinated, step-like movements at the age of two months when supine or if held erect, before the capacity disappeared and returned at eight to ten months. Why, she asked, did they "lose" their capacity to walk during this gap? Through a simple experiment, Thelen demonstrated that the infant stepping movement was not lost, because when she held these infants up in torso-deep water, stepping movements returned in number and vigor. The lack of non-stepping behavior in infants between two months and eight to ten months of age came from an increase in infant weight that was not matched by an increase in muscle strength, and this had temporarily interfered with an infant's stepping. Thelen further supported her view that stepping movements were not lost when she demonstrated that seven-month-old infants (who normally did not step) walked on a slowly moving treadmill if supported. In this experiment she showed that the voluntary use of legs is tied to context. She revealed how "systems of action" are self-organizing and do not follow rigidly formed patterns of fixed preconceived stages.

(4) Developmental Psychotherapy Theory

The concept of self-organizing in the development of an organism has recently emerged in psychotherapy theory as a challenge to the linear view of early theorists. Influenced by the views of Spencer and Jackson (1881, 1884), a linear, stage-like view of development emerged in the twentieth century. In first outlining developmental theory (1905D), Freud insisted on the ubiquity of a childhood sexual drive (Gay, 1988), which he saw as being connected to the erogenous zones (Fenichel, 1945)—the mouth, anus, and genitals. These erogenous areas were posited as the source of libido and led Freud (1940A) to delineate oral, anal, and genital stages of development, followed by a latent period before a reawakening of the sexual drive in adolescence.

Evidence of reification of these stages, however, can be seen from the practice of designating ages for them. The oral stage was from birth to eighteen months, the anal stage went from eighteen months to three years, the genital period was regarded from four until six years of age, and the latent period went from seven years until puberty around fourteen years of age (English and Pearson, 1963). The fact that the word "about" is used in conjunction with these stated age periods softens the rigidity of the model, but does not lessen the criticism afforded by self-organizing theorists that development is not the unfolding of a clearly prefigured scheme. Theorists such as Ferenczi, Anna Freud, Erikson, and Piaget followed Freud in also portraying a linear view of development.

Although Ferenczi's ideas about development shifted from Freud's psychosexual stages to stages of reality, he follows the linear developmental model. He outlines five omnipotent stages by which a person gains a good grip on reality (1913): (a) unconditional omnipotence, where wishes are automatically fulfilled; (b) hallucinatory omnipotence, where the wish is fulfilled by hallucinating; (c) magical omnipotence, where magical acts take place; (d) animistic omnipotence, where all things are animated; and (e) magical thoughts and words connected to the importance of language.

Extending the ideas of her father and Ferenczi, Anna Freud presented the concept of "lines of development" (1965). Anna Freud's theory included Freud's stages of libido (oral, anal, etc.) and of aggression, expressed in the early form of biting, through to the development of adolescent antisocial behavior. Importantly, by viewing development "from the side of the ego," she included Ferenczi's idea of "levels of the sense of reality." From her expanded theoretical base, she proposed her prototype that development moved from emotional dependency to self-reliance. This model is illustrated by such behavior as feeding, sleeping, evacuation, body hygiene, and the prevention of injury and illness. To illustrate feeding, her line of development is from an infant's suckling to an adult's ability to "regulate his own food intake actively and rationally, quantitatively and qualitatively, on the basis of his own needs and appetites and irrespective of his relations to the provider of food, and of conscious and unconscious fantasies" (pp. 69–70).

Two other examples of her lines of development are socialization, which sees changes from egocentricity into companionship, and bodily interest, which shifts into toys and then into play and finally into work. Significantly, Anna Freud thought there were special situations such as entry into nursery school, the birth of a sibling, or hospitalization, that reveal how far an infant has reached in developing from emotional dependency on the mother toward self reliance. The importance of Anna Freud's idea was seen in the previous chapter, where Ainsworth used the "event" of a mother being out of a room for a few minutes as a way of testing an infant's emotional attachment to her. Yet, as significant as Anna Freud's shift from id drives to ego functions was in developmental theory, she held the assumptions of a predictable, prefigured linear, form of development. Such a linear model does not fit the accumulating evidence of a self-organizing self.

Influenced by Anna Freud, Erikson keeps the focus of development on ego functions. To become self-reliant, a human organism needs to gain self-capacities. In the first stage, formerly Freud's oral stage, an infant needs to develop trust. Envisaging each stage's capacity as a dimension, Erikson sees the trust stage as one end of a bipolar dimension, with distrust at the other. Similarly, by making all his stages dimensional and bipolar, and by extending them into young adulthood, middle age, and old age, Erikson completed the life cycle. His well known eight stages—trust verses mistrust, etc.—are described as epigenetic. By epigenetic he (1968) meant "anything that grows has a ground plan, and that out of this ground plan the parts arise, each part having its special ascendancy, until all parts have arisen to form a functioning whole" (p. 92). Clearly, Erikson's version of linear stages of development suffers from the criticism of the earlier models that it doesn't reflect evidence of nonlinear self-organizing that is in response to the environment.

Piaget's (1951, 1952, 1954, 1970) theory of cognitive development, which posited four "qualitatively distinct and invariantly ordered stages," is also conceived linearly. These stages are infancy, preschool years, school years, and adolescence. He says,

> In infancy, children are sensor motor organisms; their mental life is what is perceived and acted on. In the pre-school years, children represent their world in symbols, but these symbols are still perceptual, rigid, and cannot be mentally manipulated. In the school years, children reason logically, mentally manipulating ideas, but these ideas are concrete, not abstract. Finally in adolescence, the full power of the mind is realized in abstract mental thought [Thelen and Smith, 1998, p. 21].

From the big picture, Piaget's stages seem reasonable, but his stages faltered as a theory of development as details were studied. For example, Inhelder and Piaget (1964) conducted an experiment where children, when told that a blue rod is longer than the green rod, and the green rod is longer than the yellow rod, could not infer that the blue rod was longer than the yellow rod. It is now known that the problem for these children was not their inability to infer but their capacity to remember the two premises. After Bryant and Trabesco (1971) conducted an experiment in which they had children memorize two premises, the children, when asked if the blue rod was longer or smaller than the yellow rod, were able to make the correct inference.

We have given these examples as a background against which to portray a major shift in modern developmental theory based on the influence of nonlinear (chaos) theory from mathematics. Thelen and Smith (1998) succinctly state that

> development does not "know" where it is going from the start. There are no constraints on development that act like levies on a flooding river, keeping it from going where it ought not to go. There is no end state other than life itself. We propose instead that development is the outcome of the self-organizing processes of continually active living systems [p. 44].

Criticism of linear developmental theories from a self-organizing systems perspective does not negate the importance of developmental learning per se. Far from it. In development theory the new emphasis is on an organism's nonlinear adaptations. This was demonstrated, for example, in Thelen's studies of physical movement. Evidence accumulating from the application of chaos theory in a number of fields suggests that self-organizing is very much a part of human development. The question of how far self-organizing extends in human self-organization, however, is a significant one. Self-organizing, and the feedback capacities that go with it seem to be necessary for action (movement) and perceptual subsystems that need continuous, instantaneous decisions.

(5) Jackson's Theory of Dissolution

The nineteenth century English physiologist John Hughlings Jackson's concept of dissolution, "the reverse of evolution" (1884, p. 3), has relevance for a theory of self-organizing for psychotherapy. He had extended Herbert Spencer's application of Darwin's evolutionary theory to the nervous system by claiming that evolution developed from the lowest, simplest, automatically organized centers up to the highest, most complex, least genetically fixed, and most voluntary nervous centres. He (1884) says,

> The highest centers, which are the climax of nervous evolution, and which make up the "organ of the mind" (or physical basis of consciousness) are the

least organized, the most complex, and the most voluntary. So much for the positive process by which the nervous system is "put together"—evolution [p. 46].

Jackson (1881) illustrates dissolution with the example of "epileptic mania" (p. 7). He thinks that the temporary condition of epileptic patients after a seizure best demonstrates a dissolution that begins with the highest neural centers. He evaluates the severity of the epileptic discharge from three post-epileptic conditions of mental confusion, insensibility, or coma, and found the severest discharge resulted in the most automatic behavior. Jackson illustrates the most regressed coma condition with a "patient who acts after a fit, and remembers nothing after recovery, [yet] may, for the time, be a mere mechanism or automaton, without any consciousness" (p. 15) and with a man who, after a seizure, lit a fire and who knew nothing of it upon recovery. He thinks that dissolution can be a controlled adaptive retreat even if the self-organizing process is temporarily overburdened (p. 16).

Jackson's study of epilepsy supported Spencer's (1867) concept of nervous dissolution as reverse development. "It is a 'taking to pieces' in the order of the least [automatically] organized, the most complex and the most voluntary, towards the most organized, most simple, and most automatic" (Jackson, 1884, p. 46). It is possible to interpret Jackson's work as advocating a prefigured linear view of development and regression, but this is not necessarily so. It is possible to accept Jackson's concept of a general retreat from more voluntary behavior to more automatic behavior without going back through the exact route taken during development. Furthermore, Spencer's idea of dissolution may be conceived as a controlled retreat where the drive to self-organize leads to the most stable cohesion possible under the circumstances.

As Kohut makes cohesion-fragmentation a major dimension in his theory of self-organization (see section B), the Spencer/Jackson model suggests that a patient's "fragmentation" should not be assumed to be chaotic, because it may be a controlled retreat to more automatic, less differentiated processes, driven by a person's tendency to self-organize. Even so, the controlled retreat need not follow a prefigured strategy. The Spencer/ Jackson idea of dissolution points to a need to distinguish fragmentation as a total collapse, or as a controlled retreat to more automatic forms of self-organization, which is similar to Kris' (1952) concept of "regression in the service of the ego" and Hartmann's (1939) idea of adaptive regression. Furthermore, even with a "controlled retreat," there needs to be a distinction between a general retreat or a retreat in specific subsystems. This idea of different types of dissolution is illustrated by a comparison between two WWII battles: the complete collapse and annihilation of the German Sixth Army at Stalingrad, or the calculated withdrawal of the Australian forces along the Kokoda trail to Imita Ridge when fighting the Japanese during World War II.

In contrast to the Spencer/Jackson model of dissolution, Freud used "regression" as the idea of a retreat to earlier prefigured forms of thought. From his references in "On Aphasia" (Freud, 1891, pp. 56–58), it is evident that Freud had read the writings of Jackson, yet chose to conceptualize regression based on his own theory of dreams (1900). He claims that in a waking state mental excitations ("action potentials") traverse from perceptions to motor activity. During sleep, when thoughts found access to motor activity blocked, Freud thought they regressed into images that expressed themselves in a quasi-hallucinatory fashion as dreams. As he says (1900), "We call it regression when in a dream an idea is turned back into the sensory image from which it was originally derived" (p. 543).

Freud's predetermined psychosexual stages of development (1905D, 1940A) enabled regression to be conceived of as a return to a previous stage of development, the libido expression appropriate to the stage. As increasing empirical evidence does not support linear stages of development or Freud's concept of regression, Jackson's general idea of dissolution as a shift to a more automatic way of functioning retains a useful explanation for forms of self-organization that were not necessarily previously experienced. So, by incorporating the Spencer/Jackson idea of dissolution into a Kohutian view of fragmentation, we may be better prepared to understand specific defects in self-organization, and so increase our empathic resonance with patients.

(6) Fodor's Modular View of the Self

Fodor (1983) thinks an organism's self-organizing capacity requires modular components, a modern version of faculty psychology that was discarded by the end of the nineteenth century (Rippa, 1971). Modular components are necessary for a nonlinear theory of development. He thinks Chomsky's idea of an innate language "faculty" has helped stimulate a renewed interest in faculty psychology, but distances himself from Chomsky's belief in an innately acquired, cognitive set of rules for language. Fodor uses the example of Miller's (1956) study where an experimental subject attempted to recall unfamiliar, unrelated items. How many balls can the working memory effectively juggle at the same time? The recall limit averaged seven. As Fodor thinks that Miller's "limits" arise from the characteristics of the working memory rather than from an innate program, he avoids being aligned to any idea that could be construed as a residue of the homunculus idea.

In Fodor's modular concept of self-organizing, he concentrates on two major systems: input (perceptual) systems and central thought processing (modeling) systems. Fodor describes ten characteristics of perceptual input systems to distinguish it from modeling systems. As an example, perceptual systems are fast as demonstrated by Potter's (1975) experiment of recognizing slides of magazine photographs based on description. He found there is 70 percent accuracy when the slides are exposed for an eighth of a second. For Fodor, the dissimilarity of perception from modeling enables fast, automatic perceptual processes that save time and "computational space." As Fodor says, an "eye blink is a fast response because it is a reflex—that is, you don't have to decide whether to blink your eye when someone jabs a finger at it" (p. 64). By comparison with perception that uses sensory neurons, thinking (modeling) that involves interneurons and synaptic junctions, is relatively slow.

Fodor's comparison between the functioning of perceptual systems and central thought processing, makes an appealing contribution to a theory of self-organizing, because, the long-term planning of belief systems serve different purposes than perceptions. As he succinctly states, perceptual systems "categorize" and central processing systems "believe." Perceptual systems make quick computations, biased towards a "false positive." A "false positive" occurs because it is better to be startled by a stick, for example, mistakenly perceived as a poisonous tiger snake, than be bitten from waiting too long to be sure the percept was a snake. Perceptual bias toward "false positives" ("temporary functional perceptual delusions?") has survival value. After being startled by the stick, a central processing analysis corrects the initial "misperception" of a snake. Perceptual representations are often quick guesses that are corrected in the light of "background knowledge, . . . information in the memory, and the simultaneous results of input analyses in other domains" (Fodor, 1983, p. 102). These corrected representations lead to a "fixation of belief" and a resulting theoretical model. Indeed, in contrast to input perceptions, the functions of the central processing systems, being relatively slow and unencapsulated, don't show the typical characteristics of continuous feedback self-organizing modularity. Central processing belief systems may be considered a slow-changing mode of self-organizing.

If input systems develop perceptions from directly verifiable empirical evidence, modeling systems, by way of contrast, consist of relatively "fixed" beliefs using non-demonstrative inferences. These belief systems go through a Darwinian form of selection based on how well they predict results, not on how fast they self-organize. One difficulty with predictive models based on "best belief" is their inaccessibility to direct measurement. Fodor suggests a solution. He says, "When you run out of direct evidence, you might as well try arguing from analogies" (p. 104). Kohut follows a similar procedure. He says, "realizing that they can never get at 'the' truth, only at analogizing approximations, [creative, playful people] are satisfied to describe what they see from various points of view" (Kohut, 1977, p. 207).

We have delved into the distinction Fodor makes between input perceptual systems and belief systems because it may not be familiar to psychotherapists of an empathy-based tradition. His work reminds us that when referring to cognitive self-organizing, there are two vastly different subsystems that need to be distinguished, reflected in two different organizing styles of patients who present for psychotherapy. One patient presents material that has been carefully thought about, compared to, and influenced by the patient's beliefs, and containing little affect. Other, more spontaneous patients, are more descriptive of their impressions and senses. Fodor's distinctions remind us that both these patients present with their cognitive processes in the foreground, yet are different, and they suggest hypotheses about whether, and in what way self-organizing is over- or underdeveloped. Patients who present with a well-developed perceptual system are usually easier to engage in the initial sessions of the psychotherapy because they find it easier to talk spontaneously about matters that pop into their minds (free associate), but we have also found that thoughtful patients who focus more on central processing material may become engaged with us by associations initially focused on beliefs.

Fodor believed in the value of analogy for developing a theory of self-organization by resorting to the external model of scientific hypotheses, and to "isotropic and Quineian" properties. What are these? By isotropic, Fodor means analogies may be taken from any field where they have been empirically supported and used to confirm hypotheses. In principle, botany may influence thinking in astronomy—if a valuable analogy can connect. For example, modern physics took a major step when Ernest Rutherford (Rhodes, 1986) conceived of the atom as a miniature universe. Another example is Kohut's analogy of a eukaryote cell to conceive of the clinically useful distinction between a nuclear self and a peripheral self. From an isotropic perspective, then, an analogy helps to fix a model, especially if a number of analogies tend to converge and support the model's beliefs. The model is only retained eventually anyway after a Darwinian-like selection process for usefulness.

By a Quineian property, Fodor referred to the American philosopher Quine (1953). Fodor says, "By saying that scientific confirmation is Quineian, I mean that the degree of confirmation assigned to any given hypothesis is sensitive to properties of the entire belief system" (p. 107). The Quineian feature of a theory is that it fits as a total system. So Fodor thinks that a good theory has isotropic and Quineian features. He explains (1983):

> If scientific confirmation is isotropic, it is quite possible that some fact about photosynthesis in algae should be relevant to the confirmation of some hypothesis in astrophysics (isotropic) . . . But the point about being Quineian is that we might have two astrophysical theories, both of which make the same predictions about algae . . . but such that one of the theories is better confirmed than the other . . . on grounds of such considerations as simplicity, plausibility, or conservatism. . . . properties that theories have in virtue of their relation to the whole structure of scientific beliefs taken collectively [pp. 107–108].

The relative fixating of belief to form predictive models not only involves unencapsulated belief systems, but systems that function holistically, where considerable inter-influencing of beliefs takes place. Fodor's ideas have relevance for a psychotherapy theory of self-organization, not only because his emphasis on modularity supports a place for self-organizing in the human organism, but because he also points to relatively firm and enduring self-organizing structures as a result of central processing. As these beliefs play important, diverse functioning in an organism's self-organization, they will be discussed further in subsection 8 and in section B.

(7) Edelman's Theory of Neuronal Group Selection (TNGS)

Edelman's TNGS theory reinforces the view of a self-organizing human organism. He (1987) says,

> The neuronal group selection theory deals with adaptation to a relative, changing, polymorphous world in the same fashion as Darwinian natural selection: from the bottom up (Mayr, 1982). Typological, essentialist (or top-down) assumptions are avoided. By having the environment act dynamically on potential orderings already present in the organism, selection theories of brain function avoid the problem of the homunculus, just as evolution avoids the argument from design [p.66].

For Edelman, an epigenetic neuronal development follows a nonlinear process of constant selection. Thelen and Smith (1998) paraphrase Edelman as saying that "epigenetic processes produce brain structures that are modally similar in all members of a species, [but] these same processes also produce—through [Darwinian] selection—enormous individual variability at the level of anatomical connectivity of the individual neurons and groups" (p. 143). Thelen and Smith continue, "At both the cellular level and higher, events that lead to increased complexity and diversity of structures and functions are all dependent upon events that preceded them. This means . . . developing systems exhibit properties that are emergent from their interactions and not dependent on pre-existing codes" (p. 142).

In his Darwinian, selectionist neural development, Edelman eschews the linear view because it involves an unworkable hierarchical accretion of complex structures, based on modal performances. Such a linear view makes normative thinking the organizational center and sees any diversity from a norm as irrelevant or pathological if they are excessive. A dynamic view of development, in contrast, welcomes variability because it is the source of new forms. Not only is variability from the norm not extraneous, it becomes the motivator of change in a dynamic self-organizing system. Without diversity, the nervous system could not develop perceptual categories as described by Fodor earlier. As will be demonstrated in the next chapter, the concept of perceptual diversity is an extremely valuable one for clinical work. And as Gadamer (1993) argues, perception consists of combining the results of looking at something from a number of points of view, because perception occurs from multiple ways of measuring (sensing) the same phenomenon.

Edelman (1987) thinks the major function of perception is to form categories, which are facilitated by means of two extremely important neural characteristics: *degeneracy* (multi neural channels) and *reentry* (multi-input modes). It is through these processes of degeneracy and reentry that Edelman explains how perceptual categorization is carried out at the neuronal level "without an explicit program and without explicit prior knowledge of the categories that it develops procedures to represent" (p. 66). Degeneracy is where an input signal takes a number of pathways. As these different pathways create variances in the signal's characteristics, at the end point there is a need for an averaging-like process, an abstraction of the signal, to be of use. So, a form of signal categorizing is built into neural input architecture through the overlapping of multiple signal channels. A way to envision neural degeneracy is illustrated by Australian Aboriginal Water Dreaming paintings (from Papunya), where a stream is shown as a series of waterholes, connected by many channels. The stream, under dry conditions, "degenerates" into many streamlets, some of which eventually dry up. With neural systems, degenerate overlapping circuits create signal transmissions that have a generalized effect and a primary level of abstraction or categorizing.

Edelman (1987) also sees *degeneracy* as creating "a particular threshold condition, [where] there must in general be more than one way satisfactorily to recognize a given input signal" (p. 49). Degeneracy results from the sharing of signals as a consequence of the "overlapping dendritic and axonal arbors [that] actually enhance the possibility of combinational variance and degeneracy in the primary repertoire" of neuronal groups (p. 66). This means that degeneracy serves a special form of redundancy to make the neural system more reliable (p. 107). It also means that if one channel is damaged, the system is still able to function because of the parallelism of degenerate circuits. Degeneracy, then, creates a reliable input system that categorizes.

Llinas also discusses the question of neural reliability. He (2001) says, "In non-reliable systems, the [parallel] elements are not redundant and are therefore slightly different in their unreliability. Because they are all slightly different in their unreliability, there will never be the possibility of this unreliability adding up! These [so called] unreliable systems are therefore more reliable than reliable systems" (p. 265). Thelen and Smith (1998) also give a reason for degeneracy. They think that "the primary repertoire [of neurons] must be degenerate—sufficiently overlapping so that stimuli impinging on only part of the network would invoke a generalized response, but not so broad as to exclude highly specific properties" (p. 148).

Edelman's second characteristic, *reentry*, involves an "interrelating of several or many simultaneous perceptual and motor representations" (Thelen and Smith, 1998, p. 149). Reentry uses multi-modal sensing. For example, a piece of fruit is generally experienced by all the senses. We see, taste, smell, feel, and even hear an apple as we bite and chew it. In using a combination of sensory modes, neural reentry involves the capacity of categorizing such cross-modal perceptions, a capacity that Daniel Stern (1985) reports for infants a few days old. Cross-modal perceptions are also demonstrated by the Meltzoff and Borton's (1979) experiment, where blindfolded three-week-old infants were given one of two different pacifiers ("dummies") to suck, one smooth, the other rough. After the babies sucked on their pacifier, the blindfold was removed and, seeing two kinds of pacifiers in front of them, infants looked more at the type of pacifier they had just sucked. This result reflects a haptic-visual transfer of information. It and other studies show that infants are born with the capacity for cross-modal perception, which develops from the trant connectivity of the brain.

Edelman (1987) says that reentrant connectivity is shown "in certain species of monkey, [where] there may be as many as fifteen visual areas carrying out different functions" and concludes, "the idea of reentry is a minimal assumption necessary to account for neural representations of spatiotemporal continuity" (p. 65). Thelen and Smith also think that reentry is an essential neural requirement for perceptual categorization to occur dynamically.

To acknowledge that multi-modal perception of the senses leads to reentrant mapping is only part of the perceptual story. Perceptual categorization also occurs as a result of kinesthetic sensations provided by movement of the large limbs, trunk, head, neck, and eyes. Edelman thinks kinesthetic sensations, in addition to multi-modal sensing, assist perceptual systems in developing categorization. If different modes of observing lead to cross-modal percepts, movement enables observations of the same object from different positions, with the resulting formation of multiple images for the development of perceptual categories. Motor signals too play a part of the reentrant process. That actions have an important effect on the perceptual system is supported by the Held and Hein (1963) experiment, in which movement [by the experimenter] of kittens who remain passive, is not enough for them to develop normal vision. But when the kittens vigorously initiated their own motion, their vision improved. This important reciprocal connection between movement and perception is evident too with blind children, whose lack of sight delays locomotor development.

(8) Fast's "Selving" Theory

It is not enough to be unknowingly self-organizing as depicted in the previous subsections. A crucial component is added when a human being realizes that he/she can self-organize. Irene Fast (1998) refers to this self-awareness as developing a "sense of I-ness," which is different from Hartmann's (1950) "ego psychology" and his concepts of self and object representations that once dominated American psychoanalytic psychotherapy. Fast thinks the self and object representations of Hartmann, Kris, and Loewenstein (1947) inadequately describe the emergence of self-awareness because they are presented as impersonal functions that are derived from energic forces. In presenting them so, he presumes a non-dynamic view of the self that does not "conceptualize interactions as personal engagements." Convincingly Fast (1998) says, "A representation does not love, take pride, envy, admire, or remember" (p. 4). She claims that a sense of "I-ness" develops long before the myelination of the frontal lobes in late infancy and formation of symbolic memory, which are needed to make sense out of Hartmann's self and object representations. So, with Hartmann's representations arriving relatively late in development, Beebe and colleagues (1997) make the case for pre-symbolic representations. If Hartmann's self and object representations are to retain theoretical value, they form later than Fast's primitive sense of "I-ness."

Fast's focus on "I-ness" seems to cover what Stern (1985) calls an "emergent self." Stern sees evidence for an emergent self in infant studies soon after birth, but based on the evidence of the existence of fetal affects (see next chapter), a case can be made for the beginning of self-awareness during the fetal period. Although the onset of this selving process is very much an open question, it is clear that in conjunction with increased perceptual processing of early fetus/infant carer interactions, an initial, undifferentiated sense of "I-ness" gradually develops into a differentiated sense of awareness. Importantly, when referring to undifferentiated "I-ness" before significant perceptual awareness occurs, Fast, influenced by Schafer's (1976) action language, claims "Our thinking, feeling and acting are not what our self does; they are what our self is." With this very early undifferentiated state, she explains, "It is not that our self loves, takes pride, envies, imagines, and remembers; our loving, taking pride, envying, imagining, and remembering are self" (p. 5). Initially the actions of the body self help shape the self-organizing "I-ness" of our eventual self-awareness.

Goethe (1990) placed a similar emphasis on action—hence body self—in understanding self-organizing. Using the New Testament as a reference, he begins,

> It says, "In the beginning was the Word."
> Already I am stopped. It seems absurd.
> The Word does not deserve the highest prize,
> I must translate it otherwise
> If I am well inspired and not blind.
> It says: In the beginning was Mind.
> Ponder that first line, wait and see,
> Lest you should write too hastily.
> Is mind the all-creating source?
> It ought to say: In the beginning there was Force.
> Yet something warns me as I grasp the pen,
> That my translation must be changed again.
> The spirit helps me. Now it is exact.
> I write: In the beginning was the Act. [p. 153]

Although Fast recognized the emergence of a primitive sense of "I-ness" from a human organism's self-organizing behavior, she (1998) also acknowledged that, after the perceptual development of the fetal and infancy periods, we are "virtually compelled to notions of the self as a subject that does various things" (p. 8). In Kegan's (1982) terms, there develops a separate subjective self that does things after we develop the cognitive capacity to differentiate.

Fast thinks the increasing capacity to self-differentiate comes from what she calls "I-schemes" that are formed from patterns of interaction with the environment, especially with a primary carer. As I-scheme interactive "events" with a carer accumulate with invariant and variant themes, their features in common lead to generalizations that both integrate them and, in so doing, enable differentiation. The process of integrating and differentiating these "I-scheme events" she calls "selving." Fast finds support for her notion of interactive selving from Piaget's "action schemes" (Flavell, 1963), from Stern's (1985) "Generalized Event Structures," from Beebe et al. (1997) "interaction structures," from Fonagy et al. (1993) "internal working model," and from Nelson's (1986) "schemes." Loewald (1980) also states that "motivational forces become organized . . . through interactions within a psychic field consisting originally of a mother-child psychic unit" (pp. 127–28). These converging theoretical constructs suggest that infants internalize interactive patterns with the primary carer in conjunction with the formation of a procedural memory—associated with the basal ganglia neural circuits. Importantly, from these interactive patterns an infant eventually develops a capacity to differentiate the part of experience that is self-contingent and the part that is influenced by a "significant other."

Self-development is assisted by attuned selfobject experiences in at least two ways. Selfobject experiences help facilitate movement from a primitive, undifferentiated sense of "I-ness" to a differentiated subjective self, and concomitantly they are key to a subjective self's vitalization during temporary undifferentiated periods of "I-ness." Examples of vitalization can be seen from such daily behavioral patterns as cuddles, sharing important experiences with relatives and friends, meditation or "bush-walking" (hiking). We also recognize that although positive vitalization can occur to some extent during a differentiated subjective state, an extreme lack of vitalization may demand more drastic, undifferentiated experiences that involve a primitive sense of "I-ness" to enable more rapid "fueling" or nourishing of the self.

The concept of differentiation, which Piaget used in his theory of development, and which Fast emphasized, complements Kohut's selfobject construct. As discussed in the previous chapter, when a patient experiences a psychotherapist as a selfobject, the psychotherapist is functioning as a psychological extension of the patient. By allowing a patient to temporarily experience him/her as a selfobject, the psychotherapist is tuned into and accepts the patient's undifferentiated state of "I-ness." Such attunement helps facilitate structuralization and differentiation and explains why after new experiences, healthy people will utilize others as mature selfobjects to gain a differentiation of the self from the new experience (Kohut, 1984, p. 219). As Kohut (1979) indicated in the case of Mr. Z (p. 398) and is now reported as a common experience for practicing psychotherapists using a self-psychology approach, patients who experience a psychotherapist as a selfobject, often volunteer that they feel better, more alive, and sometimes this is reported after only one session. Initially Kohut referred to these temporary undifferentiated states, during which the psychotherapist functions as a selfobject, as merger experiences, but later reserved this term merger for the desperate efforts of archaic, depleted patients to induce a dissolution into a primitive, undifferentiated state of "I-ness" in an attempt to be revitalized as quickly as possible. It is the lack of vitality and the desperate need for refueling that can be a major trigger for a desperate merger that is a form of what Jackson called dissolution.

Eagle (1984), congruent with Fast's concept of selving, conceives of Hartmann's impersonal self and object representations as experiences of a differentiated self. He thinks Freud's "Das Ich" (traditionally translated "the ego") as an "I" experience, and "Das Es" (traditionally translated as "the id") as an "it" experience. Loewald (1980) holds a similar view. As Fast explains,

> Like Eagle, Loewald differentiates the Id and Ego in terms of those processes people experience as automatic or intrusions from outside ["it" experiences], on the one hand, and actions they experience as personal ["I" experiences], on the other. In his view, motivation becomes increasingly personalized as people make progress in development or clinical work. In analysis, for example, a woman plagued by a compulsion to murder her child might begin to understand that the feelings of hate she harbors toward the child are connected to a disturbed relationship with her husband and, in turn, to feelings towards her father (Loewald, 1980). That is, what she experienced as an impersonal, compelling force becomes part of a network of the interpersonally structured motivations that constitute the self [p. 13].

Fast's view, which involves a reinterpretation of the traditional view of Freud's "Das Ich" and "Das Es," resonates with the physiology of Jackson and his view of human evolution from more automatic to less automatic behavior, and is congruent with the philosophy of Martin Buber with his concepts of "I," "Thou," and "It," as discussed in the preceding chapter. With Buber, a differentiated sense of "I" and "It" develops from special "Thou" experiences. In Kohut's terms, selfobject experiences are essential for the emergence of a self that organizes around "Thou" and "It" experiences.

In summarizing, we have drawn upon the ideas of Gordon, Llinas, Mesulam, Thelen and Smith, Jackson, Fodor, Edelman, and Fast, to explore how, through its self-organizing capacity, a human organism may develop from neural specialization and automatic behavior into one capable of modeling (believing) and better predicting the future. We have seen what it means for a human organism to self-organize in the movement and perceptual modular systems. Such self-organizing based on the need for action forms a useful basis for understanding the emergence of self-awareness and a sense of self-agency. It is an "experience-distant" background for psychotherapy theory that develops "experience-near" concepts useful in empathically understanding the self-organization of psychotherapy patients. For more we turn now to Kohut's concepts on self-organization.

Section B. Kohut's Supraordinate Self

Kohut was acutely aware that a definition of "self" depends heavily on the point of view of the academic discipline that constructs it. Consistent with an empathic-based psychoanalytic psychotherapy that commences with the patient's point of view, he developed a theory of self-organizing to facilitate psychotherapy, especially with narcissistic patients. Many of his self-concepts were "experience-near" and heavily influenced by his theory of narcissism. He theorized that if healthy narcissistic experiences keep a person cohesive, pathological symptoms such as grandiosity and a need to be perfect, are excessive self-organizing responses in an attempt to prevent fragmentation. Hence, narcissistic symptoms reinforce the idea that patients are motivated to create a cohesive self-organization as a result of continuing joyous transactions with its environment. To understand "disorders of the self"—Kohut's later term for narcissistic disorders—is to understand how each person is uniquely organized to gain some sense of self-agency. A study of disorders of the self reveals how much self-organizing occurs to maintain self-cohesion, and how much a person is creatively adapting to any new conditions of his/her environment.

Kohut approached treatment by viewing patients as holistically as possible. As Chessick (1980) observed, Kohut began with a phenomenological self and later, similar to Kant, postulated a noumenal self that went beyond the data, and like Kant, Kohut's noumenal self had experiences of agency. For example, Kohut depicts the narcissistic self-organizing as being depleted or yearning for mirroring. Importantly, such a holistic view includes a human organism's need to self-organize, an idea which could be construed as an expression of Spinoza's drive for survival (Damasio, 2003, p. 35). Chessick thinks Kohut's ideas of self organizing reflect the

> Zeignarick phenomenon which postulates some kind of inner motivation of undeveloped structures to resume their development when given an opportunity; the energy behind this motivation has nothing to do with Freud's instinctual drives [p. 470].

Kohut called his holistic view of self-organizing as "supraordinate" in order to emphasize the organizing from as total and inclusive a point of view as possible. This supraordinate view is similar to a view that has its roots in the religious tradition of healing the psyche (Wise, 1983). In New Testament Greek the word for psyche refers not to "one part of the total person as distinguished from other parts, such as pneuma and soma, rather, it refers to the living person as a total reality or unity" (p. 3). For example, pastoral (religious) psychotherapists attract such patients as those who are "unable to pray," "no longer believe in God," or have "sacramental phobias" (fear that receiving the Eucharist would result in punishment), as well as the usual array of clinical symptoms. Professionally trained pastoral psychotherapists explore religious presenting issues as an expression of a patient's self-organizing of the total self and recognize that any increased understanding of religious and/or non-religious self-sectors generally leads to constructive self-organizing adjustments.

In contrast to this supraordinate view of self-organizing, there is symptomatic treatment. The difference between these two approaches—supraordinate and symptomatic—is illustrated by the case of K, a patient whose head pain resulted from a low-velocity rear-end car collision. K was referred to a movement specialist who also practiced psychotherapy from a self psychology perspective. Initially, the referring GP asked the movement therapist to focus on K's movements to help eradicate her pain as it was interfering with her work concentration, her working memory, and her sporting activities. It was a symptom-oriented request, not one directed to a supraordinate self-organizing tendency.

In treatment financed by an insurance company, the movement therapist joined K's "treatment team" (GP, physiologist, psychologist, and a movement therapist trained in empathy-based psychotherapy), to implement the insurance company's goal of eradicating K's "head injury" symptoms. Despite this expensive, collective effort, K's symptoms did not improve. The GP's painkillers and antidepressants made her feel worse. The physiotherapist's diagnosis of bulging disks and sciatica, and treatment using "deep muscle release procedures" and joint manipulation, only increased her distress, further exacerbated by her shame for being a rehabilitation failure. And the psychologist's attempts to hypnotize K and explore childhood traumas left her fainting, violently nauseous, blacking out, hyperventilating, resistant to "going under," and disgusted. Following these failed treatments, K was sent to a very expensive pain management program five times a week for several months, where she was given acupuncture, exercise, massage, and injections—but the pain continued. It was similar to treatment undertaken before Freud developed psychoanalysis.

The movement therapist, who initially had been given the task of "educating" K about her body, observed that K's pain was shifting around. She said, "The pain would settle into one part, . . . her back, and working there for a few weeks, her control and strength and proper movement and patterning would improve. Foolishly I thought I had succeeded, only to have the pain and dysfunction flare up severely in another part." The movement therapist realized that the team's treatment efforts and failures had not only increased the patient's distress but also increased K's belief—and K's "healers" too—that she was a hopeless case. Responding to the treatment stalemate and the despair involved, the movement therapist changed her goal from eradicating the symptom of pain to empathically understanding K's functioning as a whole human being. After the movement therapist's empathic approach diminished the pain, K terminated with the physiologist and psychologist and, supported by the GP, gained insurance company permission to enter into long-term intensive psychotherapy with her movement therapist. Eventually, after many more sessions, K experienced enough permanent reduction in pain to become functional and take up employment again. This beneficial result followed from intensive psychotherapy with an empathic approach to understanding the total supraordinate self.

Kohut's (1971) theory of self-organizing was a significant change from the classical analysis of his training. Initially he had adopted Freud's version of the mind as a mental apparatus consisting of the id, ego, and superego, as agencies of the mind. In working with narcissistic patients, however, Kohut began with a concept of self-organizing that was similar to Kant's "phenomenal self," (i.e., a succession of relatively temporary states through time that could be accessed empathically). By 1977, however, Kohut had embraced the concept of a supraordinate self, a configuration beyond the sum of its parts that achieved continuity in time (p. 177), but was only tentatively knowable empirically. Kohut made this holistic, supraordinate self-organization, which he understood as an independent center of initiative, a major postulate.

Kohut's supraordinate self, experienced as coherence and continuity, is a description that is rejected by postmodern analysts (Teicholtz, 1999), especially such radical postmoderns as Kristeva and Barratt who view it as too unified, bounded, and fixed. Kristeva (1987) writes, "We are subjects in process, ceaselessly losing our identity, destabilized by fluctuations in our relations to the other" (p. 9). Barratt (1993) emphasizes that the focus in psychotherapy should not be on the self, but on "vital contradictoriousness" and "incessant transmutation" of the "subject-in-process."

In response to these postmodern criticisms, Teicholtz (1999) argues that a fragmentary and discontinuous consciousness does not make it necessary to reject "Kohut's emphasis on a healthy sense of coherence and continuity" that arises from constant self-organizing (p. 53). The postmoderns cast the issue as a choice between unity and change, whereas for Kohut (1977) the key to an adaptive, creative life was a "sense of coherence despite change" (p. 312). Teicholtz, explicating Kohut, explains, "We need a sense of continuity because of the discontinuities in modern living and in development; and we need a sense of coherence exactly because of the complexity and multifaceted nature of our lives and our psyches, because of the multiplicity of our roles and relationships" (p. 53). She continues, the postmodern insistence on discontinuities of experience means that "the adaptive functionality or necessity of coherence and continuity often gets lost" (p. 53).

To postmodern analysts any awareness of being a self-organizing organism is based on an illusion. Mitchell (1993; Mitchell and Black, 1995) takes such a position, as does Lacan (1977), but it is particularly articulated by Barratt (1993). In response to the illusion question, Stepansky (Teicholtz, 1999, p. 55) reminds us that the ontological issue is not whether the self is illusory or not, but whether we can go about the business of living without a subjective sense of cohesion. Teicholtz (1999) is especially skeptical of Barratt's view. She concludes, "It is difficult for me to imagine that Barratt himself, for instance, without a sense of self or identity that he theoretically rejects as a foreclosure, could have decided on a project of value and interest to him, such as a book on the postmodern impulse, carried out the sustained research necessary to implement it, and motivated and organized himself to do the writing" (p. 55). What is particularly troubling about the postmodern attack on the concept of the self, a deconstruction without any replacement, arises from a destructive self-nihilistic motivation that is self-perpetuating like a "kindled" phenomena (Post, 1992).

Even in accepting the functional need for a Kohutian supraordinate self, there is some justifiable concern about its potential for reification into a static entity. A careful reading of Kohut, however, indicates his many attempts to avoid expressing the self as a "thing" by emphasizing the self as subjective experiences of continuity and coherence. Such self-experiences are regularly associated with psychic health. Concern over reification diminishes if Kohut's supraordinate self concept incorporates the type of self-organizing theory outlined in section A. As depicted there, a person has self-organizing input and output systems and relatively fixed, slowly self-organizing central belief systems that emerge as a result of an increasing awareness of a differentiating "I-ness" from others. Linked together, these input, central organizing, and output systems become components of a larger self-organizing supraordinate system, where the relatively fixed beliefs that represent structuralizing of previous experiences have a strong influence as a self-sector, but not total control. If the thoughts of central processing were in complete control, the supraordinate self would, in effect, function as if a homunculus. Instead, it is clear that reason, as understood by the thinkers of the enlightenment, does not have a direct and centralized control of a supraordinate, self-organizing self; clinicians see this daily in the failure of logic and reason to induce psychotherapeutic change in patients with serious psychopathology.

Kohut's "supraordinate self," as a changing, holistic, self-organizing system, may be referred to as a "supraordinate self-configuration" or simply as a "self-configuration." An emphasis on self-configuration—a term used by Kohut—helps mitigate the criticism of theorists such as Stolorow and Atwood (1992), that Kohut's terms "self," "supraordinate self," "peripheral self," "nuclear self," "segmental self," and "sectoral self" are vulnerable to being conceived of as being static and reified. Yet this criticism is relevant to issues of training and practice. In supervising psychotherapists, we have found that psychotherapists with a static concept of self correlates with a difficulty of empathically placing themselves in the shoes of patients, especially those with multiple personality disorders or with narcissistic behavior disorders. In working with such patients, it is an advantage for a psychotherapist to use the conceptual tools of dynamic supraordinate selves, peripheral and nuclear selves, and segmental and sectoral selves as self-configurations that are susceptible to new configurations resulting from new experiences that are included in self-organizing.

Interestingly, Kohut rejected the reification of self-concepts. He (1970s) says, "There are those [such as Levin 1969; Schafer, 1973] who would postulate that a self—the self—is the center of our being from which all initiative springs and where all experiences end" (p. 134). He did not agree with such a single agent-self, because it leads to a "de-emphasis of the importance of the unconscious" (p. 134). He was also at pains to make clear that "the concept of a unitary, central self is an axiom introduced into analysis from the outside" (1970s, p. 135). Not that its origins outside of analysis unduly troubled Kohut; his concern was that this outside view clashed with the hard-won insights from psychoanalysis. He said that from a psychoanalytic approach "we will recognize the simultaneous existence of different and even contradictory selves in the same person, of selves with various degrees of stability and of various degrees of importance" (p. 135). To Kohut, the clinical functionality of a concept took precedence over its tidiness or parsimony. And he conceded, "despite everything there is finally the possibility that a harmonious and internally consistent personality cannot be achieved, and that some deep rents in the psyche structure must remain unmended" (p. 158).

It is of considerable interest that long before the popular surge of interest in chaos theory and its influence on theories of human development, Kohut held a view of the self that had the capacity to reconfigure in a nonlinear way. He (1970s) points out,

> The discovery during analysis of various selves in the same individual is at times similar to the discovery of various configurations in the well-known experiments regarding various figure-ground configurations [such as, the Muller-Lyer experiment]. At one moment the observer discerns one configuration, which has complete validity and forms a convincing Gestalt. Yet, after an imperceptible shift in the focus of the observer's attention, there appears another fully valid configuration which crowds out the first [p. 162].

From the point of view of a Lakatosian theory of Kohut's postulates, it is of minor relevance if Kohut reified the concept of the self or not. The significant issue is whether it is possible to conceive of Kohut's supraordinate self as a dynamic self-system that is continually self-organizing so that dramatic shifts in self-configurations, as described by the nonlinear concepts of chaos theory can be more easily understood and used to foster therapeutic change. We contend that modern dynamic, self-organizing thinking can be incorporated into Kohut's theory of a supraordinate self.

Stolorow and Atwood, in another criticism of Kohut's theory of the self, point to his concept of an "innate nuclear program." As evident from a number of references, Kohut held a view of an innately unfolding developmental blueprint, a view also challenged by the cognitive theorists in section A. Accepting this criticism of Kohut's blueprint idea, we think it is possible and valuable for psychotherapy theory to retain the idea of an innate nuclear self without specific cognitive contents as implied by the idea of blueprints. Further, we propose that a theory of a supraordinate self that includes an unencapsulated module of relatively stable beliefs, undergoes a Darwinian process just as neurons select at the cellular level.

In conceiving of a supraordinate self, Kohut emphasized the need for self-constructs that would be experience-near and clinically valuable. These self-dimensions are (1) fragmentation-cohesion, (2) peripheral-nuclear, and (3) sectoral-segmental, which we will explore further. Before we do, we emphasize that these are not considered as component parts of the supraordinate self-organization, like the perceptual, motor and belief systems, but simply as functional ways of viewing the supraordinate self-organizing. Most importantly, Kohut used these organizational configurations to understand patients during psychoanalysis.

(1) Fragmentation—Cohesion Self-Configurations

Kohut noted, understandably, that dramatic signs of patient fragmentation draw more clinical attention than states of cohesion. He intended fragmentation to be a broad, encompassing term that included, for example, gross signs of a psychotic break (loss of "time, place and person") or depression (can't eat, sleep, or take action). Stated another way, fragmentation was seen as a patient's need to dissolve into a dedifferentiated, or dissociated, or hallucinating state. He also included fragmentation signs that were less severe or appeared more subtly in psychotherapy, such as when a patient becomes enraged, goes silent, or is unable to produce thoughts, share feelings, or reveal behaviors in response to a psychotherapist's empathic failure. At the cohesive end of the fragmentation-cohesion dimension, Kohut had in mind the relatively joyous, adaptive living that involves being creative, empathic, wise, humorous, and able to face the inevitability of death (Kohut, 1966).

Kohut's idea of self-cohesion has relevance in understanding attachment theory. In their research, Main and her colleagues (1985) found that an infant's secure attachment to a significant other is highly correlated to other's ability to develop self-narratives, and is especially evident as a coherence of memories, thoughts, and feelings about early attachments, despite hardships faced. Parents' autobiographical memories function as "secure" internal models that have little need for defensive functions such as denial.

The London Parent-Child Project came to a similar conclusion to Main. When Fonagy and colleagues (1991) assessed the security of parents during the third trimester of pregnancy and then assessed the infant's attachment at one year of age, as anticipated, they found that secure parents usually had securely attached children. Of significant interest was how parents transmitted their security to their children. Fonagy's analytic training influenced his explanation that security is induced in the child as a result of the other's capacity to reflect about their own and the subjective states of others. Secure children have secure parents who are able to empathically mentalize their children's experiences, especially their feelings. He calls the processes involved, a "reflective function" (Fonagy et al., 2002) where a mother holds her child's internal affective experiences in mind (Fonagy et al.) Meins and her colleagues (Meins et al., 1998; Meins and Fernyhough, 1999) came to a similar view, using the concept of "mindedness." Such explanations are sufficiently "akin" to Kohut's concept of empathy (Slade, 2005, p. 271) to add empirical support to empathy as a central postulate in psychotherapy. Furthermore, these empirical studies underline the value of Kohut's concept of cohesion in a theory of self-organizing. It is the cohesive narrative that both reflects and imparts a sense of security.

Kohut evidenced his interest in the fragmentation-cohesion continuum in his earliest papers. For example, in his paper "Enjoyment of Listening to Music" (Kohut and Levarie 1950), he refers to musical tonality as a means of "permitting the mastery of otherwise chaotic acoustical stimuli" (p. 151). He then continues, "Within each tonality one special tone is chosen as a signal, a frame of reference within which all other tones can be understood. It is commonly called the tonic. It is the fixed point from which one measures all other tones and which determines the consonant or dissonant character of all other tones" (p. 151). He then points out that the content of classical music is a movement from consonance (cohesion) to dissonance (fragmentation) to consonance (cohesion) again. As Quine would have recognized, Kohut had first reached his fragmentation-cohesion concept isotropically and then when conducting psychoanalysis, found it helped him better to understand patients. And in his early essay on Thomas Mann's "Death in Venice" (discussed in the next chapter), Kohut portrayed the frantic efforts of the aging artist Ashenbach to stave off psychological fragmentation through his idealistic attraction to Tadzio, the young boy on the beach in Venice (Kohut, 1957, p. 107f).

As Kohut's fragmentation-cohesion dimension assumes that humans are strongly oriented to prevent self-fragmentation in order to survive, he held a view similar to Spinoza's claim that a human has "a relentless endeavor . . . to preserve" (Damasio, 2003, p. 36). As discussed earlier, his fragmentation views can usefully incorporate Jackson's idea of dissolution as a controlled return to an earlier self-organizing. They can also incorporate Fast's emphasis on Piaget's concept of differentiation and integration in the initial stages of development. Kohut's view suggests that developing humans modify an innate disposition toward self-organizing into a conscious awareness of dispositions that reflect the supraordinate self-organization's need to be optimally cohesive. So, in understanding a patient, a self-psychologically-oriented psychotherapist explores with the patient the self-organizing processes he/she uses to remain cohesive. And this clinical process in turn, leads to the realization that self-survival is enhanced by both selfobject experiences (Beebe and Lachmann's [2002] "interactive regulation") and solitary self- regulating experiences (Beebe and Lachmann's [2002] "self-regulation," and Lee's [1993, 1994] "cohesive functions").

A psychotherapist notices a patient's self-organizing patterns and especially the ways he/she defensively shores up self-cohesion by engaging in activities such as compulsive rituals or the use of alcohol or drugs, when selfobject experiences are unavailable. Importantly, the psychotherapeutic bonding that develops in the initial stage of psychotherapy may indicate a patient's capacity for cohesion. Evidence for a patient's selfobject experiences with relatives and friends, indicates if these are mature or archaic. Certainly noting the effect of selfobject experiences on the fragmentation-cohesion dimension of a patient's self-organization can help a patient feel empathically understood.

(2) Peripheral—Nuclear Self-Configurations

As early as 1963, Kohut referred to a patient's "basic core of ego functions" (1966, p. 443n) before he later developed his concept of a nuclear self. He contrasted the functions of a nuclear self with such "surface attributes as social role, or religious and national affiliation." These surface attributes were called "peripheral" in a 1972 letter (Kohut, 1978, p. 866), and then "peripheral self" in Kohut's paper "On Courage" (Kohut, 1970s). An initial exposure to these peripheral and nuclear self-descriptions, it may appear that Kohut is referring to two concretely divided parts of the self. But he is not making a "split" between them—as if one is bad and the other good, as would Klein, or as would Winnicott (1960) with his concept of "true self" and "false self." This is clear from his comments on a paper by Wolf, Gedo, and Terman (1972). Instead of an actual "splitting," Kohut (1978) recognized "the simultaneous existence of contradictory selves: different selves of various degrees of stability and of various degrees of importance" (p. 660).

From the point of view of a nonlinear theory of self-organizing, it is possible to understand how such different self-states as the "peripheral" or the "nuclear" self-organization emerge. Which elements of a peripheral or nuclear self-organizing are retained in a self-configuration may be influenced by dissociated fear or closeted shame. When a patient's focus is on social functioning and social norms, the views of others will form major elements in a patient's self-organizing peripheral self. When such elements as a patient's ambitions, ideals, and skills are included in the self-organizing, a completely new configuration emerges as a result of including a nuclear self in the total self-organizing. As Kohut (1978) says of the nuclear self,

> Among these selves [read "self-configurations"], there is one that is most centrally located in the psyche; one that is experienced as basic, and most resistant to change. I like to call this self the "nuclear self." It is composed of the derivatives of the "grandiose self" (i.e., the central self-assertive goals and purposes of the individual) and the derivatives of the "idealized parent imago" (i.e., the centralized values of the individual . . .)" [p. 660].

In speculating about the influences on Kohut when formulating his view of the nuclear self, we notice the theme of ambitions and ideals in Goethe. Goethe (1990) says, "A good man in his darkling ambition remembers the right road [ideals] throughout his quest" (p. 89).

Support for a peripheral-self and nuclear-self distinction goes all the way back to Darwin (1872), who noted the difference between voluntary and involuntary smiles, based on the work of Duschenne. Duschenne discovered that a smile of joy required the combined contraction of the zygomatic major (cheek) and the orbiculus oculi (eye) facial muscles. Darwin noted that, as the zygomatic muscle (cheek) can be activated both voluntarily and involuntarily, it is the major muscle for a polite, social smile. The social smile, he would say, is a behavioral expression of the peripheral self. The smile that moves the orbiculus oculi muscle (eyes) does not participate in the polite smile. It can only be activated involuntarily from the depth within, and was referred to as the "sweet emotions of the soul." Kohut's nuclear self has a depth meaning that is not automatically controlled by the conscious needs of the social self.

Further isotropic support for the concepts of the peripheral and nuclear self comes from Damasio (2003), who explored Darwin's distinction between voluntary and involuntary smiling. He reports that patients with damage to the left frontal lobe's supplemental motor area (SMA) and the anterior cingulate gyrus have difficulty expressing the kind of natural smile (orbiculus oculi muscle) that is spontaneously induced by telling a joke. Instead, "they are limited to the fake 'say cheese' smile" (77). This neurological evidence ties in with the brain's phylogentic development along the lines of surface and depth. Kohut not only adopted this surface/depth dimension and named it peripheral/nuclear; he used it to understand his patients empathically.

The surface/depth dimension, which underlies Kohut's concepts of a peripheral/nuclear self, has a long history, of which we give a few examples. Chomsky (1972) made a distinction between "surface structures" and "deep structures" of language. He thought that deep structure was an underlying abstract form, which determines the meaning of a sentence. The surface structure, the signal we speak or hear, is generated by the deep structure. Interestingly, Chomsky later abandoned this terminology because readers misinterpreted the deep structures as metaphysical and important and the surface structures as superficial and unimportant.

Winnicott (1960), faced a similar problem when he used a false/true self dimension to express the idea of a person's surface or depth, but in doing so, inadvertently and unfortunately helped accentuate the idea of eradicating the false self configuration as a major therapeutic goal. Kohut's peripheral/nuclear self dimension, in contrast, emphasized the therapeutic goal of a more structuralized, hence, stronger nuclear self-organizing, which he argued would transform the "false self," not eradicate it. Furthermore, Kohut conceived of peripheral self-organizing as playing an essential role in the functioning of the supraordinate self-organization. Labeling this legitimate social self-organization as "false" not only denies the value of social self-organizing, but encourages attacks on the thoughts, feelings, and behavior of peripheral self-organizing activity; in psychotherapy such attacks can actually induce patient fragmentation.

The philosopher Bergson wrestled with a surface/depth distinction for the idea of a self. As Guerlac (2006) depicts him, Bergson thinks the "pressure of social life requires the doubling of the subject, the engendering of a second self that covers over the first, like a second skin made up of dead leaves, or dead cells" (p. 76). In doing so, Bergson adopts a position similar to Kant, who proposed that a phenomenological reality covers a noumenal reality that is not directly accessible to us. Kohut, who believed that sensitive artists, musicians, and philosophers foreshadowed advances in clinical theory and practice, was able to use the ideas of creative people in all these fields as a basis for working with patients in such a way that they felt empathically understood.

Kohut's (1970s) concept of a peripheral self of "easy adaptation and comfortable consistency" (p. 158) as compared with a nuclear self, is useful in understanding psychoanalytic, self-psychologically-oriented psychotherapy that aims at structural change. Counseling, as originally conceived, was a brief form of psychotherapy that focuses on a peripheral self and tackles specific goals; it was not designed to engage the nuclear self nor alter repetitive and narcissistic transferences. The differences between peripheral self and nuclear self issues can be seen in the psychotherapy of S, a separated woman in her late forties, who was the chief executive officer of a small firm. She was referred by her GP for psychotherapy because of breathing problems and stomach pains that were considered symptoms of stress and diagnosed as "psychosomatic." Her life from the outside showed all the accoutrements of success: a brilliant career, a large comfortable home, a beautiful late-model car, and a tall, fit body that she worked on in a gymnasium each morning. The only "fly in the ointment" was a conflicted relationship with her teenage daughter. A clue to deeper problems, however, was her reported subjective feeling that she was ugly, despite being seen by others as very attractive.

The beginning sessions focused on S's relationship with her daughter, and her need to "walk on eggshells" from fear of her daughter's outbursts and threats. It seemed as if the daughter used tactics similar to S's father in conducting a psychological war to exhaust S into "surrender." The daughter was "guilt-tripping" S as a means of getting her own way. When the psychotherapist eventually reflected that dealing with her daughter was like trying to fill a bottomless pit, S sighed, felt empathically understood, and began to feel less distressed. From this point in the psychotherapy, the patient experienced her life as improving. Feeling understood and mirrored, she was soon able to say "no" to her daughter, and resisted the unreasonable demands of her job where she had previously been a workaholic. Her relationship with her current boyfriend became more enjoyable. And her daughter experienced a new popularity at school.

In the twentieth session, as S had nothing pressing to talk about, she and the psychotherapist considered stopping sessions. From the view of a better functioning peripheral self, it was a good result. However, during this discussion about terminating, S became anxious because she felt there was something being held back. The psychotherapist then indicated that although S had undoubtedly significantly changed her feelings, there still remained the question of whether the improvements would be relatively permanent. The psychotherapist realized that, although the patient's peripheral self had improved in functioning, she had not explored any depth issues.

After the psychotherapist raised the issue of permanent changes, S burst into tears and said, "Something is going on under the surface. Even though I feel things are going well, I am waiting for the other shoe to drop, as a sign my life could not be ok." So she continued the sessions to explore why she felt her life could never be ok, and why she felt so ugly. As Kohut (1970s) says, an "analytic examination of the nuclear self—in contrast to the examination of peripheral selves—leads always into the psychological depths and as the deeper layers are gradually penetrated, to the discovery of the dynamically and genetically meaningful pattern" (p. 158).

In the sessions that followed, S revealed a history of verbal abuse from her father and abuse from her alcoholic husband when he was drunk. As her history was explored further, it became obvious that S had a pattern of attracting dependent, insensitive men who used her as the breadwinner, and then abused her when she asked them to pull their weight in the relationship. With the emergence of enactments of being used and abused by her father, the goal of psychotherapy became the modification of the need for this pattern. These men did not match the values and ideals of her nuclear self-organization. As the work proceeded, S soon experienced the time between sessions as too long and requested twice-weekly appointments to enable a more intense exploration of the repetitive transference material that was creating so much distress in her nuclear self. The case eventually had a successful result.

Kohut's nuclear self is deeper than the peripheral self. It consists of a person's ambitions and ideals, particularly ideals, which form its major components. Kohut thinks that courage is a "central characteristic of the nuclear self" (p. 153) as courage especially depends on the person's core values. To illustrate courage as a derivative of the ideals sector of the nuclear self, Kohut takes examples from martyr heroes against the Nazi regime, and then analyzes the role of the tragic hero in the history of drama. Of the martyr-heroes Kohut says, "It is the set of central values and ideals, the heir to the archaic idealized object, which decisively defines the nuclear self" (p. 146). He illustrates with the example of the Austrian peasant Franz Jagerstatter, whose religious beliefs (ideals) led him to refuse service in the Austrian army during World War II. Although he was offered the compromise of noncombatant service, he "calmly and serenely . . . went to the guillotine in 1943 rather than betray his Christian values." Kohut also uses the examples of Hans and Sophie Scholl, two anti-Nazi heroes of a student conspiracy in Munich in 1943, who were killed by the Nazis because their ideals clashed with Nazi ideology.

Knowing the possibility that martyr heroes could be interpreted as having a major form of psychopathology, Kohut goes to considerable lengths to discuss this issue. Although he admits that some martyr heroes have shown symptoms of psychosis, there are others who, when faced with physical death because of their opposition to an evil authority, do so with an inner serenity, continue to respond empathically, have a mental state akin to wisdom, and retain a sense of humor, all of which indicates an absence of fragmentation. In addition to Kohut's examples above, there was the German Lutheran theologian Dietrich Bonhoeffer (Bethge, 1967) during World War II who helped lead the Lutheran Confessing Church to resist the state supported Lutheran Church, which had accommodated the Nazis. The outspoken Bonhoeffer was eventually imprisoned and killed before the Allied forces captured his prison.

Bonhoeffer's resistance arose from the clash between theological values residing in his nuclear self and the beliefs of Nazi ideology. As his "Letters and Papers From Prison" (1953) shows, he creatively used his imprisonment to strengthen his nuclear self to the end of his life. To Kohut, "such heroic individuals are not psychotic" (p. 141). What they show is their determination to remain faithful to their nuclear selves, because to them, fragmentation, hence psychological death, is worse than biological death. Forced to choose between the two, they decide on psychological life and face physical death with a quiet sense of triumph over their chief enemy, which to them is the fragmentation accompanying a total collapse.

In discussing these martyr-heroes, it is clear that Kohut (1970s) is not suggesting that the martyr-hero model is one for everyone to follow. He says, "The full assertion of our nuclear selves is thus for most of us beyond the scope of our courage" (pp. 168–69). But extreme examples of courage highlight the importance of values and ideal beliefs in the functioning of everyone's nuclear self. The tragic heroes of art, literature, and drama attest further to this importance. Kohut says,

> The art of the tragic—whether sung, told, or written as in the great epics; whether through music, on canvas, in stone, or on the stage—is concerned with man's attempt to live out the ideals of his nuclear self. And the tragic hero who is the protagonist of great tragedies, which must be counted as among the most precious cultural possessions of mankind, is a man who, despite the breakdown of his physical and mental powers (e.g., Oedipus) and even despite his biological death (e.g., Hamlet), is triumphant because his nuclear self achieved an ascendancy which never will, indeed, which never can, be undone. [p. 166].

For the tragic person, biological death is a psychological triumph if the nuclear self remains cohesive.

The tragic hero plays an important role in a group or in broader society. The tragic hero, through his/her personal triumph, has a vitalizing influence on any group to which he/she belongs, when the values and life of the group, the subculture, or the culture are threatened. Tragedy, according to Kohut, "gives the spectator, reader, listener, or beholder the opportunity to experience, in temporary identification with the tragic hero, the unfolding, expansion and triumph of his own nuclear self" (p. 168). Tragedy is not the story of a happy ending. It is generally full of unsolvable conflicts and loose ends. A tragic death usually does not traverse through Kubler-Ross's (1969) five stages of dying, but ends in a triumphal, cohesive nuclear self that creates a stronger, more vitalized group or subculture.

As a major illustration of the tragic hero, Kohut (1970s) refers to Hamlet. "Hamlet's death," he says, "is the triumphant fulfillment of his reconstituted nuclear self, and his weaknesses, hesitations, and temporary failures are like the climber's toils and sighs as he struggles to reach the peak" (p. 172). Why was Hamlet so triumphant? Kohut saw that Hamlet was a person who had faced the inadequacies of his old style of self-organizing, the idealistic innocence of his late adolescence, and transformed himself into a new person who could accept the presence of evil in the world. Although the populace liked the "pureness of Hamlet's idealism," the murder of his father and the complicity of his mother shattered his idealistic worldview, built entirely around goodness. What Hamlet faced was the realization that royalty, which represented power at that time in history, could live a life of ruthless evil. The new Hamlet is personally triumphant over evil, as evil did not reduce him, through self-fragmentation, into groveling self-destructiveness.

As Kohut depicts it, the nuclear self consists of more than ideals. He uses the personality of Winston Churchill to demonstrate how the nuclear self also contains ambitions. Churchill, as a war correspondent during the Boer War, was famous for escaping his captors. Kohut (1970s) envisions escape as a model scene (Lichtenberg, 1989) for Churchill, who "had a compelling need to be entrapped in order to prove his ability to escape" (p. 136). His nuclear self seems to have crystallized around the visions of a grandiose self. He was susceptible to flying fantasies. Not being committed to lofty ideals, he was imbued instead with the conviction that he possessed an unconquerable power. As Tolpin (1974) affirms, it eventually became a transformed grandiosity. In exhorting England in its struggle against Nazi tyranny in 1940, he captured the imagination of Britons with his expansive description of their crucial struggle, the most important for "a thousand years." Churchill saw England's crisis, refused to minimize the danger, and promised his countrymen the reward of "their finest hour." "Thus for Churchill," says Kohut, "as is undoubtedly true for many great leaders, it was the grandiose self and not the derivatives of the idealized imago that was the important ingredient of his nuclear self" (p. 137).

Tolpin (1974) describes how Tolstoy transformed the grandiosity of his grandiose nuclear self. As a nine-year-old, Tolstoy too thought he could fly, took off from the window sill of the upstairs study of his home and ended up unconscious on the ground eighteen feet below. Tolstoy's grandiosity was one of two major configurations that alternated between background and foreground. The other configuration was "leaden, bleak" and always "on the brink of despair," as shown by Tolstoy's failed studies at university and his life as a drifter. In an effort at self-repair, Tolstoy mirrored himself in his diary by writing fiction. An aunt, who served as a selfobject during his late teens and early twenties, encouraged him to write novels. In these he kept recreating himself. For example, in his *War and Peace*, when Natasha rhapsodizes about what it would be like to fly to the moon, Tolstoy's grandiosity has been transformed into an "as if" quality. This transformation is also seen in the same novel when Dolokov sits on the sill of a third story window and downs rum to win a bet. Pierre, in representing Tolstoy, is tempted to emulate him, but dances with the officer's cub bear instead, showing that Tolstoy has learned to curb his grandiosity.

This theme of transformed grandiosity is contained in the Greek myth of Daedalus (Tolpin, 1974). This myth depicts the difference between Daedalus and his son Icarus. Trapped on an island, they make wings from feathers and wax, to escape by flying. Although the father, Daedalus, was successful, his son Icarus, carried away with the excitement of flying, soared toward the sun where the heat melted his wings and he fell into the sea and drowned.

Kohut clearly conceived of the nuclear self-organization as consisting primarily of ambitions, skills, and ideals, but it is composed of more than these three things. It seems that any in-depth belief involves the functioning of a nuclear self-organization. Kohut's nuclear self-organization as a concept had a clear focus, but away from this focus the edges were left undefined. The nuclear self-organization is certainly larger than just ambitions, ideals, and skills, but seems to us to be not as large as Fodor's concept of a central modeling/predicting system. What Fodor and Kohut's concepts have in common, however, is the idea that these systems have slowly self-organizing, relatively fixed beliefs. The tenacity with which the beliefs of Kohut's martyr-heroes are held is beyond dispute. Ultimately, whether or not Kohut's concepts of peripheral self and nuclear self survive as ways of conceiving of self-organizing, will depend on their clinical usefulness. As long as patients with narcissistic disorders and other forms of self-pathology seek therapeutic treatment, the concept of a nuclear self will take precedence over many other ways of conceptualizing self-organizing.

(3) Sectoral—Segmental Configurations

Kohut's ideas of sectoral and segmental self-configurations have languished on the edges of modern self psychology theory. Kohut's use of these terms seems synonymous with special images of the self, or what Atwood and Stolorow refer to as "structures of experience" (1984, p. 33) to avoid concretizing the image. Segments are presented as larger areas than sectors. Kohut referred frequently to a narcissistic sector and, after he developed his concept of a vertical split, referred to elements of such a split as sectors. For example, in the case of Mr. X, Kohut (1977) observed that

> personality was divided into two sectors by a vertical split. In one sector, characterized by a sense of superiority, arrogant behavior, unworldly and religious aims, and identification with Christ, he maintained the old merger with his mother who permitted and even encouraged, his expression of ideas of greatness—and his pursuit of life goals that were in harmony with them. [Then there was the second sector] of the structure that yearned for merger with the idealized parent imago and contained some rudimentary foci of already internalized nuclear ideals" [pp. 207–8].

Such use of "sector" to designate an element of the vertical split, however, does not frequently appear in clinical write-ups today.

Although it may be theoretically useful to think of segmental and sectoral self-configurations, using Kohut's terms "sector" and "segment" have the advantage of being user-friendly. For example, in working with patients with a strong religious sector, some have rejected the term "self-configuration" because it was not concrete enough and felt better understood when we switched to the term "self-sector." We also found that patients could readily grasp such ideas as musical, artistic, mathematical, or philosophical self-sectors. Especially in supervision, the notion of a professional sectoral configuration has proven useful (R. Lee, 2005) to distinguish the role of supervision from training psychotherapy. It is the task of supervision to develop significant structuralization in the professional self-sector.

Self-sectors involve more than a patient's interests. For a self-sector to function in a supraordinate self-organization, the interest must be relatively sustained and permanent. Moreover, the interest must reach from the peripheral surface to the nuclear depths of the functioning self. A self-sector, therefore, links the peripheral and nuclear selves in a thematic area of the total self-organizing. To Kohut, a self-sector involves nuclear self-organizing when interest stimulates ambitions, develops skills, and is guided by ideals. The proportion of ambitions, skills, and ideals in the functioning of nuclear self-organizing will vary with each individual, but interest limited to the peripheral self-organizing, without reaching nuclear self-organizing, suggests that the patient will feel ill-nourished by the interest. An interest limited to the peripheral self-organizing, according to Kohut, does not become sectoral.

The concept of a sectoral connectivity that links peripheral self-organizing to ambitions, ideals and skills of nuclear self-organizing, suggests Edelman's understanding of a "degenerate," multichanneled approach to patients in order to gain therapeutic movement. There are multiple ways to reach a patient's nuclear self-organization, such as through a history of family relationships or the emergence of behavioral patterns embedded in procedural memory. For some, however, the connection to their nuclear self-organization comes through an interest in one aspect of self-functioning. Although there is no single road to nuclear self-organizing—dreams form only one path—the sectoral road is an important one. Kohut (1984) calls it a "sectoral continuum" (p. 205). One patient, who was cruelly abused as a child, and who found it traumatic to talk about the past, illustrated the usefulness of a sectoral approach to engage the nuclear self. She refused to talk about her traumas for a long time, but as she had a passionate interest in philosophy, and this interest involved ambitions, skills, and ideals, the psychotherapist successfully encouraged her to share her philosophical ideas as a way of steadily deepening the therapeutic relationship.

An example of a person with an interesting sectoral self comes from Virginia Wolf's character Mrs. Dalloway (Wolf, 1925; H. Lee, 1996). Parties were the rage in upper class London after World War I, and Mrs. Dalloway is portrayed as gaining a reputation as a superb hostess. With all the social glitter of these events, Mrs. Dalloway may appear to have lived shallowly in her peripheral self. But she didn't. She turned her parties into experiences that engaged the ambitions and skills of her nuclear self-organizing to bringing the "right" people together, all done while adhering to the values and ideals of her own social class. Although she was married and had a child, her parties formed a major sectoral path for her life, seemingly as an attempt to heal unresolved trauma associated with the losses of the war. These parties helped keep her cohesive because they gave meaning to her life.

Kohut's concept of self-sectors has implications for the way we conceive of a person's mental health. How is it, we may ask, that some persons born with genetic and/or environmental disadvantages—Stephen Hawking, for example—live productive and creative lives, and yet others, "born with silver spoons in their mouths" commit suicide? Kohut's idea of self-sectors helps provide an answer. He says (1978b) that mental health is fostered when

> at least one sector in personality has established itself in which ambitions, skills, and idealized goals, form an unbroken functioning continuum. . . . The ambitions, the skills and talents, and the ideals of different people have, however, different aims and contents. Furthermore, the functional preponderance of one or the other of these constituents of the self varies from person to person, both with regard to the choice of the leading constituent and with regard to the degree of dominance of any single constituent [p.265].

In defining mental health sectorally, Kohut's views differ sharply with the ideas that mental health comes from emptying a person's unconscious of all unresolved, dark thoughts and feelings, or perfectionistically seeking a complete integration of a person's experiences. To Kohut, the key to mental health depends on deepening areas of interest into sectoral connections rather than on a general self-integration that, however desirable, is not essential. As long as at least one sectoral connection is functioning, a person's life can be healthy and meaningful, even if limited in scope. Kohut staunchly resisted the concept of a normative person as an example of mental health.

Kohut's concept of sectoral self-organizing significantly alters the goal of psychotherapy. In one sense we can say that the purpose of psychotherapy is to weaken the need for repetitive, archaic selfobject transferences through the development of new self-structures. Such a view is further developed through Kohut's concept of sectoral self-organizing. Not all potential sectors need new structuralization in order for the supraordinate self to function with vitality and adaptiveness in encounters with its environment. After having developed or strengthened one sectoral connection, a patient may lose motivation for further psychotherapeutic work with other potential self-sectoral organizing, and terminate, even though unresolved matters and loose ends remain. On the other hand, there are others who seek psychotherapy with at least one reasonably functioning sectoral connection; and want their self-organizing to include new self-sectors that link new dimensions of peripheral and nuclear self-organizing. In undertaking psychotherapy they seek to make themselves less vulnerable, so that if unforeseen circumstances interfere with a vital connection to nuclear self-organizing in one sector, other sectors are available as a source of vitalization for the total self-organization.

Summary

In this chapter we have attempted to demonstrate that humans develop self-organizing visceral and sensory motor systems out of a need to act as a survival strategy. This means that therapeutic exploration with a patient involves understanding the uniqueness of his/her self-organizing as a holistically functioning system that Kohut refers to as "supraordinate." Kohut also demonstrates how attention to such self-organizing dimensions as fragmentation/cohesion, peripheral/nuclear, and sectoral connectivity, aid the psychotherapist in such exploration. But in presenting a self-organizing view of a supraordinate self we have thus far deliberately left an exploration of feelings that develop from a human's visceral self. Such a theory of feelings is another important auxiliary postulate of Kohut's self psychology. In the next chapter, we consider this postulate of a feeling self.

Note

1. Such use is open to Searle's criticism that a person cannot be viewer and viewed at the same time (see chapter 2). The concept of perceiving assumes the use of sight and, therefore, a point of view, and reflects the predominance of sight among the senses in gaining information about the outer world.

CHAPTER FIVE

Feeling States and Affects

Since the beginning of psychotherapy, patients have sought relief from such feelings as distress, fear and anger. By paying close attention to a patient's feelings and responding to them with understanding, psychotherapists soon realized the critical role that feelings play in bringing about therapeutic change. Significant feelings that emerged during training therapy and supervision also alerted Freudian pioneers to the importance of feelings. Yet, despite this recognition, the conduct of psychotherapy has not resulted in a well-formulated theory of feelings, even though successful practice typically leads to theorizing in hopes of repeating successful results or reducing future failures. A theory of feelings for the practice of psychotherapy is far overdue.

The "feeling theory" examined here is tentative and relatively unformed. In the past it has been a theory beset with terminological confusion and limited by a relative paucity of neurological research, especially into the limbic system. Thankfully, this research drought has ended and results are challenging psychotherapy theorists to develop a better theory of feelings for the practice of psychotherapy. For any theory that takes us beyond the idea that psychotherapy simply makes a patient feel good, must be an improvement. As William James (1902) says, "If merely 'feeling good' could decide, drunkenness would be the extremely valid human experience" (p. 16).

On the matter of feelings, Freud (1917) had the idea of a feeling self when he referred to "ego-feeling," but as Chessick (1977) points out, by "ego-feeling" Freud meant "something akin to self-esteem" (p. 284). Federn (1926, 1952) gave Freud's term "ego-feeling" a different meaning from treating patients who presented with symptoms of depersonalization. He writes, "Ego feeling is the sensation, constantly present, of one's own person," an experience that he thinks is different from the more cognitive process of ego consciousness. But once the concept of "ego-feeling" is used outside the context of Freud's structural theory (id, ego, superego), the term becomes self-feeling. In Kohut's self-psychology theory, self-feelings became a key postulate as a consequence of his empathic method. He found clinically that in order to be experienced as empathic, he had to give priority to a patient's specific feeling states, states referred to by Darwin (1872) such as fear and anger, and further developed by Tomkins (1962; 1963; 1991; 1992). So, in self psychology, the postulates of empathy and self-feelings are linked, as indeed are the self-organizing and selfobject postulates that interface with empathy and with each other.

An overlap between the feeling and self-organizing postulates was demonstrated in the previous chapter, where Kohut consistently attempted to understand a patient from the position of the patient's supraordinate self-organization. This involved viewing the patient holistically, at the highest possible level of functioning. So by giving priority to understanding a patient's feelings in response to whatever has happened, a psychotherapist is actually taking a holistic point of view. It is the *whole self that feels* a specific feeling, so that focusing on feelings tends to engage the patient's whole self. Feelings, then, are a royal road to understanding the self-organization of a patient.

A theoretical connection between the feeling and selfobject postulates is evident from patients who need to regulate under- or overstimulated (Schore 1994; 1997) feeling states. Overaroused patients frequently present as distressed ("upset"), fearful, angry, ashamed or overexuberant; underaroused patients generally present with a non-agitated form of depression. As Beebe and Lachmann (2002) indicate, by focusing on patients' feelings, psychotherapists engage their patients in an "intersubjective field of continuous, reciprocal mutual influence" (xiii). For patients with non-calibrated or inadequately calibrated feelings because of an absence of suitable selfobject experiences during development, a psychotherapist's consistent functioning as a selfobject offers the opportunity for a patient to become conscious of feelings or to have them calibrated to an optimal range.

In what follows, we present a psychotherapeutically relevant theory of feelings in three sections. In section A we outline a developmental theory of affects, using the ideas of Denton, Panksepp, Llinas, and Tomkins to biologically underpin a feeling theory for psychotherapy. Then in section B we seek to articulate Kohut's ideas about feelings as he applied them to psychoanalytic psychotherapy. And in section C we examine ideas about affects that can hinder an effective psychotherapy theory of feelings. Finally, in section D we present a case of a patient whose treatment helped him gain an awareness of his feelings.

A. Affect Theory

A neuroscientific approach to affect theory took a hundred and fifty years to develop from Darwin's observations, which were his principle method. In this section we will (1) sketch a very brief history of affect theory, and then outline a developmental line of (2) primordial affects, (3) primary affects, and (4) complex affects.

(1) Brief History of Affects

As the acknowledged pioneer of affect theory, Charles Darwin, influenced by physiologist Charles Bell (1806), developed his theory of "emotions" from five resources: observations of infants, the insane, the aged, master paintings, and such native communities as Australian aborigines, New Zealand Maoris, and Borneo Dyaks. Questions sent to observers of these native communities reveal Darwin's interest in the details of a person's facial features, which were involved in the expression of feelings. He asks, for example, "Does shame excite a blush when the color of the skin is visible?" Or, "When a man is indignant or defiant, does he frown?" Or, "When low in spirits, are the corners of the mouth depressed, and the inner corner of his eyebrows raised by the muscle which the French call the 'grief muscle'?" (p. 15).

Convinced that the face was the body's major expressive organ, Darwin studied the fine facial muscles. He was helped to understand a face's expression of feelings through the patterns of the French anatomist Gratiolet, by Duschenne's facial photographs, and by Henle's detailed sketches on anatomy. Darwin (1872) then wrote on "expressive actions," covering the feelings discussed by Kohut in section B of this chapter—fear, rage, shame, and joy—and three other feelings: disgust, startle, and distress. This last one he called "grieving and crying." Not only did Darwin refer to these expressive behaviors as emotions, importantly, he portrayed them as body-brain-action responses of a person viewed supraordinately.

Darwin's observations of behaviors expressive of emotions convinced him that these had an innate component. He gives evidence of this from the behavior of his eldest son. He (1872) observes,

> When a few days over six months old, his nurse pretended to cry, and I saw that his face instantly assumed a melancholy expression, with the corners of the

> mouth strongly depressed; now this child could rarely have seen any other child crying, and never a grown-up person crying, and I should doubt whether at so early an age he could have reasoned on the subject. Therefore it seems to me that an innate feeling must have told him that the pretended crying of his nurse expressed grief [distress]; and this through the instinct of sympathy [empathy] excited grief in him [p. 358].

From this description, Darwin not only demonstrates his awareness of the significance of feelings, but also shows his understanding of the importance of empathy as a human connection. It is also an inadvertent example of Kohut's twinship selfobject experience.

Darwin's theory of emotions languished until James Papez , Professor of Anatomy at Cornell University (Papez, 1937), discovered an interconnecting circle of mid-brain neural circuits ("the Papez circuit"). Influenced by the evolutionary idea that the medial (inner) layers of the cortex were older than the lateral (outer) layers, Papez proposed that circuits connecting the hypothalamus to the medial cortex generated emotions—now called affects. More specifically, he focused on a subregion of the hypothalamus called the mammillary bodies—these protrude like breasts—because the circuits of this anatomical structure were believed to channel sensory information into the thalamus, where he thought this information split into "stream of thought" and "stream of feeling" before going to the cingulate gyrus.

Later, when Papez realized that the hippocampus also received information from the cingulate gyrus, his "affect circuit" was complete. It was an inspired piece of speculation about the brain. When Papez presented this concept to his faculty colleagues, however, they vehemently rejected it because they thought feelings were an inappropriate subject for academic work. As Papez's investigations were interpreted as challenging the privileging of reason in academia, an attempt was made to remove him from the faculty, but failed.

After World War II the experimental psychologist Tomkins (1962, 1963, 1991, 1992) built a theory of affects beginning with Darwin's observations. He used evidence from psychological experiments to support and extend Darwin's theory of emotions, which he called affects. Importantly, Tomkins used Darwin's research as the basis for creating a theory of eight or nine primary affects, which he viewed as combining into a rich and seemingly unlimited plethora of affect complexes. It was a remarkable advance in theory without the help of significant discoveries from a neural biochemistry that, thanks to Katz and Eccles (Kandel, 2006), was only just discovering synaptic potential and the excitatory (Glutamate) and inhibitory (GABA) neurotransmitters. Without the advantages of the modern studies on the neural system of the brain, Tomkins' theory was, perforce, limited to the general explanatory idea of "neural firing patterns."

Even as Tomkins developed his theory, neuroscience was beginning to pay more attention to understanding the brain's functioning in affects. Paul MacLean, the Director of Research at the U.S. National Institutes of Mental Health, revived Papez's idea of affect neural circuits. In his research, MacLean focused on the rhinecephalon, an older part of the cortex involved in sense of smell, and noted its substantial connections to the hypothalamus, which was relatively large in humans, even though smell played a smaller role with humans than other species. So MacLean borrowed the term "limbic" (Fr. "ring") from the French anatomist Brocca, to refer to the ring-like shape of the circuits of the medial cortex. To Papez's anatomical structures, MacLean added the amygdala, the septum, and parts of the prefrontal cortex to form this limbic system.

It was only after the publication of MacLean's (1970) concept of the "triune brain" that the idea of a distinct part of the brain responsible for emotions took hold. MacLean used Haekle's principle (ontogeny follows phylogeny) to propose an evolutionary theory of affects as a part of brain development. He believed that the limbic system was the inheritor of an old mammalian brain, whereas the brain stem was the inheritor of a reptilian brain. He conceived the modern human brain as an old mammalian brain containing a modified reptilian brain and further modified by the addition of the cerebral cortex. To oversimplify, MacLean believed that the three brains coexist in human beings; in primitive mammals the old mammalian and reptilian brains coexist; in birds, reptiles, amphibians and fish there is only a reptilian brain. Although MacLean's ideas captured the imagination of the neurosciences and stimulated research, his concept of an old mammalian, "emotional brain" did not survive careful scrutiny.

In the 1960s and 1970s, new staining techniques enabled researchers to discover brain structures that support cognitive functioning in birds and reptiles (LeDoux, 2002, p. 5). These structures, such as the insula, had remained undetected earlier because they were located in areas other than on the top of the brain, as with humans. As further evidence of early phylogenetic cognitive functioning, behavioral observations of the modern inheritor of the reptilian brain, the crocodile, show they possess both feelings (affects) and planning (cognitions) ability. For example, angry female crocodiles will defend their babies from being eaten by hungry male crocodiles, and hungry crocodiles, after noting drinking patterns of animals along a riverbank, will plan an attack from bushes beside the stream. Evidence suggests that reptiles, mammals, and humans all use complex, but different combinations of reflexes, affects, and thoughts in order to survive and thrive. So, the idea of a discrete limbic system consisting of just affective circuits has fallen into disuse.

The concept of a limbic system originally relied heavily on the "localization" of sensation, feeling, language, and memory into separate brain areas, a residue of the long discredited view of phrenology (based on skull bumps). And the hippocampus does not belong to an "emotional brain" as it primarily consists of processes involved in facilitating long-term memory, not affect circuits. Convincingly, damage to the hippocampus, the mammillary bodies, and the anterior thalamus, which were all considered part of MacLean's limbic system, has little effect on the ability to express emotions (LeDoux 1996). A more adequate model is one where neural circuits from different locations influence each other across the reptilian, old mammalian, and new mammalian "brains." The differences among reptiles, mammals and humans have more to do with complex inter-influencing among neural circuits than with specific neural locations. For the purposes of psychotherapy theory, these circuits are better understood as functioning in a complex feeling system within the perspective of a supraordinate self-organization.

Modern affect theory now covers an extensive and growing area of research. In what follows we have selected ideas from Denton, Panksepp, Llinas, and Tomkins because they help demonstrate a biological underpinning to a psychotherapy theory of feelings. They also are our principal resources for advocating the idea of a three-layered affect system in humans as a result of phylogenetic and ontogenic development. These three layers are the primordial affects of startle, interest, and distress that become available during the fetal period, the primary affects of fear, rage, and joy that become available during early infancy, and the complex affects involving the humiliation affects of shame, disgust, and dissmell that become activated during the toddler period of development after the frontal lobes have myelinated.

(2) Primordial ("Fetal") Affects

The phylogenetic emergence of affects—and the beginning of feelings—is tied into the issue of consciousness. The physiologist Denton (2005) notes that the neurosciences see the "when" and "how" of consciousness as the crowning achievement of evolution. Edelman (1992) believes that "the evolutionary development of the ability to create a scene . . . led to the emergence of primary consciousness" (p. 118). Edelman reasons that the ability to create a scene is contingent on circuits with reentrant signaling that are connected to exteroceptors (see Edelman subsection chapter 4). From this he means that cold-blooded animals without a cortex or its equivalent, lack consciousness. So to Edelman, "snakes are in, but lobsters are out. . . . Consciousness is about 300 million years old" (p. 123). But Denton thinks this is too late in development for conscious feelings.

Agreeing with Denton, Llinas (2002) thinks "Emotions [affects] in general are among the oldest of our brain properties" (p. 156). In contrast to Edelman's emphasis on exteroceptors, Denton thinks "consciousness emerged in animal evolution as . . . primordial emotions mostly driven by internal sensors (interoceptors)" (p. 3). By primordial emotions Denton means that hunger for food, thirst for water, need for air, and the experience of pain are signals by which organisms become acutely conscious of distress and the need to act. A fetus shows signs of the primal affects of interest, startle, and distress.

In comparison to Denton's theory, Edelman's concept of consciousness depends on perceptual categorizing and the degenerative neural architecture of the caudal brain as it processes sensory information from the outside world using exteroceptors. Edelman refers to Herrenstein who demonstrated the cognitive abilities of pigeons by having them recognize humans. Experimentally, if pigeons pecked a picture of a human, they were fed, but if they pecked a picture without a human in it, they weren't fed. Then by presenting pictures of an infant, a human side face, a human back, a naked human, and a clothed human, who were all pecked, Herrenstein made a compelling case for a general image of humans in pigeons. Denton (2005) accepts that pigeons have the ability to categorize, but argues that Edelman's theory is not the basis of consciousness because it depends on "a distance receptor theory of neurophysiological organization" (p. 7). By distance receptor Denton means such senses as eyes, ears, and nose. Edelman's theory depends on these exteroceptors and the channel neural features (Mesulam, 1998) of the caudal (posterior) brain (see chapter 4).

Differing with Edelman, Denton (2005) thinks "the imperious states of arousal and compelling intentions to act that characterize the *primal [primordial] emotions* were the origins of consciousness" (p. 7). These primordial emotions describe the "subjective element to the instinctive behavior, which subserves control of the vegetative systems of the body" (p. 7). He claims support from the ideas of William James (1890) who says, "In speaking of instincts it is impossible to keep them separate from the emotional excitements that go with them" (II, p. 442). Succinctly, when our body's physiological system is out of balance because it is depleted of water, we *feel* thirsty. We become conscious of our thirst as "overwhelming sensations that commandeer the whole stream of consciousness [and] are choreographed from the lower or basal areas of the brain" (Denton, 2005, p. 7). Tomkins (1962) too, reflecting the experimental psychology of his time, says that the distress of thirst signals the urgency of corrective action to the attentional circuits (p. 21).

Denton describes how interoceptors monitor the physiochemical composition of the blood that is reaching the base (basal area) of the brain. These interoceptors "regulate and maintain the constancy of the internal environment of all the cells of the body" (Denton, 2005, p. 7). They detect the salt concentration of the blood reaching the brain, the carbon dioxide content of it, its temperature, and its sugar content. He then reminds us that these vegetative interoceptors are in the basement of the brain that is organized to communicate primarily with axons that project into the anterior (rostal) brain areas. In contrast, the exteroceptors are organized in the gray matter of the neocortex of the upper brain, principally in posterior (caudal) areas. So Denton argues that conscious awareness developed first in the interoceptive system. It is a primordial affective system that functioned prior to the development of primary affects that utilize the exteroceptors of fear, anger, and joy (Tomkins 1962, 1963, 1991, 1992), that later integrate with the primordial affect system during infancy.

In the primordial affect system, distress is aroused in conjunction with a consciousness of thirst, hunger, suffocation, or pain. Its strength determines how urgently corrective action is needed. Clinical experience supports Denton's idea of distress as a primordial affect before the emergence of the capacity for fear, anger, and joy in human development. For example, persons who experience excessive levels of fear, anger, or joy, also experience distress as a result of a persistent excessiveness in their primary affects. And the everyday management of surgical patients demonstrates the importance of relieving the distress of pain. Also it is a common experience in psychotherapy sessions that until a patient's distress is acknowledged in an empathic way, and thereby reduced, the therapeutic bond is weakened.

Tomkins' distinction between distress and fear supports Denton's contention that primordial affects precede primary affects. Such a distinction is demonstrated by Kandel's experimental distressing of the sea slug *Aplysia californicus* through repeatedly touching its gills. A human fetus too will show signs of distress if, for example, it is exposed to light in utero, suggesting that distress experienced as a fetus is earlier than an awareness of fear and anger. And a distinction between primordial and primary affects is supported by experiences that reducing patients' fears may not reduce patients' distress if distress comes from sources other than fear (R. Lee, 1998). In a grieving situation, for example, a patient may experience attempts at soothing as unempathic. This may be because crying, as a sign of distress during grieving, is a healthy response that needs to run its course and not be soothed away. In grief work, as Bowlby (1980) emphasizes, "it is not so much the crying itself, but a facilitating context in which crying and distress behaviors are encouraged (p. 228) . . . that clients report as an empathic experience" (R. Lee, 1998, p. 130–31).

Stern's (1985) idea of "vitality affects" may be linked to Tomkins' highlighting of the significance of distress as an affect. Stern thinks these are elusive, early feelings of aliveness that are not covered by the primary affects of Darwin and Tomkins. He references the philosophy of Langer who points to a sense of vitality expressed in art or music. Langer (1967) says, "'aesthetic' covers two different psychological processes, . . . the one tending to place emphasis on vitality, the other discovering the still center, the balance and harmony of beauty" (p. 122). As Stern (1985) indicates, interest in vitalizing is "inextricably involved with all the vital processes of life, such as breathing, getting hungry, eliminating, falling asleep and emerging out of sleep, or feeling the coming and going of emotions and thoughts" (p. 4). This suggests that when the body's homeostatic processes using the interoceptive affect system are in "vital balance" (Menninger, 1963), and when the circuits of primary affects of the exteroceptive system are in an optimal range, there is a feeling of "well being." If either of these primordial or primary affect systems are ineffective, distress is activated. As it is possible to conceive of distress as the negative side of vitality, twinning a person's distress may be the most effective way to facilitate the return of a patient's vitality.

Other than distress, two other Tomkins' affects may be viewed as primordial. One is the interest affect, which indicates an ability to attend to distress. This capacity may come from an early precursor to the search system of the HPA (hypothalamic pituitary adrenal) axis using interoceptive signals rather than exteroceptive ones. An awareness of primordial distress signals needs an elementary perceptual system appropriate to interoceptive signaling, to create a sense of awareness. This primordial perceptive system probably developed before Edelman's complex perceptual system of reentrant circuits were selected to take advantage of the multi-modal sensing of the exteroceptive system. Evidence of the need for primordial cognitive ability to accompany feelings of thirst or salt deficiency is seen from the example of elephants digging for salt in a cave of Mount Elgon in Kenya (Denton, 2005, p. 75). This suggests that "the evolutionary ancient cerebral cortex of the brain, the cingulate gyrus, the insula and the parahippocampus, are the most likely to encode the memory of the location of salt as well as an awareness of thirst.

"Startle" is the other primordial affect that Tomkins included in his list of primary affects but is better conceived as primordial. Although Tomkins considers startle an affect, its major component is a reflex response that short-circuits the attentional system and activates emergency bodily reactions before an awareness of distress in the primordial feeling system. Startle, therefore, is a primitive attentional and distress system that rapidly responds to unexpected pain, noise, sight, touch or smell, before there is a focused conscious awareness. It is considered an early ontogenetic experience of feeling.

The primordial startle affect has clinical relevance because its capacity to "habituate" with repeated experience is generally damaged if patients have been severely traumatized. Van der Kolk (1996) goes so far as to suggest that an inability of post traumatic stress disorder (PTSD) patients to habituate on an acoustic startle test be used as "a marker of, or a vulnerability factor for, developing PTSD" (p. 221). It seems significant, then, that damage to the most primitive and least cognitized of the affects occurs in the self-organization of patients with one of the most difficult disorders to treat psychotherapeutically or biotherapeutically. If the most primitive affective system is damaged in such patients, surely their treatment needs to focus on the primordial affects, especially feelings of distress.

(3) Primary ("Infant") Affects

Although primary affects were observed by Darwin and studied as nine discrete affects by Tomkins (1991, p. 50), Jaak Panksepp has made a significant contribution to understanding the neural circuits of these affects by identifying them through their neuromodulators. So far, he details four primary circuits: (a) the catacholamine (epinephrine-norepinephrene-dopamine) circuits activated during "interest/searching," (b) the "P substance" circuits associated with "anger," (c) the glutamate circuits involved with "fear," and (d) the oxytocin circuits involved with joy. He thinks that other neuromodulator circuits remain to be discovered. We explore these four of his studied affect circuits, one primordial and three primary, in more detail.

(a) Catacholamine Circuits (Primordial Affect of Interest/Search)

Although Panksepp (1998) prefers to describe these circuits as a seeking system, in the literature it has been described in many different ways. As he says, "I will pursue the idea that the mammalian brain contains a 'foraging-exploration-investigation-curiosity-interest-expectancy-SEEKING system that leads organisms to eagerly pursue the fruits of their environment—from nuts to knowledge, so to speak" (p. 145). This seeking system involves catacholamine arousal, which has been extensively researched during the last fifty years to understand the functioning of the HPA (hypothalamic pituitary adrenal) axis. Affect theory's growing awareness of the importance of the interest affect—and not just the negative affects of fear and anger—coincides with an increased emphasis on psychotherapists focusing on "leading [forward] edge" (Tolpin 2002) material as it appears in psychoanalytic psychotherapy.

The catacholamine circuits are heavily involved in the clinical disorders of mania and depression. It is easy to believe that a manic patient is coping with underlying distress or affective overstimulation by going through frantic searching patterns of behavior. Nor is it difficult to believe that if patients become depleted they can lose interest in their environment. Although psychotherapy is generally not effective in producing long-term gains through direct efforts to influence the interests of manic or major depressive patients, the more a psychotherapist is experienced as empathically understanding, the more likely a manic patient will calm down, or a depressed patient will renew an interest in something. Although psychotherapy aimed at permanent changes and new structuralization does not attempt to alter the catacholamine system directly, its attention to a patient's interest affect will be a significant indicator of general adaptive functioning. From the evidence of fetal learning, this affect is best considered primordial.

(b) P Substance Circuits (Primary Affect of Anger)

Modern research has traced the anger-rage response of the medial circuits of the amygdala, through the discrete zones of the hypothalamus and into the periaquaductal gray area of the brain stem. Electrical stimulus of the brain (ESB) in the anger-rage circuits creates rage reactions, which can trigger aggressive behavior. This circuit is particularly activated by frustration and offers a biological underpinning to Kohut's "reactive aggression." Panksepp (1998) cautions: "aggression is not always accompanied by anger, and anger does not necessarily lead to aggression, especially in mature persons who can control such impulses" (p. 187). He reminds us that ESB has discovered two other circuits that trigger aggression, but are not associated with frustration-anger. These are the predatory aggression circuits connected to hunger, and to intermale aggression circuits triggered by competition for females. Panksepp emphasizes that these findings do not support a general Freudian aggressive drive.

The P substance neuromodulator for the frustration-anger circuit is a small, short peptide chain of amino acids. When P substance is injected into anger circuits, ESB leads to increased anger displays, but when a P substance antagonist such as serotonin is introduced, it reduces the ESB stimulated anger. Important for psychotherapy, stimulating the oxytocin circuits of the cingulate gyrus inhibits the firing of anger circuits. This suggests that when a psychotherapist calmly seeks to understand the circumstances and sources of a patient's rage and the patient is soothed from the resulting stimulation of the oxytocin circuits, there is reduced neural firing in the anger circuits. Another consequence of psychotherapy is that expectations (cognitions) function to increase or decrease the anger affect. This is consistent with the experiences of narcissistic persons whose archaic, grandiose ambitions and unrealistic expectations intensify rage, as Kohut reports (1966, 1972a). Kohut also described how feelings could be attenuated by other feelings, which Panksepp's research now supports.

Research into the anger circuits has a bearing on biotherapy. Panksepp and colleagues (2002) point to the use of chlorpromazine (Thorazine) in the mental hospitals in the 1950s as an anti-aggressive agent. It was effective in high doses (with side effects) in reducing the broad catacholamine activity of most of the brain circuits, not just the anger circuits. This means that although antipsychotic drugs reduce violent behavior, "they are still little more than [general] chemical straight jackets." He continues, "To this day there is still no highly specific way to treat pathological anger pharmacologically" (p. 202). If this is so, research into the P Substance anger circuits underscores the need for an effective empathically-based psychotherapy as a viable option for regulating patient feelings of anger, as biotherapy treatment of rage in patients, especially nonpsychotic narcissistic patients, creates the image of an ant being hit by a sledgehammer.

(c) Glutamate Circuits (Primary Affect of Fear)

The fear-terror circuits, as with the anger-rage circuits, involve parts of the amygdala, hypothalamus, and periaquaductal gray areas of the brain that are in close proximity to each other. This close proximity of circuits enables inter-influencing between them as they activate in response to emergency situations. In their neurochemistry, the fear-terror circuits include the excitatory amino acid glutamate and a variety of neuropeptide neuromodulators that instigate specific fears, such as heights or predators. Minor tranquilizers of the benzodiazepine class dampen this glutamate system through GABA mediated neural inhibition. As Panksepp (1998) elucidates, benzodiazepine receptors have been discovered to be concentrated along the whole trajectory of the fear circuits, from the central amygdala, through the hypothalamus to the periaquaductal gray area of the brain stem. He says, "Just as glutamate is the brain's most prolific excitatory transmitter, its metabolic product GABA, . . . is the most pervasive inhibitory transmitter" (p. 217).

In an important distinction that is clinically relevant, Panksepp explains that what is referred to as separation anxiety in psychotherapy does not involve the glutamate circuits, but circuits of the oxytocin system. This finding suggests that the glutamate fear circuits of the amygdala are linked to exteroceptors (of the eyes, ears, nose, and skin) that are specialized to detect events outside the body, while the oxytocin circuits are altered by fears of the interoceptor sensing system of events within the body (Denton, 2005). This view coincides with clinical experience that patients with "disintergration anxiety" (Kohut, 1977) and "depletion anxiety" (Tolpin, 1978) fear the loss of the vitalizing function that is provided by the joyful mirroring of a nurturing selfobject.

(d) Oxytocin Circuits (Primary Affect of Joy)

Panksepp states that research has discovered three subcircuits that use the neuropeptide neuromodulator oxytocin. These are the sexual, nurturing, and play circuits, mainly located in the pre-optic area of the anterior cingulate gyrus and the bed nucleus of the stria terminalis. These circuits descend, partly through the habenula to the brain stem, and partly through the hypothalamus to the ventral tegmental area of the dopamine system. These three oxytocin circuits are clearly involved in the creation and early development of infants.

Studies of the oxytocin circuits suggest that successful bonding and social interaction leads to increased expression of oxytocin in the joy circuits. As Panksepp (1998) says, "Animal research indicates that both brain opioid and oxytocin circuits are activated by various pleasurable pro-social activities, such as grooming, play, and sexual exchange" (p. 248). Further, there is evidence that *activation of the oxytocin circuits and feelings of joy regulate all the other primary affects*. Oxytocin circuits are clearly activated when selfobject-hungry patients are enabled to have a selfobject experience, particularly the mirror experience. The ability of these circuits to be activated in an empathy-based psychotherapy goes a long way to explaining why accepting the importance of selfobject experiences for a patient, lowers distress and helps create therapeutic success.

Panksepp's studies are supported by the research of Taylor and colleagues (2002) who think the female stress response is one of "tend and befriend " of the oxytocin circuits, not the "fight or flight" arousal of the sympathetic nervous system. Taylor asks, "How would a female responding to stress with sympathetic arousal . . . quiet and calm down offspring" (p. 415)? They wouldn't, if their sympathetic system was aroused. But females don't respond with sympathetic arousal because, with their high oxytocin levels, they are able to calm their infants. Taylor supports the premise that "tend and befriend" is a built-in female response, by listing studies of nursing mothers whose oxytocin levels stimulate milk to reduce crying in infants (Blass, 1997) or when they don't have milk, enjoying nipple sucking to calm infants (Field and Goldson, 1984). These and many other studies make it clear that the activation of oxytocin circuits, which is the biological basis of the feelings of joy, has an inhibitory effect on the catecholamine circuits of the HPA axis and the cortisol stress response.

What also supports the oxytocin response to stress in women is the way they befriend each other to gain mutual comfort. Social contact not only comforts women, but also enhances their collective behavior to cope with dangerous situations. A small pride of tigresses, especially accompanied by their young, create such a formidable challenge for any foe that they rarely need to fight or flee. Furthermore, this idea of oxytocin circuits being involved in a social response is reinforced by studies in such animals as voles, a mouse-size rodent of the American Midwest, of which there are two major types. One, the prairie vole, is monogamous, pair bonds, and creates multigenerational family groups. But the Montane vole, found in isolated burrows of high meadows in the Rocky Mountains, shows little interest in social or parental care activities and abandons the young after two weeks. Significantly, "Montane pups at day 5 do not respond to social separation with either distress calls or corticosterone release" (Inse l, 2000, p. 179), the latter being equivalent to a cortisol stress response in humans. Importantly, although there was no difference in the oxytocin responses of these two types of voles, there was a major difference where the oxytocin receptors were distributed in their brains. The prairie vole's receptors are distributed in the dopamine circuits to induce positive feelings of reward; as the Montane vole's oxytocin receptors are not distributed in the dopamine circuits, they are not rewarded for pair bonding and social behavior.

The importance of these oxytocin circuits also helps understand "panic attacks." Psychoanalytic tradition interpreted panic as a "phobia"—an unrealistic fear. Panksepp's designation of two fear circuits that use two entirely different neuromodulators in two different areas of the brain, makes the case for two kinds of fear: an emergency fear that mobilizes a defense against attack and a panic fear of losing the person on whom one is dependent for nurturance. These two fears are connected to a person's need to survive against the threats of slaughter and starvation. Panic at the prospect of losing a mother is very understandable because until the relatively recent ability to refrigerate milk, the death of a mother often meant the death of an infant from starvation if a wet nurse could not be found. In psychotherapy a distinction between these two types of fear is important because panicked patients, if asked what they fear, truthfully respond that they don't know because the question presupposes an object of fear. Being unable to answer this question may make them feel foolish and intensify their feelings of shame. In contrast, if feelings of panic focus on an anticipated loss or actual loss of someone who functioned as a selfobject, patients generally feel like they have been empathically understood.

These differences between the affect circuits described by Panksepp encourage a creative responding to engage patients with these feeling states. The results of neurosciences do not offer direct clinical answers, but suggest why some psychotherapist responses are experienced as empathic and some responses are not. And, the oxytocin studies support the importance of Kohut's concept of a psychotherapist's selfobject function in producing therapeutic change.

As important as neuromodulators are to modern affect theory, the involvement of Tinbergen's "fixed action patterns" (FAPs) can't be ignored in the development of primordial and primary affects. According to Llinas, these FAPs consist of reflexive behavior patterns in the brain stem and spinal cord (Whelan, 1996) and are not modifiable by learning. As well, there are the more complex, less reflexive FAPs associated with the basal ganglia (Hikosaka, 1998) that are able to store automated-like motor programs as a result of learning and using their intrinsic circuitry.

The role of these genetically derived, learning-modified, fixed action patterns of the basal ganglia is confirmed by studies of bird singing. As Llinas (2002) says, "Genotypically speaking, this means that a particular type of Robin would have a specific song that characterizes the family [species]. The males sing and the female recognizes the song, choosing a male on the quality of the song" (p. 138). Reducing the testosterone in the male bird's brain reduces the size of the basal ganglia and the production of the song (Arnold, 1975a, b). If testosterone is given to female birds, they sing because of new neurons and synaptic connections in the basal ganglia (Schlinger and Arnold, 1991). Conclusively, damage to the basal ganglia means the birds are incapable of generating normal song (Doupe and Konishi, 1991).

What have these bird song patterns to do with affects? The short answer is that affects form a special class of FAPs. Llinas (2002) says these affective FAPs evolved as premotor patterns (p. 155) and "states of readiness for action." These modifiable FAPs are triggered when a circuit reaches its firing threshold. For example, LeDoux (1996) has traced a neural pathway from the fear circuits of the amygdala to the basal ganglia. Although it has not been ascertained whether FAPs are stored in the basal ganglia or the cerebellum, LeDoux thinks the basal ganglia function as a control center for the triggering of these premotor fixed action systems. The amygdala's pathway to the FAPs of the basal ganglia contrasts with another neural pathway from the amygdala to the brain stem, and the reflexive freezing that can occur when startled or in situations of extreme fear. Tomkins thinks that premotor programs triggered by the affect circuits are not only modifiable through learning, but evaluate the necessity and urgency of taking different kinds of corrective action. This picture of premotor FAPs, modifiable by experience, supports the idea that affects are major components in forming the subjective self-states we refer to as feelings.

(4) Complex ("Toddler") Affects

Many of the feelings encountered in psychotherapy are not just distress, fear, anger, or joy. There are affects that involve greater cognitized components and have subtle nuances, rich colorations, and exquisite meanings that not only require admixtures of primordial and primary affects but also the fine discriminations of the cognitive circuits of the prefrontal lobes. These highly cognitized feelings are associated with Tomkins' "affect complexes." Ontogentically they become available during the toddler period of development. Weinberg and Tronick (1994) call these complexes "affect configurations" because they include vocalizations and body postures, behavior that Darwin had included in his study. So, although the face is important in communicating affects, the expression of affects is broader than the face and more extensive than just primary affects. For example, Tomkins (1963) thinks that feelings of humiliation, which involve admixtures of shame, disgust, and dissmell, can develop into paranoia (p. 455). In another example, he thinks jealousy and envy come from a combination of rage and humiliation (p. 381).

A colleague once asked Tomkins for a dictionary of affect words, coded according to various combinations of complex affects. Tomkins (1991) confessed, "I studied several thousand English words for two years and had to eventually give up the attempt because of the great variety of admixtures of affect with cognitive, behavioral, and event references" (p. 51). Of all the affect complexes, Tomkins' concept of depression may have the most clinical relevance. Tomkins saw shame as the core depressive experience, combined with an admixture of all the negative affects: distress, fear, anger, disgust, and dissmell. His concept of depression suggests why antidepressive medications have such a variable treatment effect. Unipolar depression does not appear to be a single unitary "disease" because it consists of a broad complex of negative affects. Complementing Tomkins' view of depression as a negative complex of affects, there is the neurological evidence that depression correlates with lower levels of neural activation in the left frontal lobes and higher levels in the right frontal cortex (Baxter and colleagues, 1985). And Davidson and Fox (1982) showed that by ten months an infant's brain is lateralized into positive and negative affects. If an infant watched a video of an actress laughing there is EEG activation of the left frontal lobe, whereas if the actress cried, the EEG activity took place in the right prefrontal lobe.

An example of how one affect can modify another is seen in "The Prophet" where Khalil Gibran reveals how joy modifies fear. He says, "Your fear of death, is but the trembling of a shepherd who stands before the king—whose hand is laid upon him in honor. Is the shepherd not joyful beneath his trembling, that he shall wear the mark of a king?" And yet another example comes from the hymn "Praise my soul the king of heaven" where joyous praise is used to modify distress, especially in one verse where the words are "Praise him for his grace and favor to his people in distress." From such examples Tomkins thinks that, compared to a limited number of primary affects, affect complexes consist of an almost inexhaustible number of combinations and permutations. So for clinicians to focus just on primordial or primary affects is, to Tomkins, a mistake. Tomkins' affect complexes include not only combinations of affects, but cognitive beliefs and physiological responses, as well. Affect circuits amplify the urgency for an organism to act. They are the biological "heart" of subjective experiences that motivates a person to act. As stated by Kohut, feelings are an experience of the whole person, to which affects give an appropriate sense of urgency.

Orange (1995) is critical of Tomkins, Spezzano, and Krystal, for their "atomistic treatment of single affective states" (p. 94). But an understanding of Tomkins' affect complexes reveals that his theory is far more than this. True, as Orange states, "these views suggest the existence of original or fundamental affects, which like the elements of the periodic table, may combine" into a theory that developed "bottom up." But why is such "bottom up" theorizing detrimental if, in so doing, Tomkins reinforces the importance of the feeling state of the whole person? As affects, especially in their complex admixtures, add a sense of urgency and amplification to subjective feeling states, they are the key to the human motivational system.

In describing the complexity of a human feeling system involving affect complexes as motivators, we also have been touching on affect regulation. This is an idea based on the Yerkes and Dodson (1908) law that a right level of affect arousal is needed for optimal adaptation of the human organism. But as affects are embedded in a total feeling system of cognitive, sensory, and motor circuits, affect regulation is better described as regulation of the self-organization. As Schore (1994) indicates, "the ontogeny of the emergent function of self-regulation [that is, regulation of the self] is perhaps the most fundamental problem of development" (p. 9). Krystal (1988) and Sander (1977) hold a similar view.

Lachmann (2000) uses the idea of "solitary regulation" to specify a person's use of non-dyadic "self-directed regulatory behaviors" (Gianino and Tronick, 1988) to distinguish it from interactive, "other-directed regulation" (Beebe and Lachmann, 2002) of selfobject experiences. A key issue is how regulation of the self occurs, namely, whether an infant is forced to resort to rigid, nonadaptive solitary regulation to compensate for failures of interactive self-regulation, or whether an infant is regulated by interaction with a responding mother, and then, internalizing the interaction.

As Tronick and colleagues (1998) claim, an adaptive self-organization develops from the patterns of interaction in early childhood, particularly in infancy. Adaptive self-regulation begins first as a mother-infant relationship that develops an interactive regulatory pattern and then is internalized. Earlier Kohut described an example of interactive regulation, where an infant is made anxious by a bee, and how the mother's containment of her own anxiety helped the infant contain his/her anxiety. As similar situations occur many times during infancy, the pattern of interactive regulation is internalized in infants as self-regulation. Sroufe and colleagues (2005) have reached a similar conclusion: "Research has confirmed, effective regulation of the infant is only possible within a supportive care-giving system. By providing appropriate and changing stimulation in response to perceptions of infant state, moods, and interests, caregivers not only help keep arousal within manageable bounds, but they also entrain the infant's own capacities for regulation" (pp. 87–88).

This brief overview of a developmental theory of affects provides a biological underpinning to a theory of feelings for psychotherapy. It supports the idea that feelings have evolved to induce the level of urgency needed to act for the survival of the organism. Through conscious feeling and its actions, the total self is able to gain a sense of agency. Such feelings form a consciousness that serves the larger self-organizing system as its most important characteristic.

B. Heinz Kohut's Theory of Feelings

Kohut used a relatively undeveloped, "experience-near" theory of feelings in his clinical work. In his theory of narcissism he initially followed classical theory by assuming the primacy of libidinal and aggressive drives and interpreted fear and anger as derivatives of these drives. Working with narcissistic patients and discovering their yearning for selfobject experiences, Kohut made a patient's self-cohesion as a result of selfobject experiences his major organizing construct and demoted classical drives to a peripheral role. Loewald (1960) took a similar view. As Teicholtz (1999) summarizes, "Ultimately, Kohut (1959, 1966) and Loewald (1960) placed self and relationship at the center of human motivation and narrative and questioned Freud's notion of sexual and aggressive drives as the primary organizers of personality, experience, and psychopathology" (p. 6).

Kohut also thought that such feelings as fear and anger were better understood, not as the drive derivatives of classical theory (Tomkins 1962), but as independent motivators. In rejecting Freud's theory of feelings as auxiliary (and subservient) to drives, Kohut took a position about feelings and drives similar to Denton's (2005) presentation of primordial affects and Tomkins' (1962, 1963, 1991, 1992) view of primary affects, where drives are in the service of affects. In what follows we elaborate more specifically about Kohut's ideas on (1) fear and (2) anger, (3) joy and (4) shame.

(1) Fear

Influenced by Hartmann's emphasis on an organism's adaptive functions, Kohut recognized that feelings of fear were necessary for survival and, if not excessive, were a motivating component to accomplishments in many fields of endeavor. To Kohut, patients who presented for psychotherapy with excessive fear (Freud's "anxiety") needed the psychotherapist to function as a soothing selfobject, reduce fear, and lessen the constrictions that high levels of fear imposed on the working memory (see chapter 6). A less restricted working memory facilitates increased therapeutic exploration, understanding, and acceptance of the sources of excessive fear. Kohut saw high levels of fear as creating self-fragmentation. This Kohutian view contrasts with Freud's (1926D) later theory of signal anxiety that arose from conflicts between the agencies of the self (id, ego, superego) and facilitated the repression of the conflict. Incomplete or failed repression led to symptoms as substitute formations for conflicts. In conceiving of anxiety as signaling repression and symptom formation, Freud associated anxiety with psychopathology.

Kohut's concept of fear acknowledged it as only pathological when it was excessive. He gives such examples as "disintegration anxiety" (Kohut, 1977, p. 97), "depletion anxiety" (Tolpin, 1978), and "hypomanic overstimulation anxiety" (Kohut, 1968). But he always thought that fear was a necessary part of healthy adaptation. His emphasis was on lessening excessive fear through a patient's selfobject experience. He illustrates with a mother's calm responding to her infant's feelings of fear so as to modify them, clearly revealing that he assumed some form of optimal feeling states in his treatment of patients. Kohut (1996) explains,

> [a child] becomes anxious, for whatever reason—a buzzing bee, a noise that won't stop, that type of thing, a pregenital phobia. The child's anxiety is transmitted to the mother sufficiently so that the mother becomes a little anxious, but not very much; she knows it is just a bee or a fly or whatever. . . . She will handle [appraise] it as an anxiety signal meaning "My child is anxious, and there is a little anxiety in me, but there is no reason to be anxious," and her anxiety will subside. What she does, is pick up the child and put the child close to herself, underlining the fact that they are one unit. And the one unit moves from anxiety signal to the absence of anxiety [p. 360].

With the excessively fearful child consistently and repeatedly experiencing the mother's calming presence, the calming pattern becomes internalized as an important part of the child's memories, both "symbolic" and "procedural" (Grigsby and Hartlaub, 1994; Clyman, 1991). These memories eventually help regulate the potentially excessive levels of a child's fear even when the mother is no longer physically present.

Kohut (1949) also revealed familiarity with the idea of an optimal level of fear from a story of his first training analyst, August Aichhorn. When a student told Aichhorn of failing an examination because of a paralyzing fear, Aichhorn arranged to see the student just before the next examination. "Aichorn was at first friendly but then proceeded to needle and offend him so skillfully and systematically that the student finally jumped up in a fury, slammed the door behind him without saying a word, and walked in a rage to his examination, which he passed with flying colors" (p. 33). Kohut revealed in this example his belief that feelings elide. As persons overstimulated by fear are also inhibited in expressing anger, stimulating their anger decreases their fear and releases the brake on their performance inhibitions. This link between fear and rage seems to be facilitated by the close proximity of their circuits in the brain's amygdala and hypothalamus (Panksepp, 1998, p. 207–8).

(2) Anger

From the beginning of Kohut's efforts to understand narcissism, he made distinctions between anger, rage, and aggression. In his early writings Kohut referred more to anger than rage, but after his important article on narcissistic rage (1972), anger is no longer mentioned in his theoretical papers. This is because he conceived of rage as more than a severe form of anger; it was a qualitative transformation of angry feelings into something fundamentally different. It is as if Kohut assumed a quantum-like shift between relatively mild anger to a more severe level of rage. This shift to rage is contingent on the angry patient's type of attachment. Losses of persons, places, or things experienced as extensions of self ("narcissistic objects"), result in "narcissistic wounds" and rage states. Patients in need of archaic selfobject experiences are particularly susceptible to rage if these relationships become ruptured or cease. In comparison, other frustrating situations or people tend to induce anger rather than rage because a selfobject loss is not involved. Such anger is generally more manageable than feelings of rage.

Just as with fear, Kohut took the position that mild, perhaps moderate feelings of anger could facilitate adaptive human behavior, a view proposed by psychologists Yerkes and Dodson (1908). In its initial development, an infant's feeling system is regulated by the mother's own feelings and responsiveness to form an optimal range of feelings for the infant's functioning in the environment. Schore (1996) and Perry (1996) give evidence that a mother's insensitivity to her infant's feeling state leaves the infant with defective circuits in the brain's prefrontal lobes, which then fail to regulate the "limbic" circuits of the brain at optimal levels of functioning. Successful selfobject experiences in psychotherapy with narcissistic patients who are prone to rage, develop new structuralizations in the prefrontal lobes that help diminish these rage states.

Kohut was clear that rage did not derive from an aggressive drive. He (1977) says, "The child's rage and destructiveness should not be conceptualized as the expression of a primary instinct that strives towards its goal or searches for an outlet. They should be defined as regression products, as fragments of broader psychological configurations" (p. 118). He conceived of rage as a "breakdown product" following the dissolution of a self-organization. This in turn directed the psychotherapist to explore the perceptual "triggers" of the breakdown and facilitate selfobject experiences to foster new self-structuralization. With new self-structuralization, hence firmer self-cohesion and less fragmentation, there is less expression of rage.

Kohut was aware that narcissistic rage emerged as a result of feeling wounded. He (1972) gave the example of the German Emperor Wilhelm II whose birth with a withered arm and need for psychological compensation was widely believed to be an important factor leading to the outbreak of World War I. Kohut adopted Freud's view that it was not Wilhelm's birth injury that had created his sensitivity to slights, as Adler claimed, but Wilhelm's rejection by his proud mother, who could not tolerate an imperfect child (p. 629). To Kohut, such a narcissistic wound led to feelings of revenge in conjunction with rage. He says,

> The need for revenge, for righting wrong, for undoing a hurt by whatever means, and a deeply anchored, unrelenting compulsion in the pursuit of all these aims, which gives no rest to those who have suffered narcissistic injury—these are the characteristic features of narcissistic rage in all its forms and which set it apart from other kinds of aggression [p. 638].

Rageful patients often need managing in the initial stage of psychotherapy until a selfobject bond forms. Such patients often present for treatment because family or employers are becoming increasingly intolerant of their "temper tantrums" or because there is a medical concern about potential somatic damage from rage-induced high blood pressure. Panksepp (1998) indicates that increased anger leads to a corresponding increase in heart rate, blood pressure, and muscular blood flow. With rage, this is more so. Rage-prone patients sent to anger management seminars, may learn to inhibit rage behaviors—often they don't—but even when successful, often do so without reorganizing underlying feeling states. This "containing" approach means changing the peripheral self-organization into a "policeman," suppressing rageful states emanating from the nuclear self-organization, and increasing the risk of somatization. If the rage of these patients becomes difficult to control, they may end up with "anti-psychotic" medications to "quieten" (tranquilize) them.

In contrast to these direct attempts at controlling rage, Kohut (early 1970s) understood that archaic rage states arose from structural defects in the nuclear self (p. 158). Although there may be an immediate, temporary need to use direct methods such as medication or restraint, Kohut thought that the major goal of working with enraged patients therapeutically was repairing the nuclear self. This means eventually inducing greater self-cohesion through selfobject experiences, and then persisting until the experience is internalized. Indirect containment of rage may be achieved by exploring failures, where the patient's feelings are heavily invested, such as relationship failures or failures to achieve goals. By "heavy investment" of feeling, Kohut meant situations in which a patient experienced persons or goals as self-extensions, that is, as narcissistic objects. The unexpected wrenching of these extensions from such patients leaves gaping holes—narcissistic wounds—that need soothing calmness and the bandage of understanding.

Anger, transformed into rage, may be vociferously expressed or trigger aggressive physical behavior that can be very violent. Kohut (1972) recognized "that narcissistic rage belongs to the large psychological field of aggression, anger, and destructiveness" (p. 636). To Kohut, mild to moderate levels of anger lead to healthy assertive, goal-directed behavior, but when anger becomes narcissistic rage, it may explode into irrational, aggressive acts because "the need for revenge, for the righting a wrong, for undoing a hurt . . . gives no rest to those who have suffered a narcissistic injury" (p. 637). This need for revenge may result in "reactive aggression." So, with his 1972 paper Kohut not only shifted theoretical attention from anger to rage; but demonstrated it was unnecessary to hold aggression as the second drive in Freud's dual drive theory and as a death instinct (Stepansky, 1977) to depict human destructiveness.

In an important extension of Kohut's ideas on anger, rage, and aggression, the self psychologist Lachmann (2000) explores the transformation of reactive aggression into the extreme destructiveness that he calls "eruptive aggression." This is where aggression blasts "from the person like a volcano" (p. 232). Transformation from reactive to eruptive aggression takes another quantum-like leap. Lachmann illustrates this from examples of serial killers who portray an "after-the-fact, dry, affectless description of the killing with little regard for an explanation" (p. 138), and in so doing, demonstrate no self-reflection. He says, "I am placing the serial killer off the end of the range of eruptions of aggression. There is no context with which the killer is in touch and to which we can relate or can grasp empathically in order to understand the meaning of the behavior" (p. 138). The implications of this Kohutian understanding of anger is that narcissistic personalities transform it into rage and into reactive aggression, which in very extreme cases, may turn it into eruptive aggression.

Kohut's understanding of transformed anger and his theoretical shift away from an aggressive or death instinct to a theory of anger and its transformations, have led psychoanalytic psychotherapists of other theoretical perspectives to accuse Kohut of being ignorant or avoidant of the issue of aggression. From what we have presented, we clearly think this is not so. What Kohut has demonstrated is that a theory of aggression is better served through a new understanding of a theory of anger. His theory holds that angry feelings, unless successfully regulated by inhibitory neural circuits connected to beliefs of the nuclear self, can result in severe violence. To Lachmann, successful regulation avoids eruptive aggression by using three processes: first, regulation from internalized patterns resulting from selfobject experiences; second, interactive regulation from current selfobject experiences; and third, regulation from solitary activities. These solitary activities, Lachmann (2000) says, "include symbolic elaborations, fantasies, identifications, and defenses" (p. 33).

They are similar to Tolpin's (1978) idea of symptom formation (p. 174). Lee (1994) calls them "cohesive functions." Killers who erupt with aggression have little if any of the first two regulatory processes available to them, so they increasingly resort to such extreme solitary forms of regulation as "S & M" sexual behavior to prevent fragmentation. But if these extreme solitary forms of regulation are insufficient to contain their self-fragmentation, they may erupt in violence to stave off complete deadness or madness.

(3) Joy

References to joy saturate Kohut's writings. One of the earliest was in his paper on Thomas Mann's *Death In Venice* (Kohut, 1957). Kohut describes Aschenbach's stay in Venice during a deadly plague as a decision made "triumphantly and with a reckless joy, motivated by his fascination with a fourteen-year-old Polish boy of 'perfect beauty' called 'Tadzio.'" Interpreters of this story tend to see Aschenbach's attraction to Tadzio as homosexual, but Childs (2003) suggests that the attraction was "homolimerance," that is, an attraction to a person of the same sex, more like the craving for an idealized selfobject experience than a sexual desire. What supports Childs' position is Kohut 's suggestion that Aschenbach was fascinated by Tadzio's experience of being favored by his mother and governess, as reflected in his beautiful clothing, and his "pure and godlike serenity"—a description of idealization if ever there was one. If Kohut had written his paper on "Death in Venice" a quarter of a century later, he may have interpreted "homolimerance" as a joyous twinship experience. Through this twinship, Aschenbach may have been attempting to repair a defective self-sector from his own childhood. As an aging artist, Aschenbach was finding it difficult to maintain his self-cohesion without a vitalizing selfobject experience, such as the twinship experience with Tadzio. Feelings of joy, then, may have been connected to his twinship selfobject experience and the temporary alleviation of a defect in his self-organization.

Not only did Kohut think that joy accompanies repairs to a self-organization; joy blossoms with any significant self-development. Kohut (1977) refers to a "warm glow of joy—a joy that has all the earmarks of an emotionality that accompanies a maturational or a developmental achievement" (p. 229). This is the joy that is a byproduct of any forward move in personal growth. For example, Kohut thinks that the Oedipal phase of development need not be a bitter rivalry between the father and son over the mother. He thinks, "the healthy child of healthy parents enters the oedipal phase joyfully" (pp. 245–48). As he says,

> the affectionate desire and the assertive-competitive rivalry of the oedipal child will be responded to by normal empathic parents in two ways. The parents will react to the sexual desires and competitive rivalry of the child by becoming sexually stimulated and counter-aggressive, and, at the same time, they will react with joy and pride to the child's developmental achievement, to his vigor and assertiveness [p. 230].

Kohut takes pains to distinguish feelings of joy from those of pleasure. He sees joy as an encompassing emotion evoked by success whereas pleasure is limited to sensual satisfaction. He (1977) says,

> From the point of view of depth psychology, . . . the experience of joy has a generic root different from that of the experience of pleasure; that each of these modes of affect has its own developmental line and that joy is not sublimated pleasure. Joy relates to the total self whereas pleasure . . . relates to experiences of parts and constituents of the self [p. 45].

He (1974) also thinks the distinction between joy and pleasure is important because pleasure is linked to discharging a drive, whereas triumph and joy are linked to the fulfillment of the nuclear self-organization's ambitions and ideals. Further support for his view is that blocking ambitions and breaking ideals do not evoke anxiety but feelings of despair, shame, and empty depression (p. 757).

The usefulness of distinguishing between pleasurable experiences and joyous feelings is illustrated by the clinical problem of pathological overeating and obesity. Kohut (1977) says,

> It is not . . . the child's wish for food that is the primal psychological configuration. Seen from the point of view of the psychology of the self, we will affirm instead that, from the beginning, the child asserts his need for a food-giving selfobject—however dimly recognized the selfobject might be. (In behavioral terms, we might say that the child needs empathically modulated food giving, not food.) If this need remains unfulfilled (to a traumatic degree) then the broader psychological configuration—the joyful experience of being a whole, appropriately responded to self—disintegrates and the child retreats to a fragment of the larger psychological unit, i.e., to pleasure-seeking oral stimulation . . . or . . . to depressive eating [p. 81].

A psychotherapist's feeling of joy during a session is often an indication that the patient is experiencing a forward movement in the psychotherapy. This may indicate that a psychotherapist is responding to "leading edge" [now "forward edge"] material (Tolpin, 2002) that is, to the "crushed tendrils of a mobilizable selfobject transference in a manifestly pathological adult system" (p. 174). By recognizing and responding to forward edge material with joy and pride, a psychotherapist enables the patient to have a growth-enhancing, selfobject experience. Tolpin illustrates this from one of Guntrip's (1961) failures, in which the patient fled the analysis. This shy, professional patient had sought analysis because he had a compulsion to look at breasts, which he was able to link to his cold, unresponsive wife and a mother who buttoned herself up tight to her neck. After Guntrip interpreted that the patient's compulsive attention to breasts was a regression to the security of the breast, the compulsion subsided, but was replaced by fantasies of a very strong, secure house. Then the patient broke off the analysis. Belatedly, Guntrip realized that the compulsion to look at breasts was not a backward step to more secure times, but a constructive search for a warm selfobject experience to protect himself from self-fragmentation (p. 175). When constructive forward moves occur and are recognized, joy soon emerges as part of the intersubjective process of the psychotherapy.

As Kohut developed his self psychology theory, it became clearer to him that feelings of joy were a byproduct that accompanied the structuralization of a person's new self-experience, just as anger and shame were byproducts of a fragmenting self-organization. Although he had shifted his theoretical attention from drives to subjective feelings, it was his shift to feelings of joy, as well as his theory of empathic understanding with its associated concepts of a selfobject experience, the supraordinate self, and internalization/structuralization that represented key elements to his new psychotherapy paradigm. Perhaps even more importantly, in emphasizing the importance of joy in his theory, Kohut clearly understood that feelings were the experience of the whole (supraordinate) self-organization. For him, feelings do not occur in an isolated part of the self as if an isolated Leibnitzian monad. When a person is fearful, the total self is fearful. Although rage is a breakdown product, it is still the response of the whole person who is experiencing the breaking down. And even though feelings of shame lead to a walling off—splitting doesn't really describe it as well—it is still the whole self that feels ashamed and cooperates in walling off the need for mirroring so it can continue to function.

It was primarily with his emphasis on joy that Kohut revealed his understanding that feelings are the response of the total (supraordinate) self-organization. Joy comes from healthy communications and interactions with others, and from an inner sense of cohesion as one fulfills the ambitions and ideals of the nuclear self with skill. Reflecting about joy in a letter to a colleague a few months before he died, Kohut (1981c) asked the rhetorical question, "Will we be able to shift from committing ourselves to trust in the voice of the intellect as our ultimate salvation, to the trust in man's ability to experience the joy of existing in a matrix of nurturing selfobjects and the correlated ability to experience the joy of providing such a matrix for others?" (p. 696). So, Kohut's holistic approach, with a special focus on joy, forms the foreground to our "experience-distant" view of affects in the neurosciences. We argue that a modern theory of affects derived from scientific studies has insights to guide the exploration of the feelings generated by the intersubjective process of psychotherapy, but affect theory may also be misused as "objective" knowledge and so create case-destroying empathic failures and disjunctions, especially if affect theory leads to a view of emotions as competitive with, rather than cooperating with, perceptual, cognitive, and memory processes.

(4) Shame

Feelings of shame as well as rage emerge as "breakdown products" when narcissistic wounding and self-fragmentation occur. Of these two "ubiquitous" (Kohut, 1969–1970, p. 110) feeling states, Kohut thought that shame emerged earlier in the breakdown process than rage, which is an observation that we have found to be very useful clinically. He (1966) explains,

> The disturbances of narcissistic balance to which we refer as "narcissistic injury" appear to offer a particularly promising access to the problems of narcissism, not only because of the frequency with which they occur in a broad spectrum of normal and abnormal psychological states, but also because they are usually easily recognized by the painful effect of embarrassment or shame that accompanies them and by their ideological elaboration—known as inferiority feelings or hurt pride [p. 428].

As a clear example of an extreme admixture of rage and shame, Kohut (1969–1970) refers to Melville's symbolic tale of the white whale "Moby Dick" to "demonstrate the enormity and restlessness of the rage which may ensue subsequent to the shameful experience of a narcissistic injury in the narcissistically vulnerable individual" (p. 105). In this tale, the great white whale Moby Dick had severed the leg of Captain Ahab, and Captain Ahab is obsessed with killing the whale, with getting revenge at any cost.

Kohut (1966) thinks shame is a feeling that arises when a person who is functioning as a self-extension does not respond to a patient's exhibitionistic needs (p. 441). He says, "Instead of a pleasurable confirmation of the value, beauty, and loveliness of the self, there is painful shame" (p. 439). These shameful states may be signaled physiologically with blushing. Darwin (1872), for example, points to the connection between blushing and shame in the Old Testament, where Ezra cries out (Ezra, 9:6) "Oh, my God! I am ashamed, and blush to lift up my head to thee, my God" (p. 321). Kohut (1987), for example, mentions a twenty-two-year-old patient, a second-year graduate student, who was distressed over a breakup with her boyfriend. Her pattern was to form an intense relational bond, make heavy demands that alienated the boyfriend, then become depressed when they broke up. These relationship failures made her feel foolish and ashamed (p. 115). Yet the patient's story suggested she was shame-prone long before her break-up experiences with boyfriends. For example, she revealed feeling shame from a reluctance to use the psychotherapist's valuable time on her dating problem. Exploring this with the psychotherapist led her to remembering the lack of availability of her mother to her when she was a child.

The patient's mother was an energetic person who spent much of her time busily working as a volunteer in community organizations. As a result of twinning the mother's values, the patient had developed the altruistic ideal of privileging the serving of others over her own needs, an excessive form of a "reverse selfobject experience" (R. Lee, 1988, 1999). One shameful incident as a child, remembered as a model scene (Lichtenberg 1989, pp. 253–55), was a family trip (Freud's "screen memory"). The other children brought their bags downstairs, but she had left hers in her room. The mother said sarcastically, "Do you expect us to bring your stuff down?" The patient then felt overwhelmed by shame for expecting others to carry her bag instead of doing her share (Kohut, 1987, p. 116). Kohut considered this incident a sequel to earlier experiences of shaming by the mother.

In treating a narcissistic patient, it is necessary to understand that early experiences of shame may result in what Kohut called a "vertical split" in the nuclear self (Kohut, 1971, pp. 176–88). Kohut's concept of a "vertical split," which is linked to feelings of shame, needs to be addressed in some detail, because the cohort of narcissistic patients presenting with a hunger to idealize, to be mirrored or be twinned, or some combination of these, may have a developmental arrests that comes predominantly from an absence of a needed selfobject experience without excessive feelings of shame and a "vertical split." Any shame is a relatively minor component in these cases.

In contrast, however, another cohort of narcissistic patients present with a chronic catalogue of failures, misery, and shame, have a "vertical split" as a major component to their self-organization (Goldberg, 1995, 1999, 2000). Their "split" self-development resulted from not just an absence of mirroring, but a persistent humiliating parental response that has left them feeling ashamed for seeking the mirroring. The unique inhibiting bind of this second group of patients is their *feeling ashamed for not wanting to feel ashamed.* In order to reduce these feelings, the patients wall off their exhibitionistic desires. They do not repress them; they know they have a wish to exhibit. But they wall off these exhibitionistic desires to prevent shaming feelings as a result of these desires being activated. By walling off their desires and preventing conscious shame, they are able to continue functioning adaptively. Their walling off, then, reflects a policy of containing exhibitionistic desires.

The concept of shame as "walling off desire," rather than repressing it, suggests the difference between looking and knowing. This difference reflects Kohut's emphasis on healing through selfobject responsiveness leading to the re-calibration of feelings, compared with Freud's original concept of healing through the expanding knowledge that comes from making the unconscious conscious. Kohut's focus on shame is on the experience of "not looking" rather than "not knowing." We are reminded of this by the story of the Old Testament prophet Elijah (I Kings, 19:9–13). Threatened with a loss of his life, Elijah fled from King Ahab and Queen Jezebel after his opposition to their Baal religion failed. Defeated, discouraged, and ashamed, he sought the solitude of a remote cave on the historic Mount Horab. According to the story, when God called from outside the cave, Elijah came to the entrance, his face wrapped in his cloak, to avoid seeing God. This act of eye covering is the symbol of "dislook" that defends against the intensification of shame in the presence of the "perfect one." As Darwin (1872) observes, "Under a keen sense of shame there is a strong desire for concealment. We turn away the whole body, more especially the face, which we endeavor in some manner to hide" (p. 320).

Patients who present with a walled off, shame-prone self-organization have developed a strategy of living as perfectly as possible according to ideal models of how to behave, think, or feel. By adhering to the norms these models generate, patients seek to prevent criticism and avoid exacerbating their walled-off feelings of shame. A patient's strivings to be perfect suggests a dyadic developmental experience with a parent who, as a perfect other, was never at fault about anything. Such a transference to the therapist as a perfect one suggests that the idealizing involved is not the vitalizing kind of Kohut's idealizing transference, but the defensive kind that induces feelings of shame and inferiority. So, retriggered by the therapeutic relationship, strategies of attempted perfectionism and walling off are ways of containing feelings of shame. By living cautious, fear-ridden lives, and by being vigilant against mistakes, their narcissism takes a constrictive, self-righteous form rather than grandiose expansiveness (R. Lee, 1993) in order to prevent self-fragmentation.

Moderate to excessive levels of shame help create a distinct "vertical split" in a patient's self-organization. Such patients in the presence of an idealized, perfectly experienced psychotherapist, feel inferior and ashamed and resort to a "vertical split" to cope with these feelings, but this split blocks internalization of the psychotherapist's mirroring of healthy present-day assertiveness of the nuclear self that has, in the past, been structuralized to inhibit internalizing responses of non-attuned significant others (Kohut and Wolf, 1978, p. 377). Another reason for a vertical split may come from progress in creating a therapeutic bond that may reawaken an intense wish for empathic understanding along with deep feelings of shame for this wish. Unless this potential to evoke shame and trigger a vertical split is understood by the psychotherapist and, eventually the patient, treatment of vertically split patients may trigger a depressed, hopeless withdrawal from the treatment. Yet, as Kohut indicated, psychotherapy with such patients invariably involves non-empathic responding by the psychotherapist, and when this happens, becomes an opportunity to openly discuss the psychotherapist's fallibility. So, the goal of treating such patients is transforming a patient's defensive, perfectionistic, idealizing transference into a twinship with a fallible but humane person. In order for this to happen, the psychotherapist has to be comfortable with his/her own fallibility and not respond to mistakes with excessive feelings of shame.

Kohut also describes how a patient may relieve shame by using outbursts of rage or making revenge-substituting, reparative demands that the "wrongs" and wounding be set right. In sessions with patients who manifest shameful, constricted narcissistic disorders, a psychotherapist needs the capacity to empathically understand both the socially aware self-sector and the walled-off grandiose self-sector, and the role of shame in this walling off.

In treating shameful, constricted narcissistic disorders, the psychotherapist is in a bind similar to that confronted by the patient. Any attempt to bring into the open the core issue of feeling ashamed for desiring mirroring only intensifies the shame. Nor does pressure to be less perfectionistic succeed because, as this implies criticism, and this challenges the patient's constricted strategy, it only makes them feel more distressed. Until the results of the psychotherapist's efforts to be seen as more humane take root, the psychotherapist may need to adopt, at first, the patient's own strategy of finding ways to contain the shame. As the patient shifts the brittle idealization of the psychotherapist to a more humane relationship, it opens the way for a twinship experience that is capable of modifying the structuralized feelings of shame that have been embedded in the procedural memory.

Goldberg (2007) offers an important insight into working with vertically split patients. He claims that in working with these narcissistic behavior disorders that it helps if the psychotherapist is able to match the patient by experiencing a complementary split. When this complementary split is present, the psychotherapist is able to be empathic with both sides of the patient's split. Goldberg (2007) says,

> Just as some analysts work better with some patients than with others, it seems without question that some analysts will be incapable of allowing such a split transference to develop and be recognized. Rather than attribute this sort of failing to a deficiency or resistance in the analyst, it may be the case that his or her own psychic organization does not allow for this complementary state [p. 129].

A clinical case illustrates. A treatment session with a shame-ridden W, a divorced male in his late thirties, reveals strong feelings of shame. In his seventy-fifth session he entered the consulting room of the female psychotherapist, settled into his chair, looked at her for about half a minute, and then did his usual glancing downward. It was this regular "dislook" that suggested he felt ashamed in the presence of the psychotherapist. This was not interpreted to him because it would have probably reinforced his feelings of shame and resulted in denial, his major defense against shame. The patient's shame feelings seem to have been activated by the desire to be mirrored by the psychotherapist, suggesting a narcissistic transference. After noting the glancing downward behavior, the psychotherapist said that she was happy to see him after the long Christmas holiday period (of the Australian summer). He nodded, and then with a touch of anger, said that he had gone through a meaningless Christmas ritual.

The psychotherapist then asked W what the meaningless Christmas ritual felt like for him. Contemptuously, he said the psychotherapist was stupid in not realizing that every Christmas was the same for him. He then explained, "As soon as I make one plan or another, my ex-wife ensures that it is thwarted." He continued, "I had planned to get some projects accomplished this January, but my ex-wife dumped my son on me. As I love my son, I can't turn around and say, 'No I am busy,' can I? So I just have to accept what she hands out. I have no choice." As W said this, he kept opening and closing his fists. There was a pause, and then he said, "I would just like to get my hands on her!" The psychotherapist then pointed out that although he was outwardly calm, inside he was furious. He then exploded with, "Yes, I think one day I will kill her!" The shame had turned into feelings of rage, which the psychotherapist silently accepted as understandable.

W then associated to memories of a family court hearing when, although he had been abiding by the divorce agreement, his ex-wife was demanding more money and threatening not to give him access to his child. The court made a judgment that made him feel wrong and his wife right, in effect shaming him. He paused. The psychotherapist said, "The court does not always get it right and may not have been right in your case" (which was the possibility of fallibility of the "other"). He then shared, "I think that was the day I decided to just give in. I had no other option." Smiling oddly, he said, "This is all old stuff that I have gone over many times. It doesn't really matter anymore. There is nothing I can do. I am probably wasting my time talking about it." The psychotherapist thought that maybe his feelings of helplessness induced some self-fragmentation and hence fueled his rage.

The psychotherapist replied that W's concerns, although old stuff, were having a marked effect on his motivation in life, particularly his work. She then interpreted that his lack of energy was a consequence of his need to prevent his rage at his wife from being expressed in behavior. W seemed to accept this interpretation by confirming that he just lay around the previous weekend. He then added, "But I am not depressed!" The psychotherapist mirrored this with, "Just de-motivated." After a short silence, W said, "I have interests and ideas, and want to do them, but then I shy away from them." The psychotherapist thought to herself that this was evidence of his deeply structuralized "monopolistic" (Tomkins) shame that was holding back his life. So she indicated that she would like to know more about what it feels like to "shy away." She also playfully indicated that she was glad he was willing to speak about this "ancient history."

W began to smile ever so slightly at the psychotherapist's interest. When she wondered aloud if the "shying away" had started with the family court experience, W began by saying "Yes," but, upon reflection, corrected himself by saying that it had been happening for a long time. The psychotherapist had the image of a small child who had to give up and not make demands. He had to pull himself together and get on with his life. She also knew that when he was five years old, his disabled brother was born. She could imagine (vicarious extrospection) that this disabled child demanded all the resources of W's parents, and she could also imagine (vicarious introspection) his feelings of helplessness as the interest and attention that he vitally needed were given to his brother. So in response to W the psychotherapist said, "You had to figure these things out previously, by yourself, without help. Now," she said, "I am glad you are talking to me about your feelings because I am interested in working with you to figure out these feelings together."

In response to this idea of working together, W's face brightened. In fact he started to laugh. He said that he had thought of himself as weak, and that he should be tough with his wife and not let her get away with her bullying, but he can't. He then indicated that he had smiled because of a memory of his son. The psychotherapist asked if he would say more. W shared that his son had recalled his mother saying that she would never marry again, because life was so awful with his father. The memory of his son's statement led W to say, "Maybe I am capable of giving someone a hard time. That's nice to think about." Both he and the psychotherapist chuckled.

As the session ended, the issue of meeting twice the following week came up. When the psychotherapist asked W what he wanted to do, he replied that he did not want to take responsibility for the decision. Thinking that W was checking to see if she was still interested in him, she said, "Ok, then I will decide. Things are getting interesting. I want to see you twice next week." W smiled with relief, and said, "Good!" W then stood up and teasingly said, "Maybe I should call you a dictator." So, the psychotherapist playfully responded, "Now, you are giving me a hard time." He left with a smile on his face saying, "See you Friday."

Successful psychotherapy with constricted, shame-prone patients depends on understanding that the major generator of a patient's shame consists of a hunger for mirroring from the "perfect other." This means that failures, disappointments, and the shame of not being perfect in adulthood are derivatives of, and secondary to, childhood experiences of being rejected by "perfect parents" for wanting exhibitionistic needs met. In treatment, empathic attention to, and understanding of, a patient's current failures and disappointments are often necessary to minimize a worsening of a patient's feelings of shame and humiliation. More importantly, the patient may model the psychotherapist's acceptance of mistakes in understanding during treatment without extensive feelings of shame or blame. Such modeling helps validate the patient's strategy of shame containment. And the therapeutic relationship may create a twinship experience, without the patient consciously realizing it, as a way forward.

Clinical experience indicates that the walled-off, exhibitionistic desire, persistently seeks expression in "feeling-action," a concept akin to Kohut's idea of "action-thought" (1971, pp. 36–37). In "feeling-action" the feeling of shame, an expression of the supraordinate self-organization, is reenacted. Patients' "activity" creates shameful events to express their nuclear "monopolistic" shame (Tomkins, 1963). In order to do this, shame-ridden persons will, seemingly impulsively, break their cautious, constricted patterns and make plans where failure is virtually guaranteed. The ensuing failure activates underlying nuclear-self experiences of shame; the failure is more the expression of an underlying, already existing shameful state than the "cause" of it.

Attention to current experiences of shame, while an important beginning, is not enough. Psychotherapy is enhanced as the transference shifts toward a twinship experience because as this occurs, the psychotherapist becomes less perfect and more humanized. If the psychotherapist can be enjoyed and accepted as more human, the patient does not need to be perfect either, and the patient's hunger to exhibit, a core dynamic, is no longer shameful. Until the psychotherapist becomes experienced as a fallible human and not idealized as the "perfect one," failures by the patient can reinforce feelings of shame deeply embedded in the nuclear self.

This constricted, perfectionist, cohort of shame-ridden patients needs to be distinguished from a third group, which Kohut referred to as narcissistic behavior disorders. They too are shame-ridden. As with the second group, they have walled off a shameful sector and resorted to "action feelings." But they differ from the second group in that their "action feelings" are a stronger, more defiant expression of their need for self-agency. These patients were shamed, not because they wished to be mirrored, but because they wanted their self-agency affirmed, and were "put down." They now express their action-shame defiantly, often antisocially if not unlawfully.

Kohut includes "sociopathic personalities" in this group. According to him, they were mirrored in their development when they acted in accordance with the mother's needs, but were shamed when they presented with their own wishes and ideas (Kohut and Wolf, 1978, p. 377). Their behavior goes beyond "action feeling" to destructively "acting out" in defiance of a parent. Their treatment is similar to the second group, except that the explanations focus on the defiant acting out, the need for acceptance of their assertiveness and, most importantly, an acceptance of their need for self-agency.

C. Barriers to a Functional Feeling Theory

Although psychotherapy theory needs a theory of feeling, two extreme views may hinder rather than help the effective practice of psychotherapy. These may be stated as "Thinking without feeling and feeling without thinking" (E. Balint, 1953, p. 478) which were earlier expressed by Ferenczi (1931, p. 236). Examples of such hinderance are (1) Rene Descartes, with his emphasis on the enlightenment concept of reason, and (2) the opposite extreme of a compensatory ideal that retards the creative exploration of feelings in psychotherapy.

(1) Rene Descartes and "Reason"

Rene Descartes rejected feelings, and because his ideas have powerfully influenced the history of Western thought, an effective theory of feelings cannot avoid the influence of his ideas. What may be even more significant for psychotherapy is that patients who hold a similar opposition to feelings, as does Descartes, make a successful therapeutic outcome difficult. In Descartes' case, his opposition may have derived from his experience of his mother's death during the birth of his brother when Rene was fourteen months old (Eisenbud, 1991), and from experiences of being raised by his grandmother and a nurse, for whom he had no warm feelings later in life. These significant relationships, and everything about Descartes' life, suggest he was dominated by an effort to prevent being wounded from experiences similar to those with his "mothers." His story is one of illness in early childhood, restlessly wandering through Europe for eleven years as a single young man, and constantly shifting his residences during middle age to two dozen cities or towns of Holland over a period of twenty years. After being appointed to the Swedish court, where the Queen insisted on her lessons at five a.m. during a very severe winter, Descartes contracted pneumonia and died within a few days. In effect, he died of neglect, fifty-four years old!

From the evidence of his life and particularly his philosophy, it may be hypothesized that Descartes did everything in his power to avoid repeating the wound he had experienced as an infant, by resisting attaching to people, places, or beliefs. Before the studies of Anna Freud, Rene Spitz, John Bowlby, and modern infant researchers, infants before the age of walking and talking were thought to be relatively immune from the loss of a mother. After all, it was said, the prefrontal lobes of these infants were still unmyelinated, and therefore the loss of the mother was before conscious symbolic memory. There is now compelling evidence that although very early loss is not recoverable as a conscious symbolic memory, it is usually imprinted in the procedural memory (see chapter 6) of a self-organization. During Descartes' life, as he was self-organized to prevent being vulnerable by resisting emotional attachment, he could be considered as an example of Ainworth's insecurely attached, avoidant personality (group A).

Descartes' self-organization also utilized the process of dissociation. As a devout Roman Catholic, Descartes lived a religiously chaste life except for one sexual encounter with a domestic servant, that resulted in the birth of a daughter who died from scarlet fever when five years old. Descartes' lack of distress following his daughter's death suggested that he had not bonded to her or coped by dissociating, and is evidence to support the idea that his nuclear self was organized so that personal loss would not affect him. This dissociated organizing style is reflected in his philosophy, which, no less than a painting, a poem, or a psychotherapy theory, reflects its personal origin in the creator's life. Stolorow and Atwood (1979) demonstrate from the writings of Freud, Jung, Reich, and Rank, how a theorist's self-organizing issues are intertwined in their theories.

In his "Principles of Philosophy," Descartes' need for security took the form of a search for the certainty of knowledge, and his eventual adoption of the bias that an idea was false until he "could have no occasion to doubt it." His systematic doubting reflected a reluctance to emotionally commit to beliefs. Descartes then realized that the only thing (content) not doubted was his experience of doubting (process), a form of thinking. Only in his capacity to doubt (think, "reason") did he feel certain. Hence, his famous phrase "Cogito ergo sum" (I think [doubt] therefore I am) involved a shift from the content of thought to process thinking, from a static sense of self to a sense of self-agency through the activity of thinking, which reflected the privilege of his class and education. It did not occur to him to say, "I am sweating (process) therefore I am" (Brittain, 1963). It is ironic that Descartes' insight into his self-agency came from imagining himself as doubting, because imagining is a right frontal lobe function rather than of the mathematical, logical "reasoning," left frontal lobe function that is usually attributed to him.

In emphasizing "reason" as the privileged, disembodied left brain self, Descartes separated his thinking "I" from the material world, a dissociation consistent with defending against feeling. In doing so, he privileged mind over the body and one part of the mind, the reasoning area, over the rest. In privileging reason, he affirmed the core belief of the Enlightenment philosophy and the major organizing idea for the Western intellectual world of the last three centuries. A motive for the development of modern affect theory has been, at least partially, a reaction to privileged intellectualism of the Enlightenment, and a resulting concept of affects that is oppositional to thinking. Unfortunately, if modern psychotherapy theory of feeling is influenced by this oppositional view, a dissociative split is encouraged. An overemphasis on feelings at the expense of thought in psychotherapy reinforces the pathology of patients with "impulsive" problems. Such a dichotomy of thought and affects is contrary to a tradition of treatment that "involves unitary configurations of experience in which cognitive and affective components are virtually indivisible" (Stolorow and colleagues, 1987, p. 101). For feeling theory to be valuable in the conduct of psychotherapy, therefore, feelings need to be seen, not as antithetical to thinking, but as involving modifiable premotor responses of the whole (supraordinate) self, as reflected in the clinical work of Kohut.

(2) Feelings as a Compensatory Ideal

The concept of compensatory ideals is derived from Kohut's theorizing. As described in the previous chapter, Kohut saw ideals as a major component of a patient's nuclear self-organization. He (1977) says, "This [nuclear] structure is the basis for our sense of being an independent center of initiative and perception, integrated with our most central ambitions and ideals" (p. 177). In a well-functioning healthy family, ideal beliefs occurred as a result of transmuted micro-internalizing of an idealized selfobject. During this process children take on the values and ideals of influential persons in their lives.

Also depicted in Kohut's thinking was the concept of compensatory structures. To Kohut (1977), compensatory structures are internalized ways of adapting to situations where there is a deficit in self-structures as a result of inadequate developmental selfobject experiences (p. 3). A compensatory ideal is one type of compensatory structure. Not only are there ideals internalized as a result of idealizing a parent or selfobject experiences outside the nuclear family, but just as important are those ideas that take shape when selfobject experiences are not readily available. These ideals develop in a person in reaction to painful experiences, which disappoint or wound. Such ideals are usually the exact opposite of a patient's distressing experience.

The case of L illustrates. L grew up in a family where the father was inebriated five or six days a week. His memories of childhood were filled with loud parental arguments, shouting and verbal abuse, the smashing of dishes and furniture, and an unhappy life of misery and shame. The problems of the marital relationship went much further than the alcoholism, but as the alcohol was the trigger for the cascade of misery, it became a target for L's anger. As a result of these experiences, L formed a compensatory ideal, a silent, determined pledge that he would remain "teetotal" for the rest of his life. Then as increasing self-esteem came from successfully adhering to his "sacred" pledge, offsetting feelings of shame for the behavior of his father, the compensating ideal became an internalized component of L's nuclear self-organization.

In the development of his theory of narcissism, Kohut theorized that a key to a patient's nuclear self-organization was not so much the content of the ideal, but whether it was archaic or not. When ideals are archaic, Kohut noted an "absolutarian flavor" (1977, p. 105). During L's teens, because the smell of alcohol brought back memories of pain and shame, his revulsion to alcohol was so absolute that he could not tolerate being around those who drank. As a boy he was so "anti-drink," that when his Sunday-school teacher asked his class to sign a pledge to abstain from drinking alcohol, he refused.

To sign would be to doubt his deep commitment to his ideal and pledge already internalized in his nuclear self-organization.

To Kohut, the transformation of narcissism was not just shrinking grandiose ambitions, but the mellowing of behaviors associated with compensatory ideals. In L's case, his teetotal ideal eventually softened. To avoid a socially ostracized existence he began to attend social functions where he learned to graciously ask for a soft drink or a glass of water, when offered alcohol. He learned to unobtrusively leave if the drinking became too boisterous. He also refused to join causes that militantly sought to shame people into giving up alcohol. He never changed his ideal, but it became less archaic, less rigidly adhered to, and eventually led to a softening in his behavior as his anger and hatred for the abuse and humiliation of his childhood years declined. He also transformed his unrealistic compensatory ideal of a world where there was no consumption of alcohol.

A theory of feelings based on anti-intellectualism as a compensatory ideal does not represent an effective psychotherapy theory. One female patient, R, had been so shamed by her parents for bad handwriting and lack of intellectual accomplishments at school, that she felt unintelligent. Abhorring things "intellectual," she was constantly expressing her feelings, but as these intellectual matters were vertically split from the feeling part of herself, she was only able to express a limited total self. She eventually attended a training program for psychotherapists, rebelled against the academic work, and offered herself as a volunteer counselor in a clinic. There she discovered that her obsession with her patient's feelings prevented her from exploring many issues from her patients' points of view and created disjunctions that drove patients away. Eventually she was seen as being too "rigidly idealistic" (narcissistic) to be an effective counselor. With her strong, archaic, idealized view, monadic feelings were prioritized over the rest of her self-organization; she was in effect dominated by a feeling homunculus. Without R's compensatory ideal being modified, she had little ability to become an effective psychotherapist.

D. Cases of Increased Feelings

Increased awareness of feelings involves perceptions and the circuits of the interoceptive and exteroceptive systems. A perceptual awareness of neural firing in the affect circuits was emphasized in Basch's (1976) distinction between feelings (emotions) and affects. Through categorizing experiences that trigger affect circuits, the perceptual system transforms neural stimulations into awareness in cognitive circuits. Just as multi-modal sensing enables perceptual systems to develop perceptual categories for objects (Thelen and Smith, 1998), so repetitive experiences of affects shared with significant others, enable the development of categories of feelings from the neural activation of affect circuits. For example, the experiences of significant others as selfobjects share in the infant's feeling state and helps develop feeling awareness.

Affect awareness is an important issue for psychotherapy, where patients may present with an absence of "feelings." Enid Balint's (1953) treatment of Sarah illustrates how "the nucleus of herself was not based on feelings arising out of body-self sensations, reinforced and enriched by responses from her mother to them" (p. 479). Structuralization of healthy interactions had not occurred and so she remained isolated from reality. After five years of analysis, Sarah had a dream in which her uterus, a symbol of her total self, was experienced as "on fire," that is, "alive."

The case of Ms. M also reflects a transformation of neural signaling of the affect circuits to an awareness of feelings through the categorizing function of the perceptual input system. Ms. M, a middle-aged project leader for a team of computer programmers, sought psychotherapy on referral from a Human Resources Department, because her job was in serious jeopardy. Although she had good technical knowledge, she was facing her third project where her leadership had been challenged or undermined by members of her "team" and where she was reduced to helpless passivity and depression. Her feelings of defeat were not helped by her personal life where she lived with a dominant female partner, and had functioned for many years as a "dutiful daughter." This partnership was a repetitive pattern of a childhood spent in a "tranquilized" home under a controlling mother and a noninvolved business-focused father.

As the psychotherapy sessions proceeded, it became evident that not only did Ms. M expect to be dominated in significant relationships, including the psychotherapy, she also did not display feelings. She never experienced joy, did not express anger, and seemed unaware in situations of danger when she should have been fearful. For example, Ms. M traveled daily to work in a U.S. city on a train line that was infamous for shootings and muggings. At first she seemed insensitive to the danger, but when the psychotherapist verbalized his concern that she may eventually be mugged, Ms. M shrugged her shoulders. She accepted his prediction as highly probable, but despairingly said she could do nothing about it, just as she could do nothing about her work situation. She seemed unable to act, either because her fears were repressed, or because they were unformed perceptually.

In the session following, Ms M said that, in view of the discussion, she had decided to carry a shoulder bag with an old purse in it to act as a decoy going to and from work, and would keep her real purse in her slim briefcase. In the months that followed, the patient displayed some increased engagement with the psychotherapist in response to his genuine interest in her. One morning the patient arrived in a state of high excitement. As she entered the consulting room, she blurted out, "Look!" and swung around so the psychotherapist could see the back of her shoulder bag. The inevitable had happened. It had a large slit in it, made by an undetected thief and a sharp razor blade as she stood in a packed train. The thief had taken her purse and probably left the train at the next station. With a huge grin M shared, "He got my old purse, worth nothing, as we planned." Joining her feelings of triumph, the psychotherapist exclaimed "Won't that thief feel frustrated!" Gleefully, the patient blurted out, "That's only half of it. I had a note in it that said, 'Got you, you son of a bitch!'"

This incident around the hundreth session, and the emergence of more positive feelings in the sessions that followed, were forward edge steps in the psychotherapy. Eventually, however, the euphoria of M's triumph was replaced by a ritualistic reporting of life happenings, or by periods of silence. Attempts to explore the meaning of M's behavior, particularly the silences, did not immediately lead to new material or insights, and the barren interaction gradually created heavy feelings of hopelessness in the psychotherapist. When he eventually shared with M, how hopeless he had felt during the session, she went silent. He then asked how she felt, and she said it felt she was being criticized.

In response, the psychotherapist said that he believed that she had created a sense of hopelessness in him, but he was not criticizing her for it. He thought her unconscious ability to create feelings of hopelessness in him was just as creative as had been her handling of the handbag situation, and a step forward in the psychotherapy. When M looked puzzled, he explained that her ability to generate feelings of hopelessness in him offered a way forward. As she was not aware of her feelings, this only left her with the capacity to act on her feelings as a more primitive but important means of communication. Her growing desire to communicate feelings of which she was dimly aware, had probably developed as a result of their shared triumph over the decoy purse success. As the session ended, M said she would need to think about his interesting explanation.

In the sessions that followed, M revealed a growing appreciation for the psychotherapist's explanation. She realized that with the psychotherapist sharing his feelings in the session, she could possibly label them. After this was agreed upon, in another session when the psychotherapist became aware of his growing anger, he asked, "Are you feeling angry?" M's response was "I have feelings of heaviness." When they then explored M's experiences of the preceding day at work, where several employees undermined or ignored her authority, he shared that if he had been in her shoes in that situation he would have been very angry. This interaction where their feelings matched, was an important step in naming her feeling. Her awareness of her feelings had developed from a perceptual categorizing of a shared perspective with her psychotherapist.

On another occasion, a puzzled M said she experienced the psychotherapist as angry. Was he angry with her? After the psychotherapist explored M's immediate experiences and found nothing to make her angry, he shared that he had been in a major disagreement with a close friend and it was possible that this incident, not M, had generated some anger in him. So the exploration of feelings went on. Over the next two years of twice-a-week psychotherapy, the sharing and exploring of feelings occurred whenever M had angry, fearful, distressing, humiliating, or joyous experiences. As a result of the psychotherapist's function as a sharing twin, M became aware of and identified feelings associated with the categorizing of her affects. As this occurred, Ms. M became more aware of herself and her feelings, became a more assertive team-leader at work—and she retained the job she had been in danger of losing.

This case suggests that focusing on and understanding feelings as the patient's experience of the psychotherapist being empathic, can lead to a patient feeling more cohesive and making significant therapeutic strides. In comparison, the emergence of naked, monadic, primordial and primary feelings, freed from context, and without connections to the other self-systems, is a serious sign of dissociative forms of fragmentation. With such an understanding, the emergence of rage, for example, can't be rationalized as "It's good to express your feelings!" Instead, the emergence of such rage indicates a person in an archaic state urgently in need of selfobject experiences.

If providing psychotherapy means understanding the feelings of a patient as holistically as possible, it is evident that a developmental affect theory offers support for self psychology's ideas about feelings. In the light of modern affect theory it is blatantly obvious that past psychotherapy has been too narrowly confined in its focus on the emergency affects of fear and anger. Although one purpose of this project has been to see if affect theory can enhance a self psychology theory of feeling, the question soon became more how than if. Although this chapter offers only outlines of a tentative solution, it shows how useful an understanding of affect theory can be to a self-psychological approach to the feeling self. Stated succinctly, we rephrase Descartes' famous dictum with, "I feel, therefore I am" as a way to experiencing a functioning supraordinate self-organization.

Summary

In the last two chapters, we have portrayed the self's thought processes as involving slowly self-organizing, relatively fixed beliefs for the purpose of long-range predictions and affects as premotor programs shaped by learning and made aware of by sharing. The relatively fixed belief system of the nuclear self has the task of making predictions and decisions it could not possibly make if it functioned like an immediately responding self-organizing system, as seen with physical movement. Long-range strategizing has an indirect influence, however, as one component in the overall self-organizing of the supraordinate self-system. Even the relatively indirect role that the thought system plays, however, would be impossible if the self-organization did not have the capacity to retain memories. It is this memory capacity we examine in the next chapter.

CHAPTER SIX

The Remembering Self and Structuralization

The preceding chapters took the view that self-disordered patients—after their empathically understanding psychotherapist functions as a selfobject, accepts their feelings, and responds to them holistically—make adaptive and creative changes. Once these changes begin to occur, a primary concern of patients becomes something like, "Can these changes be sustained even when the psychotherapy ends?" Belief in the relative permanency of psychotherapy-induced changes assumes some kind of "residual self," the self that Henri Bergson saw as experiencing "duration" in creative evolution.

An enduring sense of self has long been a part of the Freudian psychoanalytic tradition with its concept of the id, ego, and superego agencies (as structures). Kohut, after training as a Freudian psychoanalyst, adopted structuralization as a major general postulate, even though he eventually rejected these Freudian agencies. Kohut's view of structuralization focused primarily on the process of internalization, as examined later in section B. Because structuralization and internalization would be impossible without an organism's capacity to remember, we initially approach the question of permanent therapeutic change by discussing memory systems in section A. Modern research on memory systems suggests that it is useful for psychotherapy theory to understand structuralization as it has developed both phylogenetically and ontogenetically. Specifically, the different remembering systems of the brain point to the dissimilar processes through which structuralization takes place.

Section A. Memory Systems

In this section we explore three major memory systems as examples of evolutionary forms of structuralization. After (a) an introduction to memory through Kandel's research into the lowly sea slug, *Aplysia californica*, we examine (b) procedural memory, (c) working memory, and (d) episodic memory, much of which is highly relevant to psychotherapy theory.

(a) Introduction

A cursory knowledge of biology makes it clear that remembering does not need a central nervous system. For example, antibodies of the immune system remember previously encountered antigens. And the sea snail (*Aplysia californica*), studied by Eric Kandel and associates (Kupfermann et al., 1970; Kandel et al., 1995), shows an early evolutionary organism remembers. This simple creature, with 20,000 neurons, withdraws its gills if they are touched. When a mild electric shock is given, the snail experiences it as unwelcome and becomes increasingly adept at withdrawing its gills. In other words, it learns: it remembers. But a key feature of Kandel's studies is that the *Aplysia*'s learning to withdraw its gills disappears after a few minutes. The learning is short-term. By killing the snails and examining their neuronal biochemistry immediately after the touching, Kandel demonstrated that the *Aplysia*'s short-term memory involves increased "cyclic AMP," that is, an enhanced release of neurotransmitters at the synapses. Neurotransmitters help form a temporary pattern of neuronal linkage that represents short-term memories.

Kandel took a further step. He significantly increased the number of unpleasant electric shocks to the gills and noted how the Aplysia were conditioned (learned) to withdraw their gills for longer and longer periods of time. Through continual stimulations, the short-term memory eventually consolidated into a relatively permanent memory from the distress-induced shocking. Kandel then killed the *Aplysia* with the long-term memories of being shocked, examined their neurons, and found evidence of protein synthesis and new dendrites and synapses. Importantly, he concluded that "on the cellular level the switch from short-term memory to long-term memory facilitation is a switch from a process-based memory to a structural-based memory" (Abel et al., 1995, p. 302). Abel views long-term learning as a form of "memory consolidation," which is new brain structuralization at the cellular level. Analogously, permanent changes to a patient's self-organization and behavior patterns effected by psychotherapy produce new brain structures that involve growth of dendrites and synapses.

Kandel's studies of the *Aplysia californica* indicate that learning in early phylogenetic organisms—and early ontogenetic learning in human development—heavily utilizes an automatic procedural type of memory, which can be either short-term or long-term. This short-term/long-term categorization of memory is only one of many used in the neuroscience literature. From a far larger group, Terr (1994), for example, lists six kinds of memories (p. 48): the immediate, brief, procedural, priming, associative, and episodic memory systems. Even this brief list is complicated by the fact that some are implicit and others explicit, some short-term and others long-term, some both (Llinas, 2001). Influenced by Tulving (1993), we think semantic memory should be added to her list. Our goal here, however, is to explore memory systems that have the potential to enhance our view of the process of structuralization as it takes place in psychotherapy.

(b) Procedural Memory

We look first at procedural memory because it explains why appeals to "reason" may not produce changes in a patient's personality or "destructive" behavior, even when the patient genuinely desires it. It offers also a cogent explanation why long-term psychotherapy needs regular, frequent sessions, for an extended period, to produce significant and lasting therapeutic change. For example, a golf swing is an encoded form of procedural memory, and as every golfer knows, if he/she resorts to a conscious effort (working memory) to correct some feature of a swing without persistent practice, the resulting score can be disastrous. From the point of view of psychotherapy, Shane, Shane, and Gales (1997) describe procedural memory as "a form of nonsymbolic encoding, wherein the memory is repeated in the individual, behaviorally or emotionally, often out of that individual's awareness" (p. 37). A procedural memory, then, can be viewed as a complex type of Tinbergen's (1966) "fixed action pattern" (FAP).

Tinbergen's best-known demonstration of an FAP is a female goose's behavior in getting an egg back into a nest. If a goose egg is placed outside the nest (the "trigger"), the female begins a repeated movement with its beak and neck to drag the egg back into the nest. If the goose loses the egg (or the researcher removes it) during this dragging procedure, the goose continues the stereotypic dragging movement, without the egg, until the nest is reached. Then the goose goes back to the missed egg and the dragging begins again. This fixed behavior pattern suggests that FAPs have neural circuitry that is elicited by the trigger of the egg being outside the nest. Similar fixed action patterns are studied as reflex behavior in infants. For example, human infants a few days old can firmly hold an object, and show even greater strength if they touch hair. FAPs use reflex behavior as seen with a primate infant's need to hold on to a mother's hair to not fall off when she moves. Importantly, reflex FAPs not susceptible to learning, are elicited by the brain stem and spinal cord (Llinas, 2001).

The more complex FAPs, modifiable by learning, involve the basal ganglia, a set of subcortical nuclei located in the center of the brain, above the brain stem. A study of the way the basal ganglia neurons directly terminate on top of each other suggests that these neurons specialize in inhibitory electrical patterns; they function as a gateway to prevent the enactment of FAPs that are stored either in the basal ganglia or the cerebellum. Llinas illustrates his point from Dante's Inferno. In one section Dante describes damned souls who are kept in a cauldron, but no one watches them to prevent escape as any time a soul had attempted to do this, the other envious souls pulled the escaping person back in. Basal ganglia neurons function similarly, inhibiting the preformed FAP functions until they are needed and then "liberating" them for action.

The important feature of the basal ganglia FAPs as compared with the brain stem and spinal cord FAPs, is their development involves learning. They use a genetic component to function automatically, to be sure, but their patterns have been modified by experiences. This modifying is demonstrated from the generation of bird songs as indicated in the previous chapter. Each species has a base song that is genetic, but in normal animals this song has regional embellishments or dialects that have been learned. The development of songs is a part of the male courting process for robins (the females don't sing). Llinas (2001) explains,

> Singing is quite a motor performance, and thus a good measure of the state of health of the animal, as well as a measure of originality of brain activity. In fact, there is brain competition, as birds will invent, copy, and steal variations of songs from each other. . . . Ornithologists have pieced together how a particular song is developed before reproduction occurs and preceding mating. They have described how song comes to fruition and maturity at mating time and then is reinvented the following year with different variations. . . . Next season the male will need a new song because he won't do so well with the old song. It is nature's planned obsolescence. The females recognize the males' song from last season and that that sperm may not be so good anymore! [p. 139].

With respect to psychotherapy, studies of basal ganglia-based FAPs not only demonstrate that behavioral procedures can be learned, but indicate *they can be forgotten*. If they are to be retained, they must be rehearsed. This means that a patient who repeats a procedural memory through behavioral enactment reinforces the experience so that it is not forgotten over time. Stern (1985) refers to such procedural memory enactment as a "motor memory" (p. 91). Bruner (1969) claims it is "memory without words," a phrase implying that memories reside in muscle patterns. Infants, in learning to sit, suck a thumb, crawl, or walk, develop skills that utilize some form of procedural memory. Later in life these skill memories are involved in throwing a ball, riding a bike, swinging a hammer, or as noted above, swinging a golf club. Because the procedural memory is a skills memory, it can be considered as a part of Kohut's nuclear self.

Motor/skill memories function very early phylogenetically and ontogenetically. Rovee-Collier and her colleagues (Rovee-Collier et al., 1980; Rovee-Collier and Fagen, 1981; Rovee-Collier and Lipsitt, 1981) have demonstrated motor memories in early infant development by connecting a mobile to an infant's leg with a piece of string. When an infant kicked, the mobile moved, and the movement gained the attention of the infant. After infants learned to move the mobile by kicking, Rovee-Collier retested their memory by repeating the procedure some days later without connecting the string. She found that the retested infants kicked from remembering the cues of the experimental setting.

Major evidence for procedural memory in humans comes from the study of Korsakoff patients, with their damaged mammillary brain circuits (hypothalamus and diencephalon areas) (Schacter, 1996, p. 146). As the mammillary neural circuits are involved in memory that uses symbolic representations, damage to them leads to an inability to remember all kinds of facts, including instructions. But their procedural memory remains intact. For example, one of the authors (RL), in giving tests to hospitalized alcoholic patients, placed a notice on the dayroom notice board requesting a named patient to please come to his office for testing. The patient soon arrived, cooperatively went through an hour's testing, and then returned to the dayroom. The test indicated there had been permanent neural damage as a result of years of excessive abuse of alcohol. Five minutes later, however, the patient returned asking, "You wanted to see me Doc?" after seeing the notice board again. He could not remember he had just been tested!

Korsakoff patients reveal important insights into the functioning of the procedural memory. Corkin (1968), who studied the well-known Korsakoff patient HM, mentions how he was just as capable of learning a mirror-tracing task and using other procedural skills as a comparison group of non-Korsakoff patients even though he needed instructions each time he took a test. This clearly pointed to HM's undamaged procedural memory. This and other studies of Korsakoff patients support the idea of a non-symbolic memory system. For example, Cermak, Lewis, Butters, and Goodglass (1973) confirm the idea that Korsakoff patients generally learn a rotary task just as well as a normal group. Cohen and Squire (1980) also found that after three consecutive daily sessions and a fourth session thirteen weeks later, eight amnesic patients learned to read mirror-reflected words at a rate equivalent to that of a matched control group. And Cohen, Eichenbaum, Decedo, and Corkin (1985) found that Korsakoff patients were able to learn a tower of Hanoi puzzle as well as a normal group. Schacter (1983) conducted a most convincing demonstration of the difference between procedural and symbolic memories. He took a patient called MT on a golf outing. Because MT lacked a symbolic memory, yet still retained his procedural memory, his golf playing was fine, but without Schacter's help he could not have played the game because he could not remember his ball position. His procedural memory remained functional because his cerebellum and basal ganglia remained undamaged after his mammillary bodies were damaged. These examples of brain damage confirm that there is a procedural memory system functioning in early childhood prior to the development of symbolic language.

What about memory studies of infants? Mandler (1988), in reviewing experiments on cognitive development in infancy, claims that in imitation, motor recognition, acquisition of manual signs, and recall of absent objects studies, the results were consistent with evidence gained from studies of Korsakoff's disease, contrary to Piaget's view that a sensorimotor stage requires a symbolic form memory. Mandler mentions, for example, Meltzoff's (1988) demonstration that nine-month-old infants could imitate simple actions with novel objects and then, when reexposed to these objects twenty-four hours later, repeat the pattern. Bauer (1996), with imitative experiments on thirteen-month-old infants, also showed they were able to remember the sequences when tested eight months later. These and other infant studies clearly point to memory long before infants develop significant symbolic capacities.

Cognitive priming also points to procedural memory. Priming assumes that concepts influence each other, so that if one concept is activated, similar concepts are activated. As an example, if a person is shown the word "nurse" in an experiment and later shown the words "doctor" or "butter," the former is read more quickly because of the priming effect of "nurse." Tulving and Schacter (1990) are convinced that such priming is "independent of explicit [symbolic] memory" (p. 302), and is connected to a "perceptual representation system" that is a form of procedural memory.

Psychoanalyst Lyons-Ruth (1998) distinguishes between procedural and semantic memory representations. Procedural memory uses "rule-based representations about how to proceed, of how to do things" (p. 284), whereas semantic memory relies on symbolic representation in language. We mention Lyons-Ruth's conceptualization of procedural memory, because she sees it as involved in the development of a nuclear self-organization. It is of particular interest to psychotherapy that procedural knowledge can be involved in doing things with others, through what Lyons-Ruth calls "*implicit relational knowledge*." She (1998) observes,

> This implicit relational knowing begins to be represented in some yet-to-be-known form long before the availability of language and continues to operate implicitly throughout life. Implicit relational knowledge typically operates outside focal attention and conscious experience, without benefit of translation into language. Language is used in the service of this knowing but the implicit knowings governing intimate interactions are not language-based and are not routinely translated into semantic form [p. 285].

Beebe and Lachmann (2002) also make a strong case for implicit relational knowledge from the relational coordination that unconsciously develops between a mother and her infant in the first few months of life. This patterning leads to expectations and rules of relating. They list impressive evidence that *moderate* levels of bidirectional coordinating at three months lead to secure attachment behavior at twelve months, and that *low* levels of coordination at three months predict insecure avoidant attachment at twelve months, and *high* levels of coordination at three months predicate insecure anxious attachment at twelve months. These studies of attachment patterns in early infancy only could have developed in the procedural memory. Psychotherapy that leads to significant changes in a patient forms new patterns of relating that are encoded in the procedural memory.

The concept of procedural memory was introduced into psychotherapy with Freud's idea of the "compulsion to repeat," which he linked to the theory of transference (1914). This is where the patient repeats, in the relationship with the psychotherapist, a characteristic pathological pattern of earlier attachment experiences, especially of childhood. By repeating this pattern in the therapeutic relationship, the patient is expressing forgotten memories. The patient is usually unaware at first that this process is going on, and even when he/she becomes aware, the awareness is usually not enough to significantly alter the patient's compulsive behavior.

Lenore Terr (1994) illustrates the automatic repeating pattern of behavior in traumatized persons by referring to the novelist Stephen King. She once watched the movie "Stand By Me" in which there is a scene where a train suddenly appears behind four boys on a railway trestle. After the movie she told her husband that the scene felt like the depiction of a trauma. Curious, she discovered that the movie had been adapted from a Stephen King novel. In King's book the *Danse Macabre*, she found what she thought was an autobiographical passage that reflected a memory "when King was four years old [and] he and another boy were playing on the railroad tracks, and a freight train hit and killed his friend. The dead boy's severed body parts were brought home in a wicker basket" (p. 55). Although King claims that he did not remember the incident and only knew of it because of his mother's telling him about it when much older, Terr points to the theme of horror being repeated in King's novels (p. 1).[1]

Why do procedural patterns seem so intractable? And why does the procedural memory need to gain expression through reenacted behavior? Freud (1920) himself attributed this repetitive process to a death instinct, but most psychoanalysts, except Klein (1957) and some of her followers (Grosskurth, 1986), rejected this idea. Hendrick (1948), however, took another position: that repetitive patterns of behavior arise from a patient's urge to achieve some kind of mastery in a similar situation in which he/she has been wounded or defeated in the past.

Terr's (1994, p. 96f) description of Gary Baker illustrates Hendrick's idea of the need for mastery as one motivation for procedural memory. In Gary's case, his mother attempted to drown him in an irrigation ditch when he was four years of age, but the conscious memory of this was repressed until he was an adult. By then, he had been able to remember such repressed incidents as his mother pushing his head into a toilet bowl, immersing him in a bathinet of water, locking him briefly in a refrigerator, and placing him on the railway line with the train coming before rescuing him at the last minute. Furthermore, his mother, who had once masturbated herself in front of him using a dildo, also anally raped him with the dildo. As these memories returned, Gary became aware of his frequent feelings of helplessness and terror.

In response to these feelings, Gary had practiced and mastered prolonged breathing without realizing he was compensating for his childhood experiences by developing a potentially lifesaving habit. For example, at high school, he used his musical interest to develop a capacity to hold a note on a saxophone longer than anybody else, so by the time he took scuba diving lessons, he had already developed the breath control of an experienced diver.

These compensatory skills led him to organize his life around diving behavior and eventually to become one of the greatest river divers in the world.

Tolpin (2002) holds a similar view to Hendrick believing that repetitive patterns can represent the hopeful, forward edge of the transference as well as the pathology of the trailing edge. In presenting her forward edge material to the 2008 Empathink Summer School, Marian Tolpin illustrated repetition of forward edge material with Kubie's (1955) description of a gaunt, five-year-old, wheeled into a clinical conference in a hospital crib. A few weeks before admission, she had been functioning as a bright, intelligent girl, but suddenly, she had changed.

> Kubie (1953) describes her behavior on coming to the hospital.
>
> First the child refused to answer her name, insisting either that her name was that of a little girl who lived down the street, or of a boy. Presently she stopped talking almost completely, and practically stopped eating. She refused to stay in bed, or to use any bed covers, or pink pajamas and robe of which she had previously been particularly fond. She would wrap herself in a dirty blanket, rolling herself up in it with her face to the wall in the corner of the bedroom, where she soon began to wet and soil as she lay mute and unresponsive [p. 290].

Wheeled into a conference room, the child remained in a blank, staring silence and unresponsive to Kubie. After Kubie drew away from the crib and smiled at her for a few minutes, the child began to rhythmically hum a sound. The nurse, having heard this a number of times on the ward, reported that she thought the child said, "SAY YOU'RE SORRY." Hearing these words, the child turned and looked at the nurse searchingly, then turned back to Kubie. Using this cue, Kubie leaned to the child, took her hand, and said, "I am sorry. I am very, very sorry." The child looked at the doctor assisting Kubie and said, "Say 'you're sorry.'" He replied, "I am sorry too." The child then turned to the other doctors in the room, and said to each in turn, "Say you're sorry," which they did.

Then the child asked Kubie for his name, and after he told her, she asked and was told each of the doctors' names. Then she smiled and gave her name. Kubie then gave her a candy and she was rolled out of the conference. Later history taking discovered that the father, whom she had idealized, in a tired and stressful state had spanked her, and this had precipitated the illness crisis. A week later, when the child returned to the clinical conference, she came running into the room and climbed on to Kubie's lap! The child's repeated asking for people to "Say you're sorry" had not been pathology, but an expression of her hope for repair.

Once a therapeutic alliance has developed with patients who have repetitive malfunctioning behavior patterns, it helps to have them understand the hold that procedural memory has over their lives. At the appropriate time, patients experience an explanation about the procedural memory as empathic. Patients may, in fact, be relieved for not being considered crazy. This was the experience of an early-middle-aged single woman named Cathy with a history of suicidal attempts and relationship failures, and repetitive experiences of misattunement with a mother who was always in crisis. Cathy's rage toward her mother had been displaced to her latest boyfriends/partners, who were all accused of being more focused on themselves—as the mother had—than on her. Although the memory of her mother's misattunement was explicit, there was an implicit procedural memory expressed by unconsciously selecting predictably "selfish" partners whose actions would keep the procedural memory alive. Yet, if Cathy's memory was explicit and semantic, why did it still need repeating procedurally? Doesn't the Freudian view of making the unconscious conscious eliminate the need for a procedural memory? In this case, it hadn't. Why not?

In her sessions Cathy continued obsessing about her former boyfriends/partners and angrily denounced their rejection of her. After some time, when signs emerged that her rage was diminishing, she became increasingly distressed, because, as she blurted out, "if I don't maintain the rage, they (former boyfriends/partners) will win"—and presumably, mother would as well. Her remark depicts a self-organizational split consisting of a reasonable-self that asks the suffering-self to forgive and forget. If the suffering-self forgives and forgets, however, it relinquishes the possibility of ever being empathically understood; no one would ever know what Cathy went through. Until this understanding for which she hungered happened, Cathy retained her need for revenge and its associated procedural memory. The latter impelled her to reenact the model scene of mother's neglect and abandonment, now reinforced by her relationships with boyfriends/partners.

Cathy's fears about her "mother winning" by her own "forgetting" echoed those uttered by another patient named Barbara. Barbara underwent a prolonged course of psychotherapy as a result of severe self-damage from childhood abuse and victimization. She had not been sexually abused, but had been brutally beaten from an early age by a bullying mother, who had induced in Barbara deep feelings of rage and revenge. By the time the psychotherapy reached 200 sessions, it was clear Barbara's images of gaining revenge on an aging mother were strong. Overshadowing treatment, however, was a concern that if feelings of revenge lessened, she would be in danger of seriously fragmenting. This fear suggested that her feelings of revenge were major self-organizing motifs in her nuclear self-organization.

One mitigating factor, possibly preventing fragmentation, was a good therapeutic relationship based on Barbara's positive childhood experiences with her father. Not usually assertive, Barbara' father, on occasions, ignored his wife's fear-ridden prohibitions and imagined dangers, and took Barbara on outings where the two of them shared enjoyment and a sense of freedom for an afternoon. After Barbara's father developed a virile cancer and her mother refused to care for him, Barbara, a trained nurse, arranged her work shifts to do so. Her mother's abandonment of her father after his illness, however, further stoked Barbara's feelings of revenge toward her mother.

A decade after her father died, Barbara sought psychotherapy. From her relationships with men, a pattern emerged in which she felt used and abused and so enraged that she provoked her male partners to physically beat and humiliate her. Eventually, however, it was not difficult for Barbara to understand her behavior as a reenactment of an early abusive relationship. Yet despite this understanding, the reenactment continued as she provoked nursing managers and operating-room doctors to humiliate her. When her behavior was explored, she realized that giving up reenactments would be tantamount to forgetting and being cheated of revenge for her mother's abusive behavior.

The death of her mother was a major turning point in Barbara' psychotherapy. She experienced relief from no longer needing to retain feelings of revenge through the reenactment of her suffering. Then she was further liberated from reenacting her pattern of misery after a conversation with her mother's sister. The aunt felt free now to share her horror at seeing Barbara's mother slap Barbara when she was a few weeks old and lay crying in the crib. This unwitting eyewitness confirmation of early abuse liberated Barbara from the guilt of feeling so revengeful! From this point, her need to reenact abusive relationship scenes disappeared. Her case suggests that procedural memory is impervious to change unless reenactments decline through exploring the deep feelings associated with them.

(c) Working Memory

Working memory, which is relevant to the conditioned fear responses of severely traumatized patients, suggests therapeutic strategies for breaking these connections. Baddeley (Baddeley and Hitch, 1974) introduced the term "working memory" as "the temporary storage of information that is being processed in any of a range of cognitive tasks" (Baddeley, 1986, p. 34). This concept is analogous to memory buffers in computers. Goldman-Rakic

(1995) reminds us that working memory is the ability to hold information "online" during the processing of a task that requires retrieval and manipulation of information in successive steps to perform associations with new, incoming information. In a similar vein, Siegel (1999) calls the working memory "the chalkboard of the mind." Clark and colleagues (2003), however, take the step of emphasizing the plurality of working memory systems. To them, "working memory systems are central to the ongoing management of information, being critical for everyday living. They involve the ability to initiate, control, or discontinue action, use information flexibly, make reasonable inferences, think abstractly, respond to novel situations and information, and determine the capacity to direct behavior in a goal-oriented manner" (p. 474).

Working memory was originally "located" in the frontal lobe circuits. LeDoux (2002) points out that "neural activity . . . increases in the frontal cortex when humans perform tasks that require temporary storage and executive function" (p. 179). Cozolino (2002) refers to this area as the dorsolateral prefrontal cortex (to the back and to the sides of the prefrontal lobes). The importance of these dorsolateral frontal lobes for the functioning of working memory is supported by Schore's (1994) observation that myelination of the dorsolateral circuits is only completed in late adolescence.

Working memory consists of several subsystems, two of which are the "phonological loop" and a "visuospatial sketchpad." The phonological loop, for example, is used in the temporary storage of a seven-digit telephone number. The loop prevents decay by silently articulating and refreshing them until the number is punched into the telephone. In addition to these two systems, an executive function coordinates these two "slave" functions. Later, influenced by the work of Tulving, Baddeley (2000) added an episodic buffer to the working memories as a temporary storage area for subjective experiences.

In recent years a trend in the neurosciences has been to enlarge the concept of a working memory to include functions from other lobes. For example, Clark and colleagues (2003) report that "functional neuroimaging studies clearly show that working memory involves the co-ordinated activity of multiple cortical regions . . . including the supplemental motor area, inferior parietal lobe, superior parietal lobe, dorsolateral prefrontal cortex, anterior cingulate, cerebellum, premotor area, and Broca's area" (p. 474). These neuroimaging studies, in expanding the working memory, parallel the contention of Ericsson and Kintish (1995) that working memory is able to retrieve and use long-term memories in its processing.

Working memory has been demonstrated to have a limited "channel" capacity. Miller (1956) noticed the limitations of the working memory when his subjects had difficulty remembering more than seven elements, whether they were digits, letters, words, or other "chunks" of information. Ericsson and Kintish (1995), however, point out that a "reliable capacity of working memory must be considerably less than a memory span of seven chunks because, even with seven chunks, perfect recall is achieved only 50 percent of the time, on average. Hence, the capacity of reliable working memory is often assumed to be only around four chunks" (p. 212). Furthermore, this reliable four-channel capacity may be constricted by fear. Using the WAIS (Weschler Adult Intelligence Scale) when patients with mild to moderate self disorders presented for psychotherapy, one of the authors not only confirmed the constricting role of fear on the working memory using the digit span test, but was also able to note the improvement in cognitive functioning once his patients bonded and experienced sufficient empathic understanding. As the patients became less distressed and fearful, their working memories were less constricted and functioned better. These clinical observations parallel the findings of Breslow, Kocsis, and Belkin (1980).

Whereas persons with mild to moderate self-disorders have limited channel capacity, persons with major self-disorders have sustained permanent (structural) damage in the prefrontal area as a result of severe trauma. The constricted channels of the working memory of such patients don't expand after a relatively brief period of psychotherapy as do the milder self-disorder patients mentioned above. How could this be? This issue was examined by Rauch, van der Kolk, and colleagues (1996), who measured regional cerebral blood flows (using PET scans) in eight patients with post traumatic stress disorder (PTSD), when they were exposed sequentially to audiotaped traumatic and neutral scripts. Compared with the neutral scripts, the traumatic scripts led to increases in normalized blood flow in the right-sided limbic, paralimbic, and visual areas, and decreases in the left inferior frontal and middle temporal cortex. Van der Kolk (2006) says, "This and subsequent research . . . demonstrated that when people are reminded of a personal trauma they activate brain regions that support intense emotions, while decreasing activity of brain structures involved in the inhibition of emotions and the translation of experience into communicable language" (p. 3). This suggests that trauma interferes with the working memory's capacity to process verbal information into long-term memory and, hence, limits new structuralization.

An Australian study (Clark et al., 2003) arrived at a similar conclusion using ten PTSD patients (motor vehicle accidents, police duty, war service, farm accident, and natural disaster) and neuroimaging (MRI and PET scans) of different regions of the brain, compared with ten outpatients. The PTSD patients activated right areas of the brain (right supramarginal gyrus of the inferior parietal lobe, the right middle frontal gyrus, the posterior superior parietal lobe bilaterally, and the right supplementary motor area), whereas the comparison group activated all these areas bilaterally. Similar to Rauch, van der Kolk, and colleagues, Clark and his colleagues (2003) conclude,

> Working memories investigating abstract verbal stimuli, such as letters and numbers, tend to produce left hemisphere activation of the dorsolateral prefrontal cortex and the inferior parietal lobe (Awh et al, 1996; Smith et al, 1996). On the other hand, studies involving nonverbal stimuli, such as faces, designs, and objects (Andreassen et al., 1995; Kosslyn et al. 1994; Smith et al., 1996) tend to activate these regions bilaterally or on the right [p. 478].

The key difference in neural functioning in PTSD patients then, is between verbal and nonverbal processes. *So, it seems that severe traumatic experiences resulting in PTSD, limit the working memory's capacity to process experiences linguistically.*

The capacity of trauma to interfere permanently with working memory may come from structuralization in ontogenetically early memory systems. DeBellis (2005), for example, suggests that traumatic interference of structuralization in symbolic memory comes from the overactivity of the amygdala in the limbic system. He refers to studies by Shin and colleagues (1999) and Bremmer and colleagues (1999), who used PET scans to compare the neural activation of PTSD women after they were asked to recall being sexually abused as children, with those sexually abused who had not developed PTSD. DeBellis (2005) summarizes the results: "participants with PTSD activated the amygdala but not the medial frontal cortex, whereas participants without PTSD activated their medial frontal cortex, but did not show the same degree of amygdala activation" (p. 163).

The potential for strong amygdala reactivation in patients with a traumatic history, especially with a childhood traumatic history, creates a therapeutic challenge. Based on Pavlovian theory, LeDoux (Amorapanth, LeDoux, and Nader, 2000) expects conditioned stimuli such as a bell, other objects, or persons, in the presence of such a traumatic experience as footshock, or sexual and/or physical abuse (unconditioned stimuli), to acquire aversive properties that later elicit terror reactions. Strictly speaking, as LeDoux reminds us, "fear conditioning does not create fear responses, but instead establishes the environmental conditions under which innate fear responses will be expressed" (p. 74). LeDoux's point is pertinent for treatment of patients who have had traumatic experiences. A male psychotherapist's attempts to establish a therapeutic relationship with a female incest victim may only reinforce terror in the patient because of feelings associated with the event, and may make it necessary for a patient to cope with the psychotherapist by dissociating, hence making the "treatment" iatrogenic unless skillfully managed, or by shifting treatment to a same gender psychotherapist who does not elicit the same fear responses.

It may help in psychotherapy with traumatized patients to understand how extinguishing their conditioned connections can occur. In their study of the amygdala, Amorapanth, LeDoux, and Nader (2000) found that a stimulus to which a rat was conditioned no longer elicited fear when they made electrolytic lesions in the lateral and central nucleus areas of the amygdala. These circuits apparently form an automatic pathway for conditioning fear memories, as demonstrated by activation of the lateral amygdala, which communicates with the central nucleus, which in turn influences the periaquaductal grey to produce behavioral "freezing." Connected to this same pathway is the paraventricular hypothalamus that controls the endocrine responses of the HPA axis. This means that fear memories associated with trauma activate the neurons of this lateral/central nucleus pathway and create an aroused but inactive physical state that leads to feelings of helpless terror and, in extreme form, "freezing" behavior.

Very importantly, LeDoux and his colleagues have experimental evidence for a second pathway in response to traumatic memories. They claim this second pathway goes from the lateral amygdala to the basal nucleus and then connects to the motor circuits of the striatum. Use of this second pathway reduces the neural firing in the reactive "freezing" pathway, and in turn, triggers endocrine and behavioral responses to conditioned stimuli. For example, in an experiment where rats learned to expect foot-shocking (LeDoux and Gorman, 2001) and were then given the option of moving to a non-shocking place in the cage, when foot-shocking occurred the rats quickly learned to move to this non-shocking area and so experienced being in control of the foot-shocking. LeDoux found that as a result of giving the rats the option of not being shocked, the rat's connection to the conditioned stimulus was weakened. As Van der Kolk (2006) explains, "When rats are given the option of physically escaping from the stimulus they lose their conditioning, even after a conditioned fear response is well established" (p. 11). This suggests that at an appropriate time in psychotherapy, encouraging a traumatized patient to strategize and then to act on that strategy, even though it will not immediately "solve" the presenting problem, may weaken the conditioned (structuralized) connections to the fearful "freezing" response anchored in procedural memory. Ritualistic religious behavior may also weaken the helplessness induced by the "freezing" circuit. LeDoux and Gorman (2001) suggest that "by engaging these alternative pathways [lateral amygdala through the basal ganglia to the motor circuits], passive fear responding is replaced with an active coping strategy" (1954).

A crucial question in conducting psychotherapy with traumatized patients is how to facilitate a shift from activating the first amygdala neural pathway to the Periaquaductal Grey–induced freezing circuitry, into activating the amygdala neural pathway to the basal ganglia and the action of the motor neurons. Such a change may require a very specific selfobject experience in which the psychotherapist accepts the patient's attempts to express self-agency through actions, sometimes small and symbolic. To facilitate this function the patient needs empathic attunement from the psychotherapist to cocreate a sense of self-agency through action. To the extent that a psychotherapist pressures or manipulates the patient, the self-agency experience of the action will be negated. Nor is there much evidence that action growing out of a mechanically applied technique for half a dozen sessions will produce lasting results, even if it temporarily frees a passive person from a "freezing" strategy. In open-ended psychotherapy with traumatized patients, the psychotherapist pays attention to the gradually emerging playful and creative behavior of the patient, and when appropriate, encourages action on a trial and error basis. As the small symbolic actions succeed or even partially succeed, the psychotherapist mirrors and affirms the patient's experience. The reason for the psychotherapist responding this way is not only to "unfreeze" the patient's passivity and sense of hopelessness, but also to alter the underlying conditioned fear associated to the psychotherapist. In classical Freudian terms, this kind of selfobject functioning of the psychotherapist weakens the negative transference.

This emphasis on action and contingency experiences in treating patients with traumatic disorders aims at repairing the subjective experience of helplessness, which seems to be the core experience of a traumatic event. A traumatic event leads to the phenomenological experience that nothing can be done to stave off the experience. In animal studies trauma is the "inescapable shock" of not being able to alter the outcome. It is the opposite to the experience of self-agency. Consequently, unable to fight or flee, the animal experiences immobilization as conditioned behavior (Van der Kolk, 2006).

Knowing that this amygdala connection to the basal ganglia offers a pathway out of traumatic immobilization helps us understand a patient called Fiona who had been abused and highly traumatized during childhood. Now in her late thirties, single, and aversive to dating, Fiona presented for treatment with a male psychotherapist, but the sessions so reawakened terror that she often fragmented for the rest of the day and considered terminating after just about each session for the first twelve months. During these early sessions the psychotherapist said very little because Fiona's fears led her to compulsively bombard him with words to keep him at bay. Nevertheless, when Fiona asked for feedback after a dozen sessions, the psychotherapist affirmed his positive prognosis because the psychotherapy was moving according to her timetable, not his. He pointed out that *they* had achieved the goal of successfully traversing the beginning sessions and had agreed that the first priority was to reduce, where possible, her excessive feelings of fear. Fiona then revealed that, as a number of previous attempts at psychotherapy never went beyond two sessions, she wanted to continue, despite intense fears of being retraumatized and increased physical symptoms of distress after the sessions. Here was a patient who appeared to exemplify LeDoux's "reactive response system" with its aroused lateral amygdala, central nucleus, and periaquaductal grey, and with its tendency to immobilize action and create endocrine arousal of the HPA (hypothalamic, pituitary, adrenal) axis.

During the first two years of psychotherapy, Fiona's fear of being retraumatized gradually receded. After the initial sessions, the psychotherapist had unsuccessfully tried to settle her into the security of twice-a-week sessions. Her response was to resist this recommendation in what would have been once considered "acting out." She kept changing and missing sessions and kept phoning between sessions with crises. When the psychotherapist asked Fiona to call only in an emergency, it became obvious that the psychotherapist's attempts to regularize the therapeutic arrangements had increased Fiona's fear. Only later was it understood that Fiona's constant changing of the arrangements was needed to affirm her experience of self-agency, to weaken her conditioned fear, and to increase her trust. She also reported feeling less helplessness and self-loathing. After her actions to prevent feelings of helplessness, her fears receded, as LeDoux predicted. It is possible, therefore, that what has been understood in Freudian psychoanalysis as acting out and a substitute for conscious thought was the very means whereby intense conditioned feelings rooted in procedural memory were severed from the verbal component of Fiona's working memory. With highly traumatized patients, a psychotherapist's acceptance of a patient's expressions of self-agency may be necessary to extinguish conditioned stimuli that inhibited the patient from using LeDoux's action pathway from the amygdala to the basal ganglia and the motor circuits.

This action strategy with traumatized patients offers another way for forming new structuralizations. It presents a view similar to Frank's (1999) belief that changing developmental deficits comes from a psychotherapist's participation in developing a patient's skills. He believes that "once a holding environment is established, analysts often need to address not only underlying motivational factors but also competencies and skills" (p. 238). What he calls a holding environment we conceive as a therapeutic bond that utilizes the attachment behavior discussed in chapter 3.

Frank thinks developmental deficits result for two reasons: lack of motivation and lack of skills. A deficit can occur from either or both conditions. These two factors suggest that if therapeutic exploration of motives does not lead to increasingly adaptive behavior, a patient's effectiveness functioning may be enhanced by strategies aimed at developing a patient's skills. Frank (1999) does not hesitate to incorporate into his "integrative" psychotherapy practice many cognitive-behavioral techniques such as encouraging "'self-talk' for self-calming, to replace counter-productive, anxiety-provoking internal dialogue" (p. 231). He gave mutually "planned homework assignments" and used such "self-monitoring techniques" as a diary. Frank believes that structuralization occurs as the patient applies to real life the exercises developed in the psychotherapy, rather than just in direct interactions with the psychotherapist.

Frank supports his views on psychotherapeutic participation with the ideas of Gedo (1988, 1991). Gedo (1991) thinks a patient's "ego deficits" [developmental deficits], which he calls "apraxias," need a remedial education that is undertaken in the context of a therapeutic relationship. Gedo (1988) says,

> When people who are grossly deficient in the psychological skills required for autonomous adaptation enter treatment, the transference most likely to develop is the repetition of their reliance on various childhood caretakers to compensate for these ego deficits. In my experience, it is not therapeutically sufficient to interpret the nature of such a transference . . . .I have found that the lack of psychic structure can be repaired only if the precise nature of the deficiency can be identified and active collaborative efforts are made to help the patient to learn the requisite skills [p. 466].

From a self psychological point of view we see the development of skills enhances the structures of the nuclear self, which Kohut thought consisted of a patient's ambitions and ideals, the "executive functions" of talents and skills (1977, pp. 49, 63). These talents and skills from the contents of ambitions and ideals that modify (transform) their development into less archaic forms (pp. 83, 177). A careful reading (Kohut, 1971, pp. 111, 212, 320; 1977, pp. 148–49), however, suggests that Kohut thought an educational approach was not "favorable" to successful structuralization of the nuclear self. Frank's distinction between motivational deficiencies and lack of skills, suggests Kohut's view supports clinical experience where skills training, without first exploring motivational issues, has a high retention failure rate. Yet clinical experience also demonstrates that any motivation from increased experiences of being understood are wasted unless skills are strengthened through education.

Frank's action-oriented techniques don't always work. He (1999) warns, "Prescriptive applications clearly are doomed to fail, and clinical judgment must always play a significant role in the therapist's functioning" (p. 239). From his clinical example, it is clear that if education is attempted without understanding the transferences of both patient and psychotherapist, it generally fails to make lasting changes. For example, Frank mentions using "response prevention" in the symptomatic treatment of hand washing where the therapist acts as "enforcer," something he admits is not compatible with an empathic stance. In our opinion, if the compulsive symptoms decline under the enforcement of "response prevention," a consequence may be a reinforcement of an underlying transference expectation of being forced by an authoritarian home environment, resulting in other symptoms. So, from a self psychology point of view, the key to a successful educational approach is whether it's experienced by the patient as empathic.

(d) Episodic Memory

The idea of episodic memory undergirds the notion of "autobiographical memory" that is essential to self-structuralization as Kohut (and Loewald) understood it. Along with the FAPs (fixed action patterns) of procedural memory, a human organism develops the capacity to store memories symbolically. In the symbolic memory, an experience is stored as encoded patterns in "higher brain centers" rather than the procedural patterns associated with the memory of motor systems. Although the idea of a symbolic memory has a long history, in the 1970s Tulving made a significant distinction between episodic and semantic types of symbolic memories, which together had been described as declarative memory (Squire, 1992; Wheeler and colleagues, 1997, p. 333). This distinction is particularly pertinent to the conduct of psychotherapy, because Tulving thinks the episodic memory is necessary for a subjective sense of self, and because effective psychotherapy tends to result from focusing on a patient's intersubjective experiences.

How does Tulving (1993) distinguish the episodic from the semantic memory? He says, "Semantic memory registers and stores knowledge about the world. . . . [It] enables individuals to represent and mentally operate on situations, objects and relations in the world that are not present in the senses" (p. 67). In comparison to semantic memory that stores and retrieves according to themes, he (1993) says, "Episodic memory enables a person to remember personally experienced events" (p. 67). In so doing, episodic memory has a subjective point of view and therefore, is capable of "mental time travel," a capacity that other forms of memory do not possess. Even with this clean distinction between semantic and episodic memories, Tulving also acknowledges an essential cooperation between them, because episodic memory "evolved out of" semantic memory and "many of its memory operations have remained dependent on, semantic memory" (p. 67). The reverse, however, is not true. "Episodic memory is not necessary for encoding and storing information into semantic memory" (p. 68). Neurologically, semantic memory develops earlier in childhood than episodic memory and involves neural firing in the temporal lobe and diencephalic brain structures, whereas the episodic memory's neural firing takes place in the frontal lobes (Schacter, 1987; Tulving, 1985). And, as suggested in the previous subsection, episodic memory is an important component of working memory.

The concept of an episodic memory is supported by neuro-imaging studies that reveal activated frontal lobes in the recalling of personal memories. In a PET (positron emission tomography) study, Tulving and colleagues (1994) found that the left frontal lobes were activated more when the episodic memory was being encoded, and that the right lobes were activated more when episodic memory was being retrieved. This distinction between the left and right frontal lobes for the episodic memory has been corroborated by additional PET studies reviewed by Nyberg and Tulving (1996).

In the episodic memory, the activation of a memory re-creates a personally experienced event. This feature means that a personal memory is not just remembered, but that in the remembering, the event is reexperienced. This reexperiencing means that feelings associated with the memory are also remembered. As James (1890) says, "remembrance is like a direct feeling; its object is suffused with a warmth and intimacy to which no object of mere condition ever attains" (Vol. 1., p. 239). In contrast, in semantic memory feelings are not associated with the memory—unless there is also an episodic component. As Tulving (1993) says, episodic memory "is characterized by a distinctive, unique awareness of re-experiencing here and now something that happened before, at another time and in another place" (p. 68).

As first presented, the episodic memory was seen as part of the short-term working memory of the prefrontal lobes. But this idea was not tenable after Tulving's discovery of encoding and retrieval processes connected with the left and right frontal lobes, which suggested that episodic memory is stored as long-term memory, a view consistent with Ericsson and Kintish's (1995) claim. Nelson (1993) also thinks that some episodic memories become long-term and are important for self-development, but she called the long-term memories "autobiographical memory." Nelson's concept of an autobiographical memory is pertinent to the conduct of psychotherapy.

Nelson (1993) describes autobiographic memory as "personal, long-lasting, and (usually) of significance to the self-system. Phenomenally, it forms one's personal life" (p. 8). Nelson's research led her to believe that autobiographical memories are noticeable in early childhood from about four years of age. She points out that while Freud termed the absence of early childhood memories "childhood amnesia," his amnesia term mistakenly implies that something had been lost, or if it still existed, could not be retrieved. In contrast to Freud, Nelson believes that children don't have the capacity for autobiographical memory until about four years of age.

In studying very young children, Nelson saw evidence of a generic memory, where a familiar event is described without providing details of a specific time or place. These generic responses suggested that these children had developed a script (Schank and Abelson, 1977) "that specifies the sequence of actions and empty slots for roles and props that may be filled in with default values, in the absence of specifications" (Nelson, 1993, p. 7). One such script, for example, is "going to McDonalds." These generic scripts may have more similarity to semantic memory, structured as they are around themes, than to episodic memory, which refers to a happening at a specific time and in a specific place. In further research, however, Nelson discovered that young children could indeed have specific episodic memories if the events were strikingly novel, *as determined by the child and not by adults*. Although most of these memories were not retained into adulthood, those retained formed a long-term autobiographical memory.

Nelson's (1993) research technique was to listen to the "crib talk" of two and half year old children before they went to sleep. Emily, for example said,

> We bought a baby, cause, the well because, when she, well, we thought it was for Christmas, but when we went to the s-s-store we didn't have our jacket on, but I saw some dolly, and I yelled at my mother and said I want one of those dolly. So after we were finished with the store, we went over to the dolly and she bought me one. So I have one [p. 9].

Clearly Emily's narrative is a well-organized, sequential episode, temporarily structured in the working memory's frontal lobes. Thus far, however, we have not addressed the issue of how such an episode becomes structuralized as part of an autobiographical memory. To do this, Nelson turned to a "social interaction model."

In the social interaction model, "children gradually learn the forms of how to talk about memories with others, and thereby also how to formulate their own memories as narratives." In Nelson's view parents play an active role in "framing and guiding their children's formulation of 'what happened'" (Nelson, 1993, p. 10). Hudson (1990), for example, came to a similar social interaction conclusion from a study of her own child, as did Pillemer and White (1989) and Fivush and Reese (1991). In the social interaction model "children gradually learn the forms of how to talk about memories with others, and thereby also how to formulate their own memories as narratives" (Nelson, 1993, p. 10). In explaining this model, Nelson's ideas about the structuralization of permanent autobiographical memories come close to the idea of a selfobject function (chapter 3). Just as Kohut thought that a parent's/therapist's affirming of a child's/patient's actions, feelings, or beliefs, was a mirroring that fostered structuralization, so the active involvement of the social interaction model of parents in constructing a memory narrative may be considered a selfobject function also.

Support for the social interaction model also came from two empirical studies. One by Engel (1986) explored two interactive mother styles—the "elaborative" and the "pragmatic"—with their infants. The "elaborative mothers," in sharing with their children, spoke about the when, where, and with whom of specific events. On the other hand, the "pragmatic mothers" focused on knowing or talking about things, such as where the child had placed his/her mittens. When Engel studied the children of these mothers, she found that those with elaborative mothers were more involved as participants in memory talk. In the second study, Tessler (1986) interviewed children who had made a trip to a natural history museum and found that the children of elaborative/narrative mothers remembered more from the trip than the children of pragmatic mothers. More significantly, none of the children who went to the museum remembered much about the objects they had seen unless they had talked with their mothers about them afterwards.

In yet another study, Tessler (1991) found that during an event there were no differences between the children from the two different elaborative/narrative and pragmatic mothering styles, in respect to describing what was currently happening. A short time after the event, however, there was a difference in what was remembered. The children of the elaborative/narrative mothers recalled significantly more, seemingly because they talked over the experience with their mothers. In summarizing these findings, Nelson (1993) says, "Adults who present the activity in a narrative format, in contrast to a focus on identification and categorization, appear to be more effective in establishing and eliciting memories with their young children" (p. 10).

The evidence suggests that sharing an experience with a significant person helps children to develop their episodic working memories. Yet it appears that the actual rehearsing of the memory alone does not significantly help develop an autobiographical memory, as a special long-term episodic memory. For example, Emily, the two-and-a-half-year-old, whose crib talk was studied and who often recounted an event many times, did not remember the event a few months later (Nelson, 1989). Hudson (Nelson, 1993) also reports that her daughter at eight years of age remembered nothing of the events that she had rehearsed with her when she was two years of age. And in an interesting study, Hudson and Fivush (1991) asked sixth grade students about a trip they took as kindergarteners, but none of the children spontaneously recalled the event. So, what does help produce a relatively permanent autobiographical memory?

One suggested reason for long-term structuralization of the autobiographical part of the episodic working memory is the process of reinstatement, suggested by the experimental work of Rovee-Collier using the mobile kicking experiment. She discovered that if the infant's learning to move the mobile by kicking is lost, a memory can be reinstated if a context similar to the original context of the mobile is represented within a short space of time (Rovee-Collier and Hayne, 1987). A study by Fivush and Hammond (1989) of two-year-old children also demonstrated the effects of reinstatement. By providing a similar experience to the original one within two weeks, the children whose memory had been reinstated remembered more than those who hadn't had the reinstatement, when tested three months later. Three months, however, is not convincing evidence that the process of "reinstatement" plays a significant part in consolidating episodic working memory into a permanent autobiographical memory. In effect, reinstatement is close to the idea of repetition or reinforcement that consolidates procedural memory. Its use of a repetitive approach reminds us of Edelman's degeneracy and reentry constructs at the neural configurational level.

Autobiographical symbolic memory relies on other processes of structuralization, one example of which comes from "one off" experiences. Special experiences help shape the identity and life of a person as they are long remembered for the strong feelings evoked by the experience. For example, one patient reported a clear autobiographical memory from four years of age. He remembered driving in the family car with his parents to visit a family friend who was dying of breast cancer. He remembered the street near a specific Melbourne suburban railway station, which he also remembered by name.

When this memory was explored, he recalled overhearing his parents discussing the tragedy of their friend's illness while they were driving home. His major memory of the event, however, was the distressed state of the parents after the visit. This experience suggests, as Tomkins (1991) claims, that high levels of affect magnification may be involved in the development of an autobiographical memory. Magnified levels of startle, distress, interest, fear, anger, humiliation, or joy may be necessary for long-term, special experiences to be woven permanently into an autobiographical self-organization. In the autobiographical memory the self is experienced not as a thing but as an unfolding narrative.

Terr (1994) is also very much aware of the importance of primary affects for memories. She says,

> Affect drives much of the episodic memory we retain or later retrieve. It may be that the neurotransmitters released with strong emotion . . . aid in fixing our long-term memories of emotional events. On the cellular level, these chemicals are probably activated at the time an affect-laden memory is planted. They may be released on retrieval of the memory. We do not know which chemically active brain substances cement these earliest memories. But we do know that early memories are very well cemented [p. 190].

If magnified affects are seen as a major factor in the permanent structuralization of an autobiographical memory, then trauma may be understood as the excessive magnification of the negative feelings evoked by an experience. Traumatic experiences are special experiences that cannot be integrated into the autobiographical memory because the feelings associated with them have been excessively amplified. Dissociated or repressed at the symbolic level, traumatic memories are nevertheless retained in a procedural form that needs reenactment. So it may be that parents—or others who function as narrative selfobjects—help share the emotions associated with an event, and in so doing, enable the memories to be permanently structuralized within the autobiographical self. How then does psychotherapy lead to appropriate structuralization in patients whose development has been impeded or arrested by inadequate structuralization? This was a major question for Kohut, to whom we now turn.

Section B. Structuralization

This section on structuralization comprises of (a) general remarks and (b) Kohut and structuralization/internalization.

(a) General Remarks

In the section on memory it is obvious that any concept of "selving" (Fast 1998) cannot avoid the idea that biological structuralization is a well-established fact. What this present section demonstrates is that any attempt to help a highly distressed or deeply disturbed mentally ill person means inevitably confronting the experience of structuralization. For those working in the old custodial mental hospitals, for example, it was evident that after warehoused patients successfully structuralized hospital routines into their procedural memories, they had little incentive to get well and leave. With these hospitalized patients, the question was not whether structuralization took place, but how to induce the development of new structures to cope with life outside the hospital walls. From their experiences with patients, psychiatrists and other professionals working in such settings easily conceived of self-structuralization as a relatively permanent self-configuration.

An example of structuralization as a result of institutionalization is depicted in the movie *Shawshank Redemption*. After forty years, the prisoner-librarian Bowles was released from incarceration, having legally served his time. As he had become so habituated to prison life—structuralized into his self-organization—and being too old to adapt to his new life upon release, he committed suicide because he lacked the internal self-structures to cope with his newly found freedom. The situation of Bowles may be viewed as a metaphor for the pathognomic mental consequences of constantly feeling spiritually empty. In democratic countries, most mental difficulties arise not from lack of freedom, but from persons with insufficient experiences of structuralization necessary to cope with and thrive under freedom. Without healthy, adaptive internal structures to cope with freedom, persons subjectively experience freedom as abandonment.

Authoritarian dictatorships present a different pathognomic picture. In order to survive in an authoritarian society, members of such a society develop relatively permanent patterns of compliant peripheral selves. Unless persons in authoritarian cultures find compensatory ways to assert their nuclear selves to maintain a sense of self-agency, depressive illnesses and self-loathing may emerge as a consequence of their monopolistic, structuralized patterns of acquiescence. With self-structuralized loathing, patients are unable to allow positive experiences to significantly modify their negative feelings and beliefs. Such pathologically accommodating patients present for psychotherapy with arrested forms of development, different, however, from those leading to emptiness in democratically run societies or institutions.

Brandchaft (1994) makes the point that such structuralized negative experiences interfere with the structuralization of new, joyful experiences later in their lives. Psychotherapy aimed at changing the process of pathological accommodation needs to be more than the provision of positive experiences, because resistance to new structuralized forms of hopefulness arises from a negatively organized nuclear self-organization functioning as if a controlling homunculus. With such people, psychotherapy is confronted with how to help such negatively organized patients to structuralize positive experiences. Unquestionably, structuralizations that result from psychotherapy are stored in both the procedural and autobiographical structures of the self.

(b) Kohut and Structuralization

When Kohut made structuralization a key postulate, he was building on Freud's important concept of internalization. In "Mourning and Melancholia" Freud (1917) noticed that following a broken emotional attachment—which he called "sudden object decathexis"—identification with the deceased person increased. Freud theorized that an increased identification was the process whereby the mourner internalized the deceased; the mourner replaced former interactions with the deceased in the world, with an inner sense of the deceased person's presence. In this way internalization became a permanent structuralization within the autobiographical self. Freud saw such internalization as a defense against the pain of loss. Eventually classical analysis narrowed the concept of internalization to structural changes that only occurred with interpretation and insight.

Heinz Hartmann (1939) accepted Freud's concept of internalization, but expanded it to include a self-regulation that grew out of regulation from the relationship with parents or authorities. As the history of psychoanalysis shows, Hartmann's views were an important theoretical advance, as they did not constrict internalization to interpretation and insight. Kohut was heavily influenced by the ideas of both Freud and Hartmann on internalization when he developed his treatment approach to narcissistic disorders. As Strozier (2001) writes, Kohut accepted Freud's view of internalization that permitted a withdrawal of feelings from the loss of a significant other in a bit by bit, fractionated way.

Kohut accepted also Hartmann's view that it was the relationship that was internalized, but believed an attuned empathic connection during frustrating experiences was the most effective way to develop it. With narcissistic patients, Kohut considered Klein's idea of internalization as a process of introjection, but he rejected it as being detrimental to psychotherapy because it encouraged gross identifications. Such identifications perpetuated the patient's dependency on the psychotherapist and undermined the patient's internal sense of self-agency. How to make internalization a liberating rather than shackling experience led Kohut to a brilliant theoretical move: he theorized that healthy internalization took the form of micro-internalization. The development of self psychology after Kohut, seemingly influenced by Schafer (1968, 1972), has discarded the metaphor of internalization and emphasized micro-structuralization.

We understand the significance of Kohut's micro-structuralization in the context of his effective treatment of narcissistic disorders. He achieved significant results by challenging the Freudian assumption that narcissism was always unhealthy; for Kohut, narcissism could be either pathological or healthy. With the idea of structuralization, Kohut took the stance that the Kleinian view of structuralization as introjection, as noted earlier, could be damaging. Traumatic experiences, for example, involve introjection that either damages self-functioning or creates maladaptive self-functioning. And, as Beebe and Lachmann (1988) point out, Klein's idea of patients introjecting a whole object (psychotherapist) creates a further problem because such introjecting may stimulate archaic grandiosity in the psychotherapist, who feels he is being cloned.

In an important article now overlooked—perhaps because it uses the ("outdated") concept of internalization to depict structuralization—Tolpin (1971) views structuralization developmentally. She says, "What the mother does for the baby when she rocks him to sleep, or later for the toddler when she reads him a story, is eventually replaced by a structure that enables him to sleep by himself" (p. 318). Evidence of structuralization is the infant's use of a transitional object (Winnicott, 1953), such as a blanket. Tolpin thinks this "treasured possession is neither missed, mourned, repressed, nor forgotten. It is no longer needed" (p. 321). It is no longer needed because the infant has acquired a "self-soothing psychic structure" from a developmental, "structural leap." The function has been "transferred" from the mother to the infant.

Tolpin thinks "phenomenologically the [infant's] behavior with the blanket is like an addiction" (p. 323) and that this means patients with addictions have defects in their capacity to structuralize. So, the addictive potential of the soothing function of the parent (and psychotherapist) raises the question of what facilitates or restricts structuralization? Stated in terms of psychotherapy, why do some patients become addictive to psychotherapy, without significant change, whereas others develop compensatory structures to function adaptively and eventually, without psychotherapy sessions? In answer to such a question, Tolpin (1971) thinks that the blanket as a transitional object involves the "creation of a soothing imago which is neither self nor mother but which combines features of both" (p. 328). The blanket image is a *cocreation* that involves a forward step that both uses and reinforces a child's sense of self-agency. Where such a sense of self-agency has not developed, been retarded, or been extinguished, a firm imago is not cocreated, and structuralization of the soothing function is insufficient and inadequate. Hence, for more permanent gains in psychotherapy, continual soothing of distress without equal attention, at least, to reinforcing the patient's self-agency, can lead to addiction-like stalemates or unsatisfactory results.

With Kohut, his treatment of narcissistic patients enabled him to see that the important issue of structuralization, is how it occurs. The inability of narcissistic patients to develop robustness and assertiveness came from their faulty macro-internalization of traumatic events. He (1975) says,

> The cure of disorders . . . is not achieved by focusing on gross events, and on the macrostructural memories of the gross traumata related to them, but by the careful scrutiny—in technical terms: the reconstructions that can gradually be obtained on the basis of working through the narcissistic transferences [pp. 791–92].

Two years later (Kohut, 1977) says, "I believe we are describing it more accurately and cogently if the focus is on the changes in the psychological 'microstructures'" (p. 31). By emphasizing micro-structuralization Kohut rejects Freud's macrostructures of id, ego, and superego, and Kleinian introjects, as unsuitable treatment theories for narcissistic disorders.

Klein not only theorized that trauma created bad "introjects," but that structuralization also involved positive introjections. But in positing good and bad introjects, Klein shifted her thinking from introjection as a process to introjects as content: "From the beginning the ego introjects [are] 'good' and 'bad,' for both of which its mother's breast is the prototype—for good objects when the child attains it and for bad when it fails him" (1935, p. 262). Kohut, however, recognized the consequences of introjection, the idea of taking in the whole object, are bad, and the key issue is not whether the object being introjected is "good" or "bad." This very process of introjection interferes with a patient's ability to recover from arrested development and creates problems for the patient's sense of self-agency. To Kohut, small, non-traumatic levels of frustration, distress, and other feelings, fostered the processes of structuralization.

Building upon Freud's "object loss and internalization," Kohut distinguished between traumatic and non-traumatic loss, both of which lead to structuralization. With trauma, however, there is a regressed form of structuralization involving the procedural memory but not the symbolic memory. This indicates that Kohut grasped the difference between traumatic startle states, and non-traumatic but distressful states. And so he believed it was "optimal frustration"—and consequently optimal distress—that produced healthy development. But we think that "optimal frustration" needs to be interpreted as *moderate* distress that allows the gradual acquiring of micro-structuralizations, rather than sudden, massive macro-internalizations (introjections) that were whole and indigestible and that remain unintegrated in the self-organization. As Kohut (1984) wrote of the micro-structuralizing process,

> the "foreign protein" of the selfobject and of selfobject functions, whether in childhood or during analysis, becomes split up after being ingested; its constituents are then re-assembled to form the self in accordance with those individual patterns that characterize the growing child's (or analysand's) specific psychic "protein" [p. 160].

And in emphasizing his concept of micro-internalization, Kohut (1996) made it clear that the structuralizing process was meant to strengthen the self-agency of the patient rather than produce a clone who was once controlled from without and is now controlled by a substitute introject that is, more or less, the homunculus encountered in the history of the neurosciences.

Kohut's concept of micro-structuralization is reflected in his ideas of idealization. He thought that a child's idealization of the parent (or the patient's idealization of the psychotherapist) would inevitably result in some disappointments (and distress). As long as these disappointments were relatively small and openly acknowledged, however, the child's idealization would gradually fade, and the response expected of the parent (or psychotherapist) would be autonomously taken up by the child. Kohut used the model scene of a baby to illustrate what he meant by "transmuting internalization" (structuralization).

> The baby initially emerges into the dimly perceived "mother-breast" that becomes a connection to a person whose functions are taken on as one's own. The subsequent "taming, neutralization, and differentiation" (or optimal frustration) of these first expressions of idealization occur because the real figure of the mother (for the most part) inevitably comes up short in her concrete emotional responses. In the best of circumstances the child makes increasingly realistic assessments of that figure, which involves a measure of disappointment, and leads to an emotional redirection of feelings from the figure

to the internalized imago that sustains the same function in the self [Strozier, 2001, p. 199].

Once Kohut had emphasized the idea of structuralization, the archaic mergers that occurred during the course of a successful analysis with narcissistic patients acquired a new meaning. The question arose: Do not these mergers have the potential, if they become permanent, to inhibit a patient's psychological growth both during psychotherapy and after termination, because they become structuralized as whole introjects? Kohut (1981d) commented, "It is sadly easy to establish a gross identification with someone else's strength in a regressive way. But it doesn't lead anywhere. That kind of identification stifles creativity" (p. 246). Fortunately, such gross identifications proved to be only a temporary defense against feelings that were triggered in psychotherapy, often because of a non-empathic response from the psychotherapist. "They are a transitional step," (p. 247) he said.

Furthermore, Kohut pointed out that the first major change in many narcissistic patients came from imitative patterns of behavior that were on loan until these patients discovered their own ideas and ways of doing things. As he (1971) observed, "Gross identifications with the analyst—his behavior, mode of speaking, attitudes, tastes—are thus frequently observed in the early part of the analysis" (p. 166). Where such gross identifications become a permanent feature of the psychotherapy, these patients become increasingly out of control, often from some gross misattunement on the part of the psychotherapist, which is then explored. If not explored, structuralization of such an unstable relationship will make the patient worse and even put him/her at risk of suicide.

Several decades earlier, Robert Knight (1953) described a relationship involving a patient's gross identification with a "psychotherapist" that became progressively more archaic as a result of the psychotherapist's misattunement with the patient. He described a female student who was seen by a self-styled psychotherapist who was the Dean of Students in a U.S. college. As the dean felt progressively cornered by the student's demands, the sessions went overtime and were conducted in her home in evenings and on weekends. At one point, the student began staying overnight with the psychotherapist, and still later, slept in bed with her. At times the student expressed an irrational hatred of the dean, whom she pounded with her fists. At the student's request, she was held on the dean's lap and fondled. The dean raised no objections to these requests until the student expressed a strong wish to suckle! When the dean said "no" the student fragmented and entered a crisis state that led to hospitalization. Here we have a dramatic example of the introjection of a "massive identification," with a resulting loss of self-agency, rather than the micro-structuralizations that Kohut described.

Since the death of Kohut, self psychology theorists have seen Kohut's notion of optimal frustration as only one facilitator of structuralization. Bacal (1985) developed the idea of "optimal responsiveness" as a means of fostering the process of structuralization during states of joy. He observed, "It has never been our intention as analysts to either traumatize or frustrate our patients, however optimally, but to understand them"(p. 207). Undoubtedly Bacal would agree that whether or not intended, patients will eventually feel frustrated and such frustration does, per Kohut, promote structuralizations. In effect, self-psychology has arrived at a position where optimal levels of feelings, whether negative or positive as described by Tomkins, are understood to be necessary for structuralization.

In accepting that both optimal frustrations and optimal responsiveness facilitate structuralization, however, it is possible for post-Kohutian self psychology to miss or dilute an important element in Kohut's theory. It is clear that Kohut understood the importance of the positive feelings of interest and joy (see chapter 5). So why did he consistently emphasize optimal frustration? As we take the position that Kohut had a clear goal in mind when he theorized about optimal frustration, it may be a mistake to think of it as a Freudian residue that should be eventually revised. Clearly Kohut's goal for psychotherapy was the utilization of repetitive and narcissistic transferences to help develop a patient's self-structuralizations so they could become more adaptive. Why optimal frustration then? Could this be because Kohut realized that narcissistic patients needed to develop a capacity for robustness? His ideal for humans was the resilient self, not the empathic self, although included in the resilient self was the capacity to be empathic in appropriate situations. Such resilience required optimal frustration. How did Kohut come to this position? We think the reason lies partly in Freud's failure to understand or treat narcissistic patients.

The answer to understanding and treating narcissistic patients was virtually under Freud's nose when, in Vienna in 1932, his daughter Anna closed the Heitzing School that she had directed for five years assisted by two teachers, Peter Blos and Erik Erikson (Burlingham, 1989). This school had from "fifteen to twenty children . . . enrolled from families of liberal, cultural backgrounds" (p. 185), the first four of whom were children of the wealthy American Tiffany heiress, Dorothy Burlingham. Remarkably, this experimental school seems to have created developmental arrests in all the Burlingham children, albeit relatively milder in the two younger, less exposed children.

Evidence of this educationally induced developmental arrest comes from Dorothy Burlingham herself, who, as the lifelong companion of Anna Freud, had a twinship relationship with her (Tolpin, 1997).

In 1937, five years after the Heitzing school closed down, Dorothy Burlingham wrote a paper about educating "protected" children. The paper describes her experiences after moving to Vienna from New York in 1925 in order to protect her young children from the chaotic behavior of her lawyer husband Robert, who had manic episodes associated with a diagnosed manic-depressive psychosis. At first Dorothy planned to have Anna analyze her eldest son Bob for six months, but after Dorothy grabbed an opportunity to be analyzed by Sigmund Freud, she placed all her children in prophylactic analysis with Anna. With the Burlingham children as a nucleus, the Heitzing school became organized around, and an extension of, the students' analyses, which encouraged exploration of their personal curiosities in an educational setting under minimal discipline and punishment. What was the result of the "optimal responsiveness" of this experimental school? According to Burlingham (1989),

> Owing to the understanding upbringing they have had . . . it is precisely these children who are especially oversensitive, who are not readily inclined to accept restrictions, who in particular can scarcely tolerate any criticism or admonition, and who frequently experience inconsiderate and unkind behavior on the part of agemates as a profound rejection [p. 230].

Burlingham had noticed that her children's increased sensitivity was at the expense of their resilience. This lack of resilience came from the consistency with which the children experienced their environment as accommodating their needs; they never learned to balance this with the accommodating of others. In this school, the custom of a child always "heeding" (accommodating) the parent was completely reversed, so that the education was guided by the opposite compensatory ideal of complete freedom. It is not surprising, therefore, that in a 1940 letter to her twenty-five-year-old son Bob, Dorothy actually called the Heitzing school "a mistake." *Their good intentions with the Heitzing school notwithstanding, it would appear that Dorothy Burlingham and Anna Freud had inadvertently demonstrated how to create narcissistic personalities.* What a wonderful natural experiment and what a tragedy that these results have been overlooked (disavowed) as an important finding of psychoanalysis.

The importance of a robust self to Kohut's theory may have developed from his own upbringing. His biographer Charles Strozier observes, "the critical first year or so . . . seemed happy" because of the good beginnings with his twenty-two-year-old mother, Else, who developed an "intense relationship" with Heinz, the "apple of her eye" (2001, p. 12). The "good-enough" response of his mother during Kohut's initial stage of life, however, developed into an inhibiting one in the next stage of development, as Kohut sought more autonomy (Erikson, 1950) than Else wanted him to have—as indicated in his autobiographical "The Analysis of Mr. Z" (Kohut, 1979). From Else's failure to mirror Heinz's self-assertion and initiative-taking, Kohut seems to have also developed an overprotected sensitivity similar to the Burlingham children in the Heitzing school, and may have struggled in his own development with an arrest in the assertive sector of his self. From personal experience, Kohut could have understood why the Heitzing children had not developed the resiliency of children in other schools. This in turn may have contributed to his understanding that *what* is selected for mirroring is the crucial process in any mirroring transference, because selection helps determine whether developmental growth, dissolution, or addiction occurs. Hence a major goal for narcissistic patients is the structuralization of an increased tolerance of frustration, which gains expression as greater self-resilience without the rigid self-hardening that results in a loss of the capacity for empathy.

Stolorow and colleagues (Stolorow, Atwood, and Orange, 2002) reject the concept of internalization as a specific form of structuralization. They accept Schafer's (1968, 1972) criticism that formulations such as internalization and externalization employ reified fantasies of bodily incorporation and expulsion as explanations of a psychological process. Schafer (1972) challenged the idea of internalization by raising the question of what it means to be "inside the self?" (p. 412). So Stolorow and his colleagues look for other ways of understanding structuralization, because internalization involves a confusing mixture of subjective with objective space and, as such, can only be a "pseudo-explanation."

Teicholtz (1999) writes that postmodern analysts think the idea of internalization is problematic as "the concept emerged from, and is integral to, the structural theory in psychoanalysis [id, ego, superego], which is no longer in ascendancy in analytic discourse" (p. 203). As Mitchell (1993) asserts, temporal metaphors are preferable to spatial ones. And as internalization has been associated with a one-person model, it is assumed by postmodern analysts that a theory of internalization is no longer needed in order to understand therapeutic change. They believe that "a broad range of interpersonal functioning in the analytic dyad and . . . the richly expressed subjectivity of the analyst will somehow contribute to a more richly elaborated subjectivity for the patient" (Teicholtz, 1999, p. 203), but it is not explained how this will come about.

Neuroscience's recent discovery of "mirror" neurons (chapter 2) suggests that imitation can lead to new self-structures as a result of what could be considered a process of internalization as a result of a two-person, intersubjective process. This mirror experiment raises such important issues that we quote more of the passage given in chapter 2.

> Gallese (1996) and colleagues, in studying the brain of two macaque monkeys, discovered a special subset of 92 neurons in the F5 region, the inferior premotor cortex—Brocca's area in humans (Nishitani, Schurmann, Amunts, and Hari, 2005)—which fired either when the monkey performed the action of grasping an object, or when the monkey saw the experimenter perform the same act. If, however, the monkey just viewed the object, or saw the experimenter miming the monkey's hand action, these "mirror" neurons did not fire. This demonstrated an interaction between the grasping hand and the object triggered the neural firing. Gallese then concluded that "mirror" neurons give humans a capacity to learn by observing as well as by doing, and that they enable imitative behavior between mother and infant, and especially, the learning of interactional patterns.

Such interactive patterns not only activate mirror neurons, they can be remembered, and if remembered, they have helped form new synaptic connections in the brain. Such synaptic connections, in effect, structuralize the behavior of someone else as if it had been an experience of the self and represents a two-person understanding of structuralization.

One way to avoid the problems of reification involved with the concept of internalization, is to see the discovery of mirror neurons providing evidence for imitative structuralization. Even so, with imitative structuralization, it may be that this form of structuralization has more effect on the procedural memory than the symbolic memory. After all, the neurons involved are in the F5 region of the inferior premotor area. To speculate further, it may be that the internalizing taking place as a result of imitating could be more aligned with the process of macro-internalization that hinders the development of autobiographical memory and therefore closer to the concept of introjection that Kohut criticized.

Loewald offered a perspective on internalization that is close to that of Kohut. For Kohut, in a relationship where one serves as a selfobject, no firm boundary is preserved and the concepts of outside and inside become meaningless. Similarly, Loewald (1973) sees internalization as akin to assimilation, where "boundaries between subject and object, distinctions between them, on pre-oedipal levels are either non-existent or only fleetingly present, fluid, blurred, so that at least no clear or constant distinction between self and object world, between inside and outside, is maintained" (p. 81). Loewald also admits that "the naïve observer sees a baby relate to his mother, one individual to another; but this clearly is not the psychological situation for the baby" (p. 81). Thus when psychological assimilation is taking place, Loewald thinks there is no significant boundary, the other person is not on the outer, and therefore the metaphor of internalization as a spatial shift from one object to another misrepresents the process. How can internalization happen, asks Loewald, when everything is experienced as internal. When he uses the term internalization, he no longer means a spatial shift but a structuralization that takes place as a result of a relationship with permeable boundaries.

We also mention Loewald's concept of repression in relation to structuralizing. Unlike Freud, Loewald thought repression and structuralization were both involved in self-organizing. He observes, "The latter [repression and structuralization] are involved in creating and increasing coherent integration and organization of the psyche as a whole, whereas repression works against such coherent psychic organization by maintaining a share of psychic processes in a less organized, more primitive state" (p. x).

Kohut and Loewald's theories of structuralization mean that psychotherapy does not only aim at obliterating old bad relationships, but at transforming them so that out of a therapeutic relationship that accepts a patient's need at times for an undifferentiated state, a reconfigured self takes shape. These reconfigurations involve using the configurations of older relationships as well as new experiences. One of the clinical benefits of this theoretical understanding is in evaluating prospective patients. It means asking about previous psychotherapeutic experiences, looking for elements of these relationships that evoked negative emotions, and seeking to understand them from the patient's point of view. It also involves noting and affirming any constructive gains that have derived from previous treatments. This communicates to the patient that the psychotherapist intends eventually to examine both sides of any vertical split.

Mr. M was a middle-aged patient who had divorced six years previously and who presented with a third failed courtship relationship after the divorce. When he began to share his negative feelings as a result of these rejections, he began to focus on his feelings of rejection by his father when growing up as the oldest son. The focus of the first fifty sessions was on his difficulties with several women he had lived with and with his ex-wife, but he then became aware that he had "solved" his relationship with his father with an overt strategy of not wanting to have anything to do with him. He was copying his father as a form of twinship. If his father had rejected him, he was rejecting his symbolic father (his psychotherapist, his women friends), so that they could feel what he had been forced to feel.

During the second year of treatment, Mr. M came to realize that he held a secret wish, long disavowed, that his father would give him the love and acceptance he had never received. He also realized that what had motivated him to seek long-term psychotherapy—after several attempts at brief counseling—was a need to "break the deadlock" between wanting to have nothing to do with his father and his secret wish to be accepted by his father. After several months of focusing on the elements of the deadlock, a new beginning emerged when Mr. M realized that his chances of achieving either of these goals was virtually zero. So, he gave up both. He decided to pursue a more practical relationship with his father. This relationship was not easy because his father continued his life-long pattern of putting Mr. M down. When the father did this, Mr. M took a "time out" from his father by going shopping or by taking a walk, but he did not storm out saying he would never talk to his father again, as he had done in the past. This new strategy did not lead to the love he had always wanted, but it decreased the father's ability to humiliate his son, and after another year or so, the father's humiliating behavior ceased altogether.

As Mr M's self-organization was reconfigured along more positive lines, he was able to attend family functions and increase the time spent with other nourishing family members. After four years of psychotherapy his relationship with his three children had improved dramatically. There came a time when Mr. M verbalized that he was thinking about terminating the psychotherapy, but had decided to continue for another year to "reinforce" the gains that had been made. He wanted them to be permanent. The psychotherapist, in turn, supported the idea of another year to foster the structuralization of his positive experiences, and so to reinforce the internalized psychotherapy process could continue without the need for formal sessions. To structuralize the gains to achieve a relative permanent personality change, the patient's last year of sessions was often a joyous sharing with the male psychotherapist, the kind he had always sought with his father. And there was a bonus. By the time Mr. M finally ended the formal psychotherapy sessions, his relationship with his ex-wife had become more friendly, even though he avoided renewing it on intimate terms.

One of the most compelling stories of success in psychotherapy comes from Breuer's original case of Anna O (Bertha Pappenheim). In a carefully researched paper Tolpin (1993) explores what she calls "the poor Breuer myth," a myth that "affirmed Freud and minimized Breuer at a crucial time in psychoanalytic history" nearly fifty years after Breuer had conducted the case, and a time when "the nuclear oedipal complex as a chief motive force in development [was] under siege" (p. 165). Trying to preserve his theory, says Tolpin (1993),

> Freud reconstructed an unconscious sexual (oedipal) transference to Breuer, Breuer's unconscious sexual (oedipal) countertransference to the patient, and an interruption precipitated by fear of sexuality and an oedipal baby fantasy (see Freud, 1932, p. 412). . . . Everything fit together—Breuer had terminated the treatment, panicked, and fled when called back to find the patient in a hysterical labor; he later was reluctant to publish the case and collaborate on *Studies in Hysteria* and finally turned away from the truths about sexuality and denied and abandoned Freud and the field of psychoanalysis he had helped create.
>
> Jones (1953) embroidered Freud's reconstruction with a fanciful account of his own. His myth is complete with jealous wife, panic and flight, a second honeymoon in Venice, where a baby girl was supposedly conceived and was said to have committed suicide in New York sixty years later, and so on [p. 165].

None of this myth is correct (read Tolpin's evidence). It is now evident that Bertha's analytic experience with Breuer began a process of building her compensatory structures and led to the establishment of an independent self. True, she had some setbacks and hospitalizations, but eventually "during the next 40 years of her life, she formed selfobject ties with members of her mother's large, extended family [in Frankfurt], some of whom became very close friends as well as supporters" (Tolpin, 1993, p. 167). Through her reading, writing, and social work, Bertha became active in helping Jewish women, particularly refugees, and eventually forged a National Association of Jewish Women. Thus, after what turned out to be a very courageous and constructive life, Bertha died in 1936, "before all she had built, and many of the young women she had loved and trained, were destroyed in the Holocaust" (p. 175).

So, because of Freud's emphasis on sexuality as the major organizing drive, it took nearly a century to value Breuer's analysis with Bertha, and the importance of the development of a patient's compensatory structures for a successful treatment with psychotherapy, thanks to Kohut and Tolpin.

Summary

In this chapter we have attempted to show how a better understanding of the memory systems enhances our understanding of structuralization as it pertains to psychotherapy. Specifically, we have cited the literature on memory to demonstrate how it is possible to incorporate a biological form of structuralization into a theory of structuralization for psychotherapy. This underpinning, we claim, supports Kohut's emphasis on structuralization as an important postulate in a psychotherapeutically relevant theory of the self. Only through psychological structuralization, which is grounded neurobiologically, can the therapeutic gains of psychotherapy be rendered relatively permanent.

The recent burst of interest in the neurosciences and in trauma, has led to the hope that these fields will greatly enrich psychotherapy theory and the future practice of psychotherapy. This will be especially so if the ideas of neuroscience can elucidate further the pathological forms of structuralization of the self-organization of our patients. Whatever new discoveries in the neurosciences may be, they promise to underscore further Kohut's understanding of the concept of structuralization for the conduct and long-term benefit of psychoanalytic psychotherapy.

Note

1. Terr (1994) gained support for her ideas about King's procedural memory being reflected in his need to repeat horrifying scenes in his books, when she overheard three persons from the movie industry discussing a film script in a hotel coffee shop. The two who were facing Terr wanted the third person (with his back to her), to stop killing people in the script. They suggested that he try killing a horse or a dog, or even have a boy fall off a bicycle. They wanted the film limited to one death. The writer replied that having a boy ruin his bike is not as strong as a death. "Why not kill more people?" he said. Then he added, "I've got to do it. . . . that's me" (p. 56). When Lenore Terr later recognized the writer as Stephen King, she became more convinced of her hypothesis that the trauma of the gruesome death of King's friend's at four years of age had been stored in King's procedural memory and was being reenacted in his novels.

CHAPTER SEVEN

Self Psychology Theory

Pathways to Future Growth

In this project, we viewed self psychology theory through the lens of a Lakatosian-like research program that takes shape when Kohut's empathic method is made the central postulate. In formulating auxiliary postulates, we noted how Kohut's empathic stance with narcissistic patients led him to derive these postulates as an extension of, and as complementary to it. When, for example, narcissistic patients experienced empathic understanding from a psychotherapist functioning as a self-extension of them, they developed new or substitute structuralizations in their nuclear selves. So he believed that if psychotherapists attended to their patients' feelings, understood their unique self-configurations, and provided a relatively stable therapeutic relationship until patients structuralized valuable aspects of it, then psychotherapy offered a reasonable chance of permanent, constructive changes. The therapeutic results that he and his colleagues achieved as a result of this treatment approach, especially involving patients who had previously been untreatable using a classical analytic approach, demonstrated the value of his new theorizing.

A Lakatosian research program evaluates self psychology—and all scientific theories—by addressing a critical issue: Are the papers and presentations of the theory mostly a haphazard, "ad-hoc" response to the problems of theory or practice? Or do its primary theoretical extensions and auxiliary postulates offer new and novel ways of generating empathic understanding to produce better treatment outcomes? Typically, Lakatos would ask the question, "Is a theory degenerative or re-generative?" Applying this question to self psychology, we ask, not whether its auxiliary postulates are predictive, but to what extent they function as guiding/supporting elements to enhance the intersubjective processes of psychotherapy and the adaptive functioning of patients.

This concluding chapter has three sections. Section A summarizes the issue of postmodern criticism that Kohut's postulates form a one-person model of psychotherapy, by selectively ignoring the evidence that self psychology functions as a two-person model. In section B we outline ideas about a psychotherapist's professional configuration as a major postulate, and in section C we explore further the idea of a twinship selfobject experience. We offer these examples of theoretical development to suggest that self psychology theory is alive and well as a two-person model.

A. Postulates as a Two-Person Model

As mentioned in earlier chapters, a case can be made that the postmodernists have misunderstood or misrepresented self psychology theory. Influenced by continental philosophy, postmodernists reject the idea of a one-person, scientific model of psychotherapy theory because it offers a positivistic, mechanical view of science and psychoanalysis. In its extreme form, as the postmodern view thinks "objective" science is responsible for most of the ills of the modern world, it rejects science. Unlike the postmodernists, Kohut accepted the "objective" scientific method that has proved valuable for many areas of knowledge; he wanted science to expand its methodology to include a science of subjectivity as a basis for the conduct of psychotherapy. So Kohut's theoretical model used empathy as the method for exploring the subjectivity of others, and conceived of it as mutual and intersubjective.

An effective two-person model of psychotherapy needs the intersubjective theory of empathy that Kohut presented. Most pertinent to this two-person model is whether the persons in it are conceived as differentiated or undifferentiated based on their disposition to take the initiative or not. Kohut thought that psychotherapy with undifferentiated persons needed an extended period of tolerating the patient's unrelenting need for priority in the relationship. Although he recognized that healthy persons developed a differentiated relationship, he was especially interested in how this differentiation could be fostered through psychotherapy. The postmodern psychotherapeutic relationship has a different view—that differentiation develops in a child/patient through exposing the child/patient to the subjectivity of the parent/psychotherapist, not from a psychotherapist's selfobject functioning.

For postmoderns, a psychotherapist's personal self-disclosures are an important component of a therapist's subjectivity. Maroda (1999a), however, thinks self-disclosures can be harmful because "once we admitted to our countertransference and our mutuality of the therapeutic relationship, we did not have a clear idea of how it should be handled" (1999b, pp. 101–2). To Maroda (1999a) "The hallmarks of a misuse of self-disclosure involve using it primarily to further the analyst's personal or professional agenda" (100). Goldberg (2007) thinks that the psychotherapist's self-disclosure "appears to move the focus from the factors that were long considered enabling to a position of central efficacy" (p. 133). And about a therapist's self-disclosure, Orange, Atwood, and Stolorow (1997) say,

> Although recognizing that the analyst is constantly unwittingly revealing his or her psychological organization to the patient (Renik, 1995), the methodology of empathic-introspective inquiry does not prescribe deliberate self-disclosure by the analyst. Instead, . . . it enjoins the analyst to make specific decisions about self-disclosures on the basis of his or her best understanding of the likely meanings of such disclosures for the patient and analyst, and on his or her assessment, arrived at with varying degrees of collaborative input from the patient, of whether such interacting meanings are likely to facilitate or obstruct the analytic process [p. 44].

What particularly makes a psychotherapist's personal sharing detrimental to psychotherapy is the ignoring of the empathic experience of the patient as a means of determining whether a psychotherapist's sharing is beneficial or not. If a psychotherapist is attuned to a patient, the patient's experience of a psychotherapist's self-disclosure will most likely be experienced as empathic. But if the psychotherapist is not attuned to the patient and self-discloses, self psychology believes this makes the interaction highly susceptible to becoming a disjunction.

Empathy, the experience of the patient, is the crucial component in a psychotherapist's decision to self-disclose. Experiences with narcissistic patients and narcissistic psychotherapists (Gabbard and Lester, 1995) suggest that without an empathic approach to psychotherapy, patients are vulnerable to a psychotherapist's "narcissistic intrusions" in the guise of disclosure used as a technique. Without an adequate theory of empathy, a two-person model may be just as detrimental to the effectiveness of long-term psychotherapy, at least, as the one-person model the postmoderns condemn. Their theory, without empathy as a central construct, does not adequately cover the potential excesses of the two-person model.

We think debates about the differences between ideal one-person and two-person models (Frank, 1999) are tangential to the major issue. Patients without a capacity for an undifferentiated relationship, if they bond, have little choice but to initially seek and engage in a one-person model. As experienced self psychologists can attest, severe narcissistically disordered patients beginning psychotherapy expect an "archaic selfobject transference" that focuses exclusively on their own need. It is only as this one-way communication is accepted by the psychotherapist that the patient experiences enough safety to gradually differentiate and allow the emergence of a two-person relationship. This experience of increasing patient differentiation typically begins in sessions, briefly at first, before the length and frequency of the differentiation begins to increase. In contrast, postmodernists think that the differentiating process is driven by the psychotherapist's self-disclosures and, while this may be so sometimes, appropriate timing based on empathic understanding is the critical issue. Patient exposure to a psychotherapist's personal revelations need monitoring to ascertain if they are being experienced by the patient as empathic.

Moderate postmoderns such as Mitchell and Aron, make an effort to include a one-person model within a two-person model, but unless the Kohutian concept of empathy is included, it is difficult to see how these two models can be integrated into an approach that benefits the patient. A psychotherapist committed to a two-person empathic approach is less likely to interfere with a patient's development, is more likely to keep his/her own narcissistic needs in the background, and only self-discloses when appropriate to the needs of the patient.

A key test for a two-person model is how the subjective involvement of the psychotherapist plays out clinically. Self psychologists don't deny that at an appropriate stage in psychotherapy the psychotherapist's disclosing of his/her subjectivity may be beneficial for the growth and development of the patient. Where a patient seeks a twinship experience with a psychotherapist, for example, he or she grows a symmetrical robustness if the psychotherapist presents a robust self to the patient. But if the patient does not hunger for a twinship experience, the patient may complement a psychotherapist's robust subjectivity by withdrawing and being passive. As an example, if marriage relationships can be symmetrical or complementary (Moss and Lee, 1976), it is clear that a patient's increased exposure to the robust subjectivity of the psychotherapist may facilitate symmetrical robustness in the patient and mutative changes. But this study also suggests that without empathic understanding such an exposure could make the patient worse, not better. So, although a postmodern emphasis on a two-person model has made a major contribution to the development of modern psychotherapy theory, the crucial question is which kind of two-person theory? As the next section seeks to demonstrate, the danger of a patient's exploitation under a two-person model will be high without an adequate theory of empathy and professionalism. Postmodernists may reject a concept of professionalism as another pillar of a one-person model if they ignore the possibility that professionalism as a postulate in Kohut's theory can be conceived intersubjectively, as indeed, the other postulates we have proposed.

B. A Psychotherapy Professional Configuration

We propose that a professional self-configuration be considered a postulate in an empathy-based psychotherapy theory. At this junction in history, the professional identity of a psychiatrist, psychologist, social worker, etc., does not in and of itself posit a "professional commitment" to a psychotherapeutic relationship. We make a distinction between professional commitment as an attitude of the peripheral self, and a commitment that has been internalized in the nuclear self as a professional configuration consisting of ambitions, ideals, and skills. Stone (1981) came somewhat close to articulating a professional configuration for psychotherapists when he considered patient/psychotherapist interactions from the point of view of a "physicianly vocation," a general idea that does not specifically capture a professional configuration in an empathy-based approach to psychotherapy. Hoffman (1994) conceives of an "analytic discipline" that is "learned and internalized in a process of professional socialization" (p. 195). Our idea of a professional configuration attempts to counter the image of a cold, uncaring, money motivated relationship.

Shane, Shane, and Gales (1997) also approach our meaning of "professional" when they emphasize a "commitment to the patient's well-being" (p. 99). We think such a commitment is just as necessary for a successful psychotherapy as the aforementioned postulates. A professional commitment contributes to psychotherapy theory by providing a key to understanding the psychotherapist's functioning in a therapeutic relationship. The therapeutic relationship, after all, is different from other relationships, whether business, romantic, or friendship. (Lampl-De Groot, 1981, p. 614). What would such a professional relationship look like? In a therapeutic relationship the professional commitment of the psychotherapist is both subjective and communal.

In its subjective approach, a professional commitment is *to the priority of the selfobject needs of the patient*. This priority follows from using empathy to help foster a patient's mature self-agency and self-organization. Of course a friend, like a psychotherapist, may be willing to be empathic and to function as a selfobject. Where this is so, what is the difference? In friendships that endure and are not de facto attempts at therapeutic relationships, there is a mutual sharing of emotional needs. But what happens if one or both persons in the friendship are not capable of such mutuality? Typically, the friendship either breaks up or turns into a nonprofessional, quasi-therapeutic relationship where the selfobject needs of one friend takes precedence over the needs of the other friend.

Such de facto therapeutic relationships in the name of friendship may function well for a time, and even permanently if the selfobject expectations are mild, but should they become too one-sided, intense, and demanding, such relationships tend to collapse under the weight of archaic enmeshment or become dysfunctional. It is well recognized that one source of psychotherapy patients is from the break up of friendships that have failed as de facto therapeutic relationships. When one friend's excessive selfobject needs exhaust the other friend, then its "time for the professional!" For some patients entering psychotherapy, it may not be that the selfobject experience is new, but what is new is the experience of the professional ability of the psychotherapist to welcome, tolerate, and sustain this selfobject experience for the patient without demanding that his or her own selfobject needs be met.

The professional concept in medicine is rooted in the Hippocratic oath. As classical psychoanalysis was heavily influenced by its emergence from medicine, it too eventually adopted a professional model. According to the one-person theory, professionalism focuses on the analyst's neutrality, adherence to a set of rules in conducting psychoanalytic sessions, and an absence of contact outside these sessions. In Kohut's theory, a strict concept of neutrality was rejected as impossible to attain and as too "sterile to be of value for mutative psychotherapy with self-disordered patients" (Marian Tolpin, personal communication). In rejecting the traditional analytic construct of neutrality, Kohut did not reject a professional attitude; he redefined it. Importantly, Kohut's attitude was defined by a professional commitment to the patient's need for a selfobject experience, a position not dissimilar to Stone's (1961). This sense of professionalism becomes clearer when we think of it in terms of Buber's constructs of the "I," "Thou," and "It" that were explicated in chapter 3.

In chapter 3 we described patients as having a special "Thou" experience when their psychotherapists functioned as selfobjects. This "Thou" experience is like a model scene (Lichtenberg, 1989) in which, as patients are having this experience, simultaneously, psychotherapists surrender their self-initiative and temporarily experience being treated as an impersonal "It" (see chapter 4, section A, subsection 8). *It is this commitment to and capacity for tolerating "It-ness" that we think needs to be a core component of a professional configuration in Kohutian theory*. The professional configuration of psychotherapists obligate them to have their mature selfobject needs met outside the therapeutic relationship, which in turn, helps them adhere to their tolerating the "It" experiences within the therapeutic relationship. Such professionalism also means that psychotherapists' relationships with their own spouses, relatives, friends, or supervisors become important sources for meeting their own selfobject needs. This is similar to Chessick's idea (2007) of a "working ego" (professional self configuration) (p. 100) that is separate from a "private personal ego" (self).

A professional configuration means that a psychotherapist is responsible for maintaining his/her own self-cohesion. With a professional commitment comes the risk of emotional exhaustion from constant "it-ness" in therapeutic relationships. With "it-ness," we recognize that such concepts as a "facilitating environment" (Winnicott, 1974) may create a new set of theoretical problems if interpreted absolutely. There comes a point where psychotherapists may reach a personal limit in functioning as an extension of a patient. Like a mother of a young infant, it may be necessary initially for psychotherapists to tolerate patient demands for variations in the conventional social arrangements, and then seek to understand them dynamically. Such demands typically abate as the patient bonds to the psychotherapist and the psychotherapist grasps the specific nature of the selfobject experience needed by the patient. A stable mode of interacting usually emerges. When patients make excessive archaic selfobject demands on psychotherapists, psychotherapists have a professional obligation to assess if they can manage their "It" experiences during such demands, to be able to sustain a long-term therapeutic relationship.

Coen (2000) takes the position that a psychotherapist's subjectivity and self-disclosure can induce regression in some patients and this patient regression tends to occur when the psychotherapist regresses because of the urgency of his/her own needs. Coen says patients regress with "any wishful movement of the analyst out of the position of thoughtful, focused attention of the analysand's needs and conflicts to a less differentiated relatedness, much more determined by the analyst's own needs and conflicts" (p. 795). If a patient archaically regresses into a dedifferentiating dissolution, he/she is counting on the psychotherapist to remain differentiated and not regress. If psychotherapists have difficulty resisting the pull of an archaic merger with regressed, dedifferentiated patient, they have a professional obligation to find selfobject resources outside the psychotherapy relationship so they have the emotional resources to keep themselves cohesive and non-regressed.

There is a need for professional limitations on the "It" experiences of the psychotherapist. This need is supported by Tronick's (1989) studies of fifty-four mother-infant pairs in chapter 3, where the "levels of co-ordination" (attunement) between the mother and infant, took place about 35 percent of the time.

Such studies support Fossage's (1997) stance that the psychotherapeutic relationship oscillates between being empathic to the patient's viewpoint (and the psychotherapist's functioning as an "It"), to looking at the patient from an outside viewpoint. With needy patients the initial demands for selfobject functioning may mean a higher percentage of session time spent by psychotherapists in "It" experiences, especially with emergencies. But patient demands for selfobject experiences that are well in excess of the 35 percent burden and exhaust psychotherapists if they become a permanent pattern of the psychotherapy. Consistent with Kohut's concept of a professional configuration, a psychotherapist engages in vitalizing processes outside of psychotherapy to maintain his functioning as a selfobject in psychotherapy sessions.

The psychotherapist's commitment to a professional configuration that tolerates an "It" experience, subserves a major goal of psychotherapy: the development of an "I-I" relationship where both patient and psychotherapist are eventually differentiated from each other as independent centers of initiative. Many patients present for psychotherapy with an inability to have an "I-I" relationship, and initially require a "Thou-It" relationship to help them develop the capacity to do so. As was observed in chapter 3, in order for an "I-I" relationship to develop and be maintained, there will be times when the "Thou-It" relationship temporarily turns into an "It-Thou" relationship. In the language of Kohut, a patient (or child) may function as a selfobject (an "It") for the psychotherapist (or parent)—a reverse selfobject experience (R. Lee, 1988, 1999). But is this healthy? And would not a patient (or child) who has functioned as a reverse selfobject during early development attempt to do so in the psychotherapy?

One of us (RL) theorized two decades ago that excessive functioning as a "reverse selfobject" was one source of arrested development (Lee, 1988), but later realized that the "reverse selfobject experience" (Lee, 1999) was not necessarily detrimental to the healthy development of patients as long as the selfobject functioning was reciprocal. So we reformulate the question of an interactive selfobject dyad (the reciprocal "Thou—It" and "It—Thou" relationship) and ask, whose selfobject experience takes *precedence* if both patients and psychotherapists seek it? Imagining such a potential conflict makes it clear that in the psychotherapist's professional configuration the commitment is not to neutrality but to the patient's "priority of need." Patients and their needs for selfobjects (a "Thou" experience) usually need to come first!

The psychotherapeutic professional commitment to privileging patients' selfobject experiences and being able to tolerate sustained "It" experiences, points to how a shift from a patient's one-person orientation to a two-person system may take place during successful psychotherapy using a self psychology approach. Patients who regularly experience the "good enough" privileging of their selfobject needs eventually seek a more interactive "I-I" relationship and a more robust sense of subjectivity that goes with it. Self psychology is misrepresented when categorized either as a one-person or two-person system. Rather, it is a theory that recognizes that severely damaged patients often present with the attitudes and assumptions of a one-person system, and it offers a way of understanding how shifts takes place from a one-person to a two-person intersubjective system. This shift is facilitated by the selfobject experiences of patients that correlate with the commitments of the psychotherapist's professional configuration. What we are emphasizing is that you can't have one (selfobject experiences) without the other ("It-ness" experiences). As noted, this professional configuration not only places the selfobject needs of a patient first, but emphasizes the capacity to tolerate the "It" experience for prolonged periods of time without fragmenting or becoming depleted. The professional configuration of the psychotherapist takes pressure off the theory of empathy to explain everything that is mutative about psychotherapy. Without a strong capacity for a professional commitment, psychotherapists are unable to deliver sustained "good enough" empathic understanding to patients who need long-term psychotherapy.

Viewed communally, a professional configuration also accepts the inevitability of moral rules for the conduct of psychotherapy. Bloch, Chodoff, and Green (1999) think a psychotherapist's ethical conduct (the Greek "ethikos") means a predisposition to act rightly or wrongly. Goldberg (2007), influenced by Ricoeur (Hahn, 1995), views ethics as living well and in harmony with others; he actually thinks the question of a psychotherapist's professional conduct engages a narrower moralistic system. Morality (B. Williams, 1985) is a system of dutifully obeying rules and prohibitions. So the "ethics" of professional practice involves psychotherapeutic morality that focuses on "duties, obligations, prohibitions, and imperatives" (p. 7).

In the moral prohibitions of conducting psychotherapy with a patient, Goldberg discusses issues such as touching, sexual behavior, confidentiality, case publication, and marriage to former patients. He thinks a key issue is the way these prohibitions are determined. A professional psychotherapy morality may appeal to the "deontology" of Immanuel Kant, which determines the rightness or wrongness of conduct from referring to such universal principles as "murder is wrong." Habermas (1993), who claims Kant's "categorical imperatives" assume a person can grasp moral validity by reflecting on action, thinks this is impossible. He believes that "moral questions can only be solved by participants finding concrete answers in particular cases through an effort to accept the perspectives of all involved" (Goldberg, 2007, p. 111).

Fletcher (1966), a modern representative of situational morality, emphasizes that correct conduct can be determined by taking into account the specific context of behavior. Goldberg's (2007) appeal along contextual lines is to a moral pragmatism where "decisions are not made by reference to a fixed standard but rather are created and re-created according to our history and experiences" (p. 137). His pragmatism builds on the intellectual history of William James, Charles Pierce, and John Dewey where moral questions cannot be solved by appeal to a fixed principle, but from being worked on in a community network. Under pragmatism, a professional configuration means working within rules that are constantly being created by a professional community. Such rules do not reflect a one-person model of Kantian absolutes, but a two-person model that involves uncertainty and struggle around moral questions.

As one example of a moral question, professional psychotherapy organizations, under heavy societal pressure have decided that sexual involvement between a psychotherapist and patient is "unethical and unprofessional." This moral prohibition has developed out of the history of psychoanalysis where, as Gabbard (1995) says,

> Many of the most prominent analysts in the profession, both historically and contemporaneously, have become sexually involved with patients, and some have married ex-patients. No [psychoanalytic] institute or society is spared these embarrassments, and most have various "family secrets" about such an activity among prominent members. The closets of our psychoanalytic institutions are filled with skeletons [p. 89].

Sexual "boundary violations" are generally believed to be damaging to patients, to the reputations of those psychotherapist's involved, and to the social prestige of the profession. Gabbard (1995), after evaluating and treating seventy psychotherapists who had sex with their patients (p. 92), believes sexual boundary violations damage patients and affirm the need for professional prohibitions against it. This is also the conclusion of the majority of psychotherapists that have worked with distressed, fearful, or angry patients who have been sexually involved with a previous psychotherapist. But material from such cases as Gabbard's is not convincing to "evidence-based" theorists. The issue for them is generalizability. M. Williams (1992), for example, reviewing the research, thinks it is difficult to generalize from case and survey approaches to widespread sexual "boundary violations" and resultant damage to patients. Even so, he concedes there is sufficient evidence of damage in patients sexually involved with one psychotherapist who continued their psychotherapy with a new psychotherapist, to justify a professional standard of no sexual involvement with patients.

> Stepansky thinks such a professional standard is warranted. He says, psychoanalytic distance from body-based therapies has been reinforced by ongoing concern with the discomforting reality of boundary violations. After all, bodies in treatment offer up the possibility of trust bodily betrayed. Instances of such professional malfeasance represent yet another unspoken (and unwanted) dimension of the analytic legacy. Scholars have long been acquainted with the recurrent violations that punctuate the history of psychoanalysis: Carl Jung's complicated embroilment with his patient Sabina Spielrein; Sandor Ferenczi's simultaneous romantic involvement with his patient (and future wife) Gizella Palos and her daughter Elma Palos; and Margaret Mahler's affair with her first analyst, August Aichhorn, among them. The redoubtable Ernest Jones has the dubious distinction of being the first analyst to settle financially with a patient who accused him of sexual misconduct. For many decades, these and other particulars occupied some dim nether region of psychoanalytic awareness. Only with the publication of Glen Gabbard and Eva Lester's *Boundary Violations in Psychoanalysis*, which documented the continuing reality of such violations, was the profession spurred to self-examination [Anderson, 2007, p. x].

The seventy psychotherapists Gabbard evaluated or treated for becoming sexually involved with patients fell into four personality types: psychotic, predatory psychopathic, narcissistic, or masochistic. Most of those he assessed or treated fell into the latter three groups, and, viewed from a self psychology perspective, have a narcissistic disorder of one kind or another. These are psychotherapists who needed their patients to function as sexual selfobjects for them. What is pertinent to some of Gabbard's cases is the manifestation of a vertical split that Kohut had associated with narcissistic behavior disorders (Kohut and Wolf, 1978), where one side of the self disavows what the other side is doing. Psychotherapists with a propensity toward a vertical split, exemplify that a professional attitude or intention is insufficient to predict unprofessional behavior, hence, the need for professional rules. Behind the breaking of these rules, we argue, may be a self-disorder and a serious split off inability to fulfill a professional commitment.

A lack of professionalism is dramatically raised by *Running with Scissors* (Burroughs, 2002). The author was a patient who lived in the chaotic home of his *laissez faire* psychiatrist, Dr Finch. Setting aside the veracity of the account or its possible exaggeration to create a "good story," Burroughs depicts Dr. Finch as not able to maintain a professional commitment. Finch's immoral behavior was not just breaking "the rules" of his professional organization, but his seeming lack of understanding or professional commitment to the nuclear needs of his patients.

Perhaps the classic illustration of the need for a professional commitment comes from Shakespeare's *Othello*, which portrays the relationships between Othello, his aide Iago, his wife Desdemona, and his lieutenant Cassius. According to Muslin (1984), the traditional psychoanalytic view is that Othello's "passing over" of Iago as his lieutenant triggered Iago's narcissistic rage and revenge against Othello. Muslin, however, takes the view that the motivation for Iago's revenge was his need for an archaic idealized selfobject that was shattered when Othello chose both Desdemona and Cassius for significant relationships.

As the play unfolds, Iago plots to have Othello believe that Desdemona is having an affair with Cassius. At first Othello refuses to accept this as happening, but because of Iago's machinations, we realize that Othello's strong peripheral belief in the faithfulness of his wife was eroded by a doubting nuclear self. After Iago contrives for Othello to see Cassius and Desdemona talking, Othello begins to fragment. In a state of fragmentation Othello archaically regresses into a dedifferentiated state with Iago. Muslin (1984) points out that "Shakespeare has the two characters celebrate in a ritual not unlike a marriage." (p. 228). Through manipulation, Iago uses the bond of this dedifferentiated merger to create in Othello revengeful rage toward Desdemona. In a pact, he orders Othello to kill Desdemona and he will kill Cassius. This they do, but when Othello eventually realizes the evil intent of this archaic relationship, he takes his own life. Muslin (1984) thinks that

> Shakespeare has described with remarkable clarity what are perhaps the most significant aspects of the drama, the transformation of the relationship between the general and his aide. Iago has become the selfobject whom Othello follows without challenge. They have merged in an archaic self/selfobject bond in which Iago functions for Othello as the idealized parental imago whose evil directions are followed in a reflexive way [p. 230].

Iago clearly used his selfobject function for his own purposes, not Othello's. When this narcissistic use of a selfobject function occurs in a psychotherapist/patient relationship the therapist has betrayed his professional commitment to the patient; this kind of betrayal is anathema to a professional approach in self psychology.

We think that with the concept of a professional self-configuration, we have shown both its potential as an auxiliary postulate and the flexibility of a Kohutian self psychology theory. Cast into a Lakatosian research program, Kohut's theory can incorporate major auxiliary postulates other than those discussed in the preceding chapters. The emergence of new auxiliary postulates helps maintain the patient's empathic experience of therapeutic relationships and therefore demonstrates the regenerative capacity of the theory.

C. Developing the Twinship Selfobject Experience

Kohut's (1984) concept of a twinship selfobject experience was presented posthumously as an idea that needed further development. The following remarks are not considered to do justice to this need, but we hope our speculative effort encourages further development of Kohut's concept of twinship. We begin with a case.

In a consultation, a psychotherapist described an obsessive-compulsive patient, a Mr. D. Since the earliest sessions of the treatment, the patient had begun every session with the ritualistic question, "Are you Sam the psychotherapist?" After Sam answered, "Yes," the patient would ask the question again, and the psychotherapist would again answer, "Yes." This pattern typically occurred three times before the session could proceed.

The psychotherapist thought of possible meanings to Mr. D's ritual. The patient, for example, had grown up in an authoritarian family where he was punished for not conforming to the wishes of his father. Based on transference fear, Mr. D may have needed assurances that the psychotherapist would remain professional and not become the "parental" enforcer of discipline, as had his father. Or perhaps the patient felt residual rage and feared that if he expressed this in the session, the psychotherapist could not tolerate it. So, maybe the ritual was as much a need to contain the rage as the fear of being punished. Curious, the psychotherapist attempted to explore the meaning of this behavior with the patient.

One day, when Mr. D asked the psychotherapist, "Are you Sam the psychotherapist?" the psychotherapist gave the expected response, "Yes." But when Mr. D repeated the question, the psychotherapist then said that as he had answered this question three times at the beginning of each session since they had begun treatment, there might be value in exploring the meaning of this behavior. He asked if the patient was interested in such an exploration, if not now, then in the future. Annoyed, the patient responded that he had talked about this before, and that his repeated asking of the question was reasonable. "After all," he said, "when a nation declares war, the question is asked three times, just to make sure."

The illusion to war suggests that the patient saw the relationship as a battle, which he had to win by gaining control and suggested a repetitive transference with the psychotherapist as the authoritarian father. As the therapist's attempts to explore this negative transference in previous sessions had been experienced as disjunctive, the psychotherapist tried a different approach. He said that all he wanted to do was explore, not battle with or control him. But the patient was dismissive. "This conversation is most unhelpful," he said. "I am having a bad day, and this is only making matters worse." Experiencing the therapist as interfering with what he wanted to do, he complained, "This week I had an incident when someone didn't move out of the way on the footpath" (as he wished the psychotherapist would do). The expectation of people getting out of this patient's way, confirmed what the psychotherapist had gleaned from previous material. The patient needed his workmates, his personal acquaintances, people in the streets, and now his psychotherapist to obey him, just as he had been forced to obey a punitive authoritarian parent who became upset when he wouldn't. Feeling that the patient's experience of the psychotherapist's attempt to explore his ritualistic behavior had been too intrusive, the psychotherapist remained quiet. Soon the patient regained his momentum and returned to his customary, one-way monologue.

Many analysts would think that Mr. D was using the psychotherapist as an object on to whom he projected anger that he felt toward his father. From a self psychology perspective the patient's peripheral self functioned as a differentiated object, while the nuclear self needed the psychotherapist as an extension to maintain his self-cohesion and, therefore, was not able to function as an assertive, differentiated self, able to take the initiative. As an undifferentiated nuclear self, however, Mr. D had not developed as a differentiated object capable of utilizing Klein's projective identification. In our view the necessity of Mr. D's ritual to maintain his cohesion, points to his need for an archaic selfobject relationship with the psychotherapist that eventually lessens his dependence on ritual and fosters growth and development.

From a self psychology perspective the case of Mr. D suggests limitations to the concept of empathy as the experience of the patient. Mr. D obviously felt less distress if the psychotherapist acquiesced to his wishes and participated in a ritualistic performance with him. It could be said that he experienced the psychotherapist's acquiescence as empathy because he was unable to distinguish between acquiescence and empathy. In such a patient if empathic understanding is accepted as the experience of the patient, misunderstandings will occur. The case suggests that empathy as privileging the experience of the patient creates a new set of challenges for understanding and exploring the intersubjective nature of psychotherapy.

Mr. D's need for control is the clearest indication he was seeking some kind of archaic selfobject experience. But what kind? This seeking may not be for idealizing, mirror, or twinship selfobject functions, or a combination of them, but for a self-extension that creates a sense of security that can eventually lead to growth. This vignette of Mr. D demonstrates a need for the selfobject construct to have a developmental trajectory of its own. Once engaged empathically by the therapist, the patient moves from his nuclear archaic configuration into a maturity that eventually renders him/her independent and more functional in the workplace, in relations, and so forth. The risk of a psychotherapist functioning as a "security selfobject," however, as long-term cases of obsessive-compulsives have shown, is that patients use these experiences to maintain cohesiveness without fostering their self-development and new growth. In such a situation, psychotherapists may have countertransference feelings of discouragement and despair from just maintaining the patient.

Patients seeking the psychotherapist as a self-extension suggest narcissistic dynamics. It has long been understood that many narcissistic disorders present with a strong overlay of obsessive-compulsive defenses, as was the case of Mr. W (Kohut, 1977, pp. 152–70) that was supervised by Kohut. In what turned out to be a significant session, the analyst reported that Mr. W began to talk about the objects that were in one of his trouser pockets, which he listened to with bored resignation. The inventory consisted of, among other things, a number of coins, a piece of crumpled paper, and a ball of fuzzy wool. As Kohut listened to the description of the session, he gradually realized that the patient was not listing his typical negative criticism about the treatment but was talking as a little child to an adult about something with which he was pleased.

Alerted by supervision to this "being pleased" explanation, when Mr. W reported similar material in the next session, the analyst no longer experienced it as "boring gibberish" and the patient responded to the analyst's aliveness by offering nonritualized, meaningful material. He shared how, when he grew up, his family had not paid much attention to him, and he was left alone while everyone worked in the fields. When Kohut wrote about Mr. W he had not yet clarified his notion of the twinship selfobject function. But in this case we see a patient who had clearly created in the analyst the very lonely, boring feeling with which he had grown up in his family of origin. Such a feeling of boredom was actively created in the analyst through the patient's mood and behavior. From the analyst's boredom we have evidence that the patient had turned the analyst into his emotional twin. By the analyst's linking together these experiences—the patient's growing up experience, and the analyst's experience of the analysis as twinship—a meaningful, nonritualistic relationship can be fostered in which such a twinship selfobject experience enables significant changes in the patient.

A similar twinship explanation could be given to the Case of Mr. D. By controlling the session with the psychotherapist and making him acquiesce, Mr. D was replicating with him what had been his acquiescing experiences when growing up in his family of origin. The eventual sharing of this understanding with the patient, and the resulting spontaneous moments in the therapeutic relationship, helped modify the archaic nature of this patient's selfobject experience. It also helped to distinguish between a psychotherapeutic response that was only acquiescing behavior without understanding, and a response that understood and accepted the patient's need for a selfobject experience. In effect Mr. D's experiences of empathy as acquiescence at the beginning of the treatment is meant to change as the treatment proceeds.

In this example the twinship experience is not that of the child or patient twinning the parent or therapist, but of the child/patient needing the parent/therapist to twin the child/patient, a form of "reverse selfobject experience" (R. Lee, 1988, 1999). This idea was hinted at in the example of a patient who attempts to humiliate Kohut. He (1971) says,

> The patient would . . . begin to see me as a person devoid of ambitions, as emotionally shallow, pathologically even-tempered, withdrawn, and inactive, and—although this image was at variance with some of my actual personality features and activities that were well-known to the patient—his sense of conviction about these fantasies was not disturbed by the co-existing contradictory information. A prolonged working-through process then ensued in which my personality was scrutinized and experienced as being torn by conflict. What was the analyst afraid of? Did he really have no ambitions? Was he really never envious? Or did he have to flee from his ambitions and from his envious feelings for fear that they might destroy him? After long periods of such doubts and worries the patient's perception of me would gradually change [pp. 194–95].

As Kohut had not developed the idea of twinship transference when he wrote this, he did not have the idea of a reverse twinship to understand why his response to such humiliating behavior could be successful.

Lee (2003) suggests that the concept of reverse twinship transference is useful in treating aggressive patients who need to humiliate their psychotherapists. He gives the example of Peggy:

> Peggy, a new middle-aged patient rang the doorbell and was greeted by a female psychotherapist saying, "Come in, come in" as Peggy entered a hallway. With annoyed face and irritated voice, Peggy responded with, "Don't say 'come in, come in' when I am already 'in.'" Feeling slightly irritated herself, the psychotherapist ushered the patient into her consulting room.
>
> After Peggy sat in the patient's chair, she looked around the room and noted its paintings and pictures. Focusing on shelves overflowing with books, she commented, "I don't like the untidy look of bookshelves stuffed to overflowing." Aware of her growing anger in response to the patient's criticisms, the psychotherapist asked why the patient was seeking help and was told she had "relationship difficulties" [p.1].

As Peggy's criticisms became a regular pattern of the psychotherapy, it became obvious that her behavior with the therapist was part of a pattern of humiliating others. The psychotherapist understood that this pattern probably developed intersubjectively during childhood when Peggy had repeatedly been humiliated by a caregiver. Peggy behaved automatically and effortlessly because mother-infant dyads involve the structuralization of reciprocal interactions in procedural memory, so that in experiencing her critical mother, Peggy learned how to be critical too. This process is similar to that of actors, who not only learn their own lines but also know those of their co-actors to be able to time their own responses.

Patients who persistently attempt to humiliate a psychotherapist generally continue with this pattern until they feel understood. They are wary of words and interpretations because they trust the message of behavior. Through their behavior, they are in effect saying to the psychotherapist something like, "Ok, hotshot, you say you want to understand me from my point of view, then lets test you out. I won't tell you what it felt like growing up, I shall create in you a similar experience to what I felt. As I was constantly bullied and humiliated as a child, I will humiliate and bully you and see if you can tolerate it as I was forced to do. If you can, then I will respect you as a worthy twin. If you can't, I will have contempt for you, your fancy words, and all your 'book learning.'"

What does the theory of reverse twinship contribute to the treatment of such a patient? A psychotherapist's initial tolerance of the bullying may not bring any significant change in the patient, but it paves the way for explaining and appreciating the patient's behavior as a creative and effective form of communication about early childhood experiences. This explanation sets the stage for a patient understanding that the psychotherapist is neither stupid nor naïve nor pathologically passive in tolerating the patient's aggressive "put downs," but does so out of understanding a process of which the patient is, at best, dimly aware. The psychotherapist cannot expect to see any immediate major change of behavior through explaining the twinship experience, and may even have a patient verbally reject the interpretation, but he will notice that the patient's aggression in later sessions begins to soften and occurs less frequently than before. The patient realizes that another human has tasted and appreciated the living hell the patient went through growing up. In making the psychotherapist a twin to him/her (the reverse of Kohut's original examples), the patient eventually is open to twinning aspects of the psychotherapist's thinking and therefore adopt some of the psychotherapist's behavior, making the twinship two-person and mutual.

The experience of the patient behaving like a parent in the psychotherapy relationship and of the psychotherapist experiencing feelings felt by the patient as a child has been long noted in the clinical literature. Lichtenberg, in describing this clinical phenomenon in a discussion group at the twenty-ninth International Conference of Self Psychology (2006), indicated that the issue was not its theoretical labeling but how a psychotherapist uses the recognition of the process to enhance growth in the patient. A response to this transference experience will depend largely on the guiding theory of the psychotherapist. For example, Klein would interpret, based on her theory of projective identification, that the patient is projecting his/her bad self onto the therapist. But the experience of many clinicians has been that a patient can experience such an interpretation as blaming and shaming, and as a consequence, the psychotherapeutic relationship will deteriorate.

Ferenczi, a gifted psychotherapist among the early psychoanalysts, experienced this kind of reverse relationship with his "difficult" patient RN, who would now be diagnosed as a severe self-disorder. Abrasive, opinionated, and strong-willed, RN created feelings in Ferenczi of being abused, similar perhaps to feelings associated with being sexually abused by her father. As a self-styled psychotherapist who had already published a book on psychotherapy, RN entered psychotherapy with Ferenczi convinced of the value of her "mutual psychotherapy" despite the fact that she had periods of severe fragmentation similar to borderline patients. Her view of psychotherapy was one where client and therapist shared and explored each other's self-organizations, and she made it her task to convert Ferenczi to her way of conducting psychotherapy and in a religious-like way, convert him to her beliefs as a disciple. These may have been her "modus operandi," not empathic understanding.

The case of RN is one where Ferenczi had the courage to explore RN's approach to the conduct of psychotherapy, but where the relational boundaries became so blurred that RN went with Ferenczi and his wife on a vacation to Spain. Ferenczi also, at RN's insistence, shared much of his own life with her ("self-disclosed"), even though the process left him humiliated because RN did not seem to function as a selfobject during the process, and Ferenczi was "flying by the seat of his pants" as he entered new therapeutic territory. After eight years, including nearly two years of "mutual analysis," the analysis terminated when Ferenczi became extremely ill with pernicious anemia, and an exhausted RN returned to practice her brand of psychotherapy in London.

Whether this heroic effort of Ferenczi is considered a failure or not will depend on the point of view from which it is approached. What is clear, however, is that as empathic as Ferenczi could be, the whole experience was hindered by a lack of a guiding theory to promote significant therapeutic change in the patient. It was as if RN had made her goal the "converting" of Ferenczi. Today, however, with Kohut's understanding of a twinship selfobject experience, and further insight into how the twinship can be reversed by patients in desperate, archaic states, RN's behavior could be seen as an attempt to create in Ferenczi a twinship experience where "what she recovered about the analyst, she must acknowledge as a distant reflection of her own sufferings" (Dupont, 1995, p. 159). But when Ferenzci did not cooperate fully, her seeking of a reverse twinship deteriorated into a defensive, archaic, dedifferentiated merger in which "two halves had combined to form a whole" (Dupont, 1995, p. 14) with the behavioral consequence of a battle of wills.

A similar understanding can be given to the case of Sue that was conducted by the empathic Jungian psychotherapist Robert Hobson. Sue too had entered psychotherapy as a practicing psychotherapist. Hobson (1985) saw her for twelve years in another heroic effort (p. 261), as reflected in the way she intruded into Hobson's life by telephoning him ten times on a weekend, overdosing on pills, sleeping in his garden, and throwing stones through his windows. Unsurprisingly, she made Hobson angry and fed up—just as she was angry and fed up—and made him feel a failure as she had been made to feel a failure in her childhood. When she eventually committed suicide, Hobson was seemingly humiliated by the task of identifying the body. This "very difficult" case, too, could have been helped by a theory that understood its dynamics, so that the patient can experience being empathically understood; perhaps the case could have been helped by an understanding of reverse twinship as an expression of Kohut's theory of empathy. Hobson, like Ferenczi, was a gifted psychotherapist, but in the absence of a suitable guiding theory his therapeutic effort floundered from exhaustion. These examples suggest that therapeutic outcomes may be improved with such difficult-to-treat patients by understanding that they may communicate through "reverse twinship" transference. This question needs more attention from self psychology theorists and practitioners.

The potential clinical usefulness of the twinship transference in its reverse form suggests there is still much to be done to extend Kohut's theory. This is especially true if we seek new, creative ways to reach narcissistic patients who are so well defended against their "split off," softer, more intimate and joyful feelings (Goldberg, 1995, 1999, 2000, 2007). Understanding and interpreting a reverse twinship is not a new postulate, but an elaboration of one of many of Kohut's creative ideas. And there are many more that could be developed to increase the clinical effectiveness of those who conduct long-term psychotherapy.

Toward the end of his Kohut Memorial Lecture at the twenty-ninth International Conference on Self Psychology, Paul Ornstein used his personal experiences of Heinz Kohut to conjecture about what Kohut would have said if he had been standing at the back of the room at the twenty-fifth anniversary of his death. Ornstein imagined Kohut proudly affirming the work of the previous quarter of a century with something like "Well done, good and faithful selfobjects!" If we could continue Ornstein's imaginary conversation with Kohut, we think that Kohut would remind us that theory is ongoing and constantly self-organizing, and there is still much to be done. Kohut may have also agreed with Lakatos that the test of a good theory is its regenerative ability. Finally, we think that Kohut would have liked Gadamer's language of horizons, and that having reached so far on the journey, he would have readily acknowledged that other horizons beckon. In concluding, we think that as much as self psychology gains from dialogue with other theories, and from the challenges of the neurosciences, it also needs to push Kohut's creative theoretical achievements to their limits. In doing so, whatever emerges will surely regenerate a more inclusive theory that enhances our patient's experiences of empathic understanding.

References

Abel, T., Alberini, C., Ghirardi, M., Huang, Y., Nguyen, P., and Kandel, E. (1995). Steps towards a molecular definition of memory consolidation. In: *Memory Distortion: How Minds, Brains, and Sciences Reconstruct the Past*, eds. D. Schacter, J. Coyle, G. Fishbach, M. Mesulam, L. Sullivan, Harvard University Press. pp. 228–328.

Adorno, T. (1973). *Negative Dialectics*. London: Routledge.

Ainsworth, M., Blehar, M., Waters, E., and Wall, S. (1978). *Patterns of Attachment*. Hillsdale NJ.: Lawrence Erlbaum.

Amorapanth, P., LeDoux, J., and Nader, K. (2000). Different lateral amygdala outputs mediate reactions and actions elicited by a fear-arousing stimulus. *Nature Neuroscience*, 3:74–79.

Anderson, F., ed. (2007). *Bodies in Treatment: The Unspoken Dimension*. Hillsdale, NJ: The Analytic Press.

Arnheim, R. (1949). The Gestalt theory of expression. *Psychological Review*, 56:156–71.

Arnold, A. (1975a). The effects of castration on song development in zebra finches (Poephilia guttata). *Journal of Experimental Zoology*, 191:261–78.

———. (1975b). The effects of castration and androgen replacement on song, courtship, and aggression in zebra finches (Poephila guttata). *Journal of Experimental Zoology*, 191:309–26.

Aron, L. (1996). *A Meeting of Minds: Mutuality in Psychoanalysis*. Hillsdale, NJ.: The Analytic Press.

Atwood, G., and Stolorow, R. (1984). *Structures of Subjectivity: Explorations in Psychoanalytic Phenomenology*. Hillsdale, NJ: The Analytic Press.

Bacal, H. (1985). Optimal responsiveness and the therapeutic process. In: *Progress in Self Psychology, Vol. 1*, ed. A. Goldberg. New York: Guilford Press, pp. 202–26.

Bacal, H., and Newman, K. (1990). *Theories of Object Relations: Bridges to Self Psychology*. New York: Columbia.

Baddeley, A. (1986). *Working Memory*. New York: Oxford University Press.

———. (2000). The episodic buffer: A new component of working memory? *Trends in Cognitive Sciences*, 4:417–23.

Baddeley, A., and Hitch, G. (1974). Human memory: A proposed system and its control processes. In: *The Psychology of Learning and Motivation, Vol. 8*. Ed. K. Spence. New York: Academic Press, pp. 47–90.

Balint, E. (1953). On being empty of oneself. *The International Journal of Psychoanalysis*, 44:470–80.

Balint, M. (1950). Changing therapeutical aims and techniques in Psycho-Analysis. *International Journal of Psycho-Analysis*, 31:117–24.

———. (1952). *Primary Love and Psycho-Analytic Technique*. First edition. London: Hogarth.

———. (1968). *The Basic Fault: Therapeutic Aspects of Regression*. New York: Bruner/Mazel.

Banai, E., Mikulincer, M., and Shaver, P. (2005). "Selfobject" needs in Kohut's self psychology. *Psychoanalytic Psychology*, 22:224–60.

Barratt, B. (1993). *Psychoanalysis and the Postmodern Impulse: Knowing and Being Since Freud's Psychology*. Baltimore, MD: John Hopkins University Press.

Basch, M. (1976). The concept of affect: A re-examination. *Journal of the American Psychoanalytic Association*, 24:759–77.

———. (1981). Psychoanalytic interpretation and cognitive transformation. *International Journal of Psycho-Analysis*, 62:151–75.

———. (1983). Affect and the analyst. *Psychoanalytic Inquiry*, 3:691–703.

———. (1988). *Understanding Psychotherapy*. New York: Basic.

———. (1992). *Practicing Psychotherapy*. New York: Basic.

———. (1995). Kohut's contribution. *Psychoanalytic Dialogues*, 5:367–73.

Bauer, P. (1996). What do infants recall of their lives? *American Psychologist*, 51:29–41.

Baxter, L., Phelps, M., Mazziotta, J., Schwartz, J., Gerner, R., Selin, C., and Sumida, R. (1985). Cerebral metabolic rates for glucose in mood disorders. Studies with positron emission tomography and fluorodeoxyglucose. *Archives of General Psychiatry*, 42:441–47.

Beebe, B., and Lachmann, F. (1988). Mother-infant influence and precursors of psychic structure. In: *Frontiers in Self Psychology: Progress in Self Psychology, Vol. 3*, ed. A. Goldberg. Hillsdale, NJ: The Analytic Press, pp. 3–26.

———. (2002). *Infant Research and Adult Treatment: Co-constructing Interactions*. Hillsdale, NJ: The Analytic Press.

Bell, Charles (1806). Anatomy and physiology of expression. Referenced in Darwin, C. (1872) *The Expression of the Emotions in Man and Animals*. Chicago: Chicago University Press. 1965.

Benjamin, J. (1988). *Bonds of Love: Psychoanalysis, Feminism, and the Problem of Domination*. New York: Pantheon.

———. (1990). An outline of subjectivity: The development of recognition. *Psychoanalytic Psychology*, 7:33–46.

Bergson, H. (1988). *Time and Free Will*. Kila, MT: Kessinger Publishing.

Berman, E. (1981). Multiple personality: Psychoanalytic perspectives. *The International Journal of Psycho-Analysis*, 62:283–300.

Bethge, E. (1967). *Dietrich Bonhoeffer: A Biography*. Minneapolis: Fortress Press. (2000).

Bettleheim, B. (1969). *The Children of the Dream*. New York: Macmillan.

Bloch, S., Chodroff, P., and Green, S. (1999). Introduction. In: *Psychiatric Ethics*. Third Edition. Oxford: Oxford University Press.

Bonhoeffer, D. (1953). *Letters and Papers from Prison*. London: SCM Press.

Bouchard, D. (1972). A conversation between M. Focault and G. Deleuze: In: *Language, Counter-Memory, Practice: Selected Essays and Interviews by Michael Foucault*. Ed. D. Bouchard. Originally published in L'Arc #49, pp. 3–10.

Bowlby, J. (1969). *Attachment and Loss: Attachment, Vol.1*. New York: Basic.

———. (1973). *Attachment and Loss: Anxiety and Anger, Vol. 2*. New York: Basic.

———. (1980). *Attachment and Loss: Sadness and Depression, Vol.3*. New York: Basic.

Boyer, L., and Giovacchini, P. (1967). *Psychoanalytic Treatment of Schizophrenic, Borderline and Characterological Disorders*. New York: Aronson.

Bandchaft, B. (1994). Structures of pathological accommodation and change in analysis. Presented at the Association for Psychoanalytic Self Psychology, New York City.

Breggin, P. (1991). *Toxic Psychiatry*. New York: St. Martin's Press.

Bremner, J., Narayan, M., Staib, L., Southwick, S., McGlashan, T., and Charney, D. (1999). Neural correlates of memories of childhood sexual abuse in women with and without posttraumatic stress disorder. *American Journal of Psychiatry*, 156: 1787–795.

Breslow, R., Kocsis, J., and Belkin, B. (1980). Memory deficits in depression: Evidence utilizing the Wechsler Memory Scale. *Perceptual and Motor Skills*, 51:541–42.

Brittain, C. (1963). *The Shaping of Modern Thought*. New York: Prentice-Hall.

Bruner, J. (1969). Modalities of memory. In: *The Pathology of Memory*, eds. G. Talland and N. Waugh. New York: Academic Press.

Bryant, P., and Trabasco, T. (1971). Transitive inferences and memory in young children. *Nature*, 232: 456–58.

Buber, M. (1937). *I and Thou*. Edinburgh: Clark.

Buie, D. (1981). Empathy: Its nature and limitations. *Journal of the American Psychoanalytic Association*, 29:281–307.

Burroughs, A. (2002). *Running with Scissors*. New York: St. Martin's Press.

Burlingham, M. (1989). *The Last Tiffany*. New York: Atheneum.

Burlingham, M., and Freud, A. (1942). *Young Children in Wartime*. London: Allen and Unwin.

———. (1944). *Infants Without Families*. London: Allen and Unwin.

Campbell, D., and Fisk, D. (1959). Convergent and discriminating validation by the multitrait-multimethod matrix. *Psychological Bulletin*, 56:81–105.

Campos, J., Barrett, K., Lamb, M., Goldsmith, H., and Sternberg, C. (1983). Socio-emotional development. In: *Handbook of Child Psychology, Vol. 2, Infancy and Psychobiology*, ed. P. Mussen. New York: Wiley, pp. 783–915.

Cermak, L., Lewis, R., Butters, N., and Goodglass, H. (1973). Role of verbal mediation in performance of motor tasks by Korsakoff patients. *Perceptual and Motor Skills*, 37:259–262.

Chappell, P., and Sander, L. (1979). Mutual regulation of the neo-natal-maternal interactive process. In: M. Bullova, ed., *Before Speech—The Beginning of Interpersonal Communication*. Cambridge: Cambridge University Press.

Chessick, R. (1977). *Intensive Psychotherapy of the Borderline Patient*. Aronson: New York.

———. (1980). The problematic self in Kant and Kohut. *Psychoanalytic Quarterly*, 49:456–73.

———. (1999). *Emotional Illness and Creativity: A Psychoanalytic and Phenomenlogic Study*. Madison, CON: International Universities Press.

———. (2007). *The Future of Psychoanalysis*. Albany, NY: State University of New York.

Childs, R. (2003). Death in Venice: A selfobject perspective on Thomas Mann's homolimerance. In: *Explorations in Self Psychology: Progess in Self Psychology, Vol. 19*, ed. M Gerhrie. Hillsdale NJ: The Analytic Press, pp. 251–68.

Chodorow, N. (1999). Toward a relational individualism: The mediation of self through psychoanalysis. In: *Relational Psychoanalysis: The Emergent Tradition*, ed. S. Mitchell and L. Aron. Hillsdale, NJ: The Analytic Press.

Chomsky, N. (1972). *Studies in Semantics in Generative Grammar*. The Hague: Mouten.

Clark, C., McFarlane, A., Morris, P., Weber, D., Sonkkilla, C., Shaw, M., Marcina, J., Tochon-Danguy, and Egan, G. (2003). Cerebral function in posttraumatic stress disorder during verbal working memory updating: A positron emission tomography study. *Biological Psychiatry*, 53:474–81.

Clyman, R. (1991). The procedural organization of emotions: A contribution from cognitive science to the psychoanalytic theory of therapeutic action. *Journal of the American Psychological Association*, 39:349–82.

Cocks, G. (1994). *The Curve of Life: Correspondence of Heinz Kohut*. Chicago: Chicago Universities Press.

Coen, S. (2000). The wish to regress in patient and analyst. *Journal of the American Psychoanalytic Association*, 48:785–810.

Cohen, M., Baker, G., Cohen, R., Fromm-Reichmann, F., and Weigert, E. (1954). An intensive study of twelve cases of manic-depressive psychosis. *Psychiatry*, 17:103–37.

Cohen, N., Eichenbaum, H., Decedo, J., and Corkin, S. (1985). Preserved learning capacity in amnesia: Evidence for multiple memory systems. In: *Neuropsychology of Memory*. Eds. L. Squire and N. Butters. New York: The Guilford Press.

Cohen, N., and Squire, L. (1980). Preserved learning and retention of pattern-analyzing skill in amnesia: Dissociation of knowing how and knowing that. *Science*, 210:207–10.

Corkin, S. (1968). Acquisition of motor skill after bilateral medial temporary lobe excision. *Neuropsychologia*, 6:255–65.

Cozolino, L. (2002). *The Neuroscience of Psychotherapy: Building and Rebuilding the Human Brain*. New York: Norton.

Crittenden, P. (1988). Relationships at risk. In, *Clinical Implications of Attachment*, eds. J. Belsky, and T. Nezworsky. New York: Lawrence Erlbaum.

Damasio, A. (1999). *The Feeling of What Happens: Body and Emotion in the Making of Consciousness*. New York: Harcourt.

———. (2003). *Looking for Spinoza*. Orlando: Harcourt.

Darwin, C. (1872). *The Expression of the Emotions in Man and Animals*. Chicago: Chicago University Press. (1965).

Davidson, R., and Fox, N. (1982). Asymmetrical brain activity discriminates between positive verses negative affective stimuli in infants. *Science*, 218:1235–237.

Dawson, G., and Fischer, K. (1994), eds. *Human Behavior and the Developing Brain*. New York: Guilford Press.

DeBellis, M. (2005). The psychobiology of neglect. *Child Maltreatment*, 10:150–72.

Denton, D. (2005). *The Primordial Emotions: The Dawning of Consciousness*. Oxford: Oxford University Press.

Detrick, D. (1985). Alterego phenomena and the alterego transferences. In: *Progess in Self Psychology, Vol. 1*, ed. A. Goldberg. New York: Guilford, pp. 240–56.

Doi, T. (1971). *The Anatomy of Dependence*. Tokyo: Kodansha.

Doupe, A., and Konishi, M. (1991). Song-selective auditory circuits in the vocal control system of the zebra finch. *Proceedings of the National Acadamy of Science USA*, 88:11339–1343.

DSM IVR (Diagnostic and Statistical Manual of Mental Disorders IV—Text Revision). (2000). Arlington, VA: American Psychiatric Association.

Dupont, J. (1995). *The Clinical Diary of Sandor Ferenczi*. Cambridge, MA: Harvard University Press.

Eagle, R. (1984). *Recent Developments in Psychoanalysis*. Cambridge, MA: The Harvard University Press.

Eccles, J. (1970). *Facing Reality: Philosophical Adventures by a Brain Scientist*. New York: Springer-Verlag.

Edelman, G. (1987). *Neural Darwinism*. New York: Basic.

———. (1992). *Bright Air, Brilliant Fire: On the Matter of the Mind*. New York: Basic Books.

Eisenbud, J. (1991). *Love and Hate in the Nursery and Beyond: Voices from the Unconscious*. New York: Psyche Press.

Ekman, P., Levenson, R., and Friesen, W. (1983). Autonomic nervous system activity distinguishes among emotions. *Science*, 221, 1208–10.

Elkin, I., Shea, M., Watkins, J., Imber, S., Sotsky, S., Collins, J., Glass, D., Pilkonis, P., Leber, W., Docherty, J., and et al. (1989). National Institute of Mental Health.

Treatment of depression collaborative research program. General effectiveness of treatments. *Archives of General Psychiatry*, 46:971–82.

Engel, S. (1986). *Learning to Reminisce: A Developmental Study of How Young Children Talk About the Past.* Unpublished doctoral publication, City University of New York Graduate Center, New York.

English, O., and Pearson, G. (1963). *Emotional Problems of Living.* New York: Norton.

Ericsson, K., and Kintish, W. (1995). Long-term working memory. *Psychological Review*, 102:211–45.

Erikson, E. (1950). *Childhood and Society*. New York: Norton.

———. (1968). *Identity: Youth and Crisis*. New York: Norton.

Eslinger, P. (1998). Neurological and neuropsychological bases of empathy. *European Neurology*, 39:193–99.

Fast, I. (1998). *Selving: A Relational Theory of Self Organization.* Hillsdale, NJ: The Analytic Press.

Federn, P. (1926). Some variations in ego-feeling. *The International Journal of Psychoanalysis*, 7:434–44.

———. (1952). *Ego Psychology and the Psychoses*. New York: Basic.

Feiner, K., and Kiersky, S. (1994a). Empathy: A common ground. *Psychoanalytic Dialogues*, 4:425–40.

———. (1994b). Empathy is perception and interpretation (and who ever said it wasn't?): Reply to Ghent and Stern. *Psychoanalytic Dialogues*, 4:487–97.

Fenichel, O. (1945). *The Psychoanalytic Theory of Neurosis*. New York: Norton.

Ferenczi, S. (1913). Stages in the development of the sense of reality. In: *Contributions to Psychoanalysis*. Vol. 1. New York: Basic. (1950).

———. (1928a). The adaption of a child into a family. *British Journal of Medical Psychology*, 8:1–13.

———. (1931). Relaxation and education. In: *Final Contributions to the Problems and Methods of Psycho-Analysis*. New York:Brunner/Mazel. (1955).

Field, T., Woodson, R., Greenberg, R., and Cohen, D. (1982). Discrimination and imitation of facial expression by neonates. *Science*, 218:179–81.

Field, T., and Goldson, E. (1984). Pacifying effects of nonnutritive sucking on term and preterm neonates during heelstick procedures. *Pediatrics*, 74:1012–10–15.

Fivush, R., and Hammond, D. (1989). Time and again: Effects of repetition and retention interval on two year olds' event recall. *Journal of Experimental Psychology*, 47:259–73.

Fivush, R., and Reese, E. (1991). Parental styles for talking about the past. *Paper presented at the International Conference on Memory*. Lancaster, England.

Flavell, J. (1963). *The Developmental Psychology of Jean Piaget*. Princeton, NJ: Van Norstrand.

Fletcher, J. (1966). *Situation Ethics*. New York: Westminister.

Fodor, J. (1983). *The Modularity of Mind.* Cambridge MA: MIT Press.

Fonagy, P., Gergely, G., Jurist, E., and Tagart, M. (2002). *Affect Regulation, Mentalization, and the Development of the Self.* New York: Other Books.

Fonagy, P., Steele, H., and Steele, M. (1991). Maternal representations of attachment during pregnancy predict the organization of infant-mother attachment at one year of age. *Child Development*, 62:891–905.

Fonagy, P., Steele, M., Steele, H., Leigh, T., Kennedy, R., Mattoon, G., et al. (1995). Attachment, the reflective self, and borderline states: The predictive specificity of the Adult Attachment Interview and pathogical emotional development. In: S. Goldberg, R. Muir, and J. Kerr eds., *Attachment Theory: Social, Developmental and Clinical Perspectives*, pp. 223–79. Hillsdale, NJ: The Analytic Press.

Fonagy, P., Steele, M., Steele, H., Leigh, T., Kennedy, R., and Target, M. (1993). The predictive specificity of Mary Main's Adult Attachment Interview: Implications for psychodynamic theories of normal and pathological development. Presented at conference on "John Bowlby's attachment theory: Historical, clinical, and social significance," Toronto.

Fossage, J. (1997). Listening/experiencing perspectives and the quest for a facilitating responsiveness. In: *Conversations in Self Psychology: Progress in Self Psychology, Vol. 13*, ed. A. Goldberg. Hillsdale, NJ: The Analytic Press, pp. 33–55.

Frank, K. (1999). *Psychoanalytic Participation: Action, Interaction, and Integration*. Hillsdale, NJ: The Analytic Press.

Freud, A. (1965). *Normality and Pathology in Childhood*. New York: International Universities Press.

———. (1968). Indications and contraindications for child analysis. *Writings of Anna Freud*, 7:110–23.

———. (1970). The infantile neurosis. *Writings of Anna Freud*, 7:189–203.

———. (1976). Changes in psychoanalytic practice and experience. *International Journal of Psychoanalysis*, 57:257–60.

Freud, A., and Dann, S. (1951). An experiment in group upbringing. *Psychoanalytic Study of the Child*, 6:127–68.

Freud, S. (1891b). *On Aphasia*. London and New York. (1953).

———. (1900). Interpretation of dreams. *Standard Edition*, 4 and 5.

———. (1905D). Three essays on the theory of sexuality. *Standard Edition*, 7:125–43.

———. (1914). Remembering, repeating and working through. *Standard Edition*, 12:145–56.

———. (1917). Mourning and melancholia. *Standard Edition*, 14:243–58.

———. (1919). Lines of advance in psycho-analytic theory. *Standard Edition*, 17:157–68.

———. (1920). Beyond the pleasure principle. *Standard Edition*, 18:3–64.

———. (1921C). Group psychology and the analysis of the ego. *Standard Edition*, 18:67–143.

———. (1926D). Inhibitions, symptoms, and anxiety. *Standard Edition*, 20:70ff.

———. (1940A). An outline of psychoanalysis. *Standard Edition*, 23:141–207.

Friedman, L. (1978). Trends in the psychoanalytic theory of treatment. *Psychoanalytic Quarterly*, 47:524–67.

Fromm-Reichmann, F. (1950). *Principles of Intensive Psychotherapy*. Chicago: Chicago Universities Press Psychology, 47:259–73.

Gabbard, G. (1997). A reconsideration of objectivity in the analyst. *International Journal of Psycho-Analysis*, 78:15–26.

Gabbard, G., and Lester, E. (1995). *Boundaries and Boundary Violations in Psychoanalysis*. Washington, D.C.: American Psychiatric Publishing, Inc.

Gadamer, H. (1993). *Truth and Method*. New York: Continuum. (1960).

Gallese, V., Eagle, M., and Migone, P. (2007). Intentional attunement: Mirror neurons and the neural underpinnings of interpersonal relations. *Journal of the American Psychoanalytic Association*, 55: 131–76.

Gallese, V., Fadiga, L., Fogassi, L., and Rizzolattie, G. (1996). Action recognition in the premotor cortex. *Brain*, 119:593–609.

Gass, K., Jenkins, J., and Dunn, J. (2007). Are sibling relationships protective? A longitudinal study. *Journal of Child Psychology and Psychiatry*, 48:167–75.

Gay, P. (1988). *Freud: A Life for Our Time*. New York: Norton.

Gazzinga, M., and LeDoux, J. (1978). *The Integrated Mind*. New York: Plenum.

Gedo, J. (1988). Character, dyadic enactments, and the need for symbiosis. *Psychoanalytic Inquiry*, 8:459–71.

———. (1991). *The Biology of Clinical Encounters: Psychoanalysis as a Science of Mind*. Hillsdale, NJ: The Analytic Press.

Gesell, A. (1939). Reciprocal interweaving in neuromotor development. *Journal of Comparative Neurology*, 70:161–80.

Gianino, A., and Tronick, E. (1988). The mutual regulation model: The infant's self and interactive regulation coping and defense. In: *Stress and Coping*. Eds. T. Field, P. McCabe, and N. Schneidermann. Hillsdale, NJ: Erlbaum, pp. 47–68.

Gibson, E., and Walk, R. (1960). The 'visual cliff.' *Scientific American*, 202:64–71.

Goethe, J. (1990). *Faust*. Translated by Walter Kaufman. New York: Anchor Books

Goldberg, A. (1983). On the scientific status of empathy. *The Annual of Psychoanalysis*, 11:155–69.

———. (1988). *A Fresh Look at Psychoanalysis: The View from Self Psychology*. Hillsdale, NJ: The Analytic Press.

———. (1990). *The Prisonhouse of Psychoanalysis*. Hillsdale NJ: The Analytic Press.

———. (1995). *The Problem of Perversion: The View from Self Psychology*. New Haven: Yale University Press.

———. (1999). *Being of Two Minds: The Vertical Split in Psychoanalysis and Psychotherapy*. Hillsdale, NJ: The Analytic Press.

———. (2000). *Errant Selves: A Casebook of Misbehavior*. Hillsdale, NJ: The Analytic Press.

———. (2007). *Moral Stealth: How "Correct Behavior" Insinuates Itself into Psychotherapeutic Practice*. Chicago: Chicago University Press.

Goldman-Rakic, P. (1995). Anatomical and functional circuits in prefrontal cortex of non-human primates. Relevence to epilepsy. *Advances in Neurology*, 66:51–63.

Gordon, D. (1999). *Ants at Work: How an Insect Colony is Organized*. New York: Norton.

Greenacre, P. (1971). Notes on the influence and contribution of ego psychology to the practice of psychoanalysis. In: *Separation-individuation*, ed. J. McDevitt and C. Settlage. New York: International Universities Press, pp. 171–200.

Greenough, W., and Black, J. (1992). Induction of brain structure by experience: Substrates for cognitive development. In: *Minnesota Symposia on Child Psychology: Developmental Neuroscience*, eds. M. Gunnar and C. Nelson. Vol. 24. Hillsdale, NJ: Lawrence Erlbaum.

Grice, H. (1975). Logic and conversation. In: *Syntax and Semantics III: Speech Acts*. New York: Academic Press, pp. 41–58.

Grigsby, J., and Hartlaub, G. (1994). Procedural learning and the development and stability of character. *Perceptual and Motor Skills*, 79:355–70.

Grosskurth, P. (1986). *Melanie Klein: Her World and Her Work*. New York: Alfred A. Knopf.

Grotstein, J. (1983). Some perspectives in self psychology. In: *The Future of Psychoanalysis*, ed. A. Goldberg. New York: International Universities Press, pp. 165–201.

Guerlac, S. (2006). *Thinking in Time: An Introduction to Henri Bergson*. Ithica: Cornell University Press.

Guntrip, H. (1961). *Personality Structure and Human Interaction*. London: Hogarth.

Habermas, J. (1993). *Justification and Application: Remarks on Discourse Ethics*. Trans. A. Cronin. Cambridge, MA: MIT Press.

Hahn, L. (1995), ed. *The Philosophy of Paul Ricoeur*. Chicago: Open Court.

Hamilton, C. (1994). Continuity and discontinuity of attachment from infancy through adolescence. Doctoral dissertation, UC-Los Angeles, Los Angeles.

Hartmann, H. (1939). *Ego Psychology and the Problem of Adaptation*. Trans. D. Rapaport. New York: International Universities Press. (1958).

———. (1950). Comments on psychoanalytic theory of the ego. *The Psychoanalytic Study of the Child*, 5:74–96. New York: International University Press.

Hartmann, H., Kris, E., and Loewenstein, R. (1947). Comments on the formation of psychic structure. *The Psychoanalytic Study of the Child*, 2:11–38. New York: International Universities Press.

Hazan, C., and Shaver, P. (1987). Romantic love conceptualized as an attachment process. *Journal of Personality and Social Psychology*, 52:511–24.

Held, R., and Hein, A. (1963). Movement produced stimulation inn the development of visually guided behavior. *Journal of Comparative and Physiological Psychology*, 56:872–76.

Heller, M., and Yaynal, V. (1997). A doctor's face: Mirror of his patient's suicidal projects. In: *The Body in Psychotherapy*. Ed. J. Guimon. Basel, Switzerland: Karger.

Hendrick, I. (1948). *Facts and Theories of Psychoanalysis*. New York: Knopf.

Hertsgaard, L., Gunnar, M., Erickson, M., Farrell, and Nachmias, M. (1995). Adrenocortical responses to the Strange Situation in infants with disorganized/disoriented attachment relationships. *Child Development*, 66:1100–1106.

Hesse, M. (1974). *The Structure of Scientific Inference*. Berkley, CA: University of California Press.

Hikosaka, O. (1998). Neural systems for control of voluntary action—A hypothesis. *Advances in Biophysiology*, 35:81–102.

Hobson, R. (1985). *Forms of Feeling: The Heart of Psychotherapy*. London: Routledge.

Hoffman, I. (1983). The patient as interpreter of the analyst's experience. *Contemporary Psychoanalysis*, 19:389–422.

———. (1994). Dialectical thinking and therapeutic action in the psychoanalytic process. *Psychoanalytic Quarterly*, 63:187–218.

Hopf, C. (1993). Rechtsextremismus und Beziehungser fahrungen. Zeitchrist for soziologic, 22: 449–63.

Horowitz, A., and Wakefield, J. (2007). *The Loss of Sadness: How Psychiatry Transformed Normal Sorrow into Depressive Disorder*. Oxford: Oxford University Press.

Hudson, J. (1990). The emergence of autobiographic memory in mother-infant conversation. In: *Knowing and Remembering in Young Children*. Eds. R. Fivush and J. Hudson. New York: Cambridge University Press, pp. 160–96.

Hudson, J., and Fivush, R. (1991). As time goes by: Sixth graders remember a kindergarten experience. *Applied Cognitive Psychology*, 5:347–60.

Inhelder, B., and Piaget, J. (1964). *The Early Growth of Logic in the Child*. London: Routledge and Kegan Paul.

Insel, T. (2000). Toward a neurobiology of attachment. *Review of General Psychology*, 4:176–85.

Jackson, J. (1881). Dissolution in post-epileptic conditions. In: *Selected Writings of John Hughlings Jackson, Vol. 2.*, ed. J. Taylor, (1931–1932). London: Hodder, pp. 3–28.

———. (1884). Evolution and dissolution of the nervous system. In: *Selected Writings of John Hughlings Jackson, Vol. 2.*, ed. J. Taylor, (1931–1932). London: Hodder, pp. 45–75.

James, W. (1890). *The Principles of Psychology, Vols. 1 and 2*, New York: Dover. (1950).

———. (1902). *The Varieties of Religious Experience*. London: Longmans, Green & Co. (1928).

Jenkins, J., and Smith, M. (1990). Factors protecting children in disharmonious homes: Material reports. *Journal of the American Academy of Child and Adolescent Psychiatry*, 29:60–69.

Jung, W. (2003). The inner eye theory of laughter: Mindreader signals cooperator value. *Evolutionary Psychology*, 1:214–53.

Kandel, E. (2006). *In Search of Memory: The Emergence of the Science of the Mind*. New York: Norton.

Kandel, E., Schwartz, J., and Jessel, T. (1995). *Essentials of Neural Science and Behavior*. (3rd ed.). Norwork, CT: Appleton & Lange.

Kantrowitz, J. (1996). *The Patient's Impact on the Analyst*. Hillsdale, NJ: The Analytic Press.

Kegan, R. (1982). *The Evolving Self*. Cambridge, MA: Harvard University Press.

Kelso, J. (1995). *Dynamic Patterns: The Self-Organization of Brain and Behavior*. Cambridge, MA: The MIT Press.

Ketelaar, T., and Ellis, B. (2000). Are evolutionary explanations unfalsifiable? Evolutionary psychology and the Lakatosian philosophy of science. *Psychological Inquiry*, 11:1–21.
Kirsch, I., Moore, T., Scoboria, A., and Nicholls, S. (2002). The emporer's new drugs: An analysis of antidepressant medication data submitted to the U.S. Food and Drug Administration. *Prevention and Treatment*. 5 (1). Article 23.
Klein, M. (1935) A contribution to the psychogenesis of manic-depressive states. In: *Love, Guilt and Reparation and Other Works 1921–1945*.
———. (1957). Envy and gratitude. In: *Envy and Gratitude and Other Works 1946–1963*, New York: Dell, pp. 176–235.
Knight, R. (1946). Psychotherapy of an adolescent catatonic schizophrenic with mutism: A study in empathy and establishing contact. *Psychiatry*, 9:323–39.
———. (1953). Borderline states. *Bulletin of the Menninger Clinic*, 17:1–12.
Kohler, W. (1947). *Gestalt Psychology*. New York: Liveright.
Kohut, H. (1949). August Aichorn—remarks after his death. In: *Search for the Self, Vol. 1*. Ed. P. Ornstein. New York: International Universities Press, pp. 131–33. (1978).
———. (1957). Death in Venice by Thomas Mann: A story about the disintegration of artistic sublimation. In: *Search for the Self, Vol. 1*, ed. P. Ornstein. New York: International Universities Press, pp. 107–30. (1978).
———. (1959). Introspection, empathy, and psychoanalysis. In: *Search for the Self, Vol. 1*, ed. P. Ornstein. New York: International Universities Press, pp. 205–32. (1978).
———. (1966). Forms and transformations of narcissism. In: *Search for the Self, Vol. 1*, ed. P. Ornstein. New York: International Universities Press, pp. 427–60. (1978).
———. (1968). The psychoanalytic treatment of narcissistic personality disorders. In: *Search for the Self, Vol. 1*, ed. P. Ornstein. New York: International Universities Press, pp. 477–509. (1978).
———. (1969–1970). On leadership. In: *Search for the Self, Vol. 3*, ed. P. Ornstein. New York: International Universities Press, pp. 103–28. (1990).
———. (1970). Psychoanalysis in a troubled world. In: *Search for the Self, Vol.2*, ed. P. Ornstein. New York: International Universities Press, pp. 511–45. (1978).
———. (1970s). On courage. In: *Search for the Self, Vol. 3*, ed. P. Ornstein. New York: International Universities Press, pp. 129–81. (1990).
———. (1971). *The Analysis of the Self*. New York: International Universities Press.
———. (1972). Thoughts on narcissism and narcissistic rage. In: *Search for the Self, Vol. 2*, ed. P. Ornstein. New York: International Universities Press, pp. 615–58. (1978).
———. (1974). Remarks about the formation of the self. In: *Search for the Self, Vol. 2*, ed. P. Ornstein. New York: International Universities Press, pp. 737–70.
———. (1975). A note of female sexuality. *The Search for the Self, Vol. 2*, ed. P. Ornstein. New York: International Universities Press, pp. 783–92.
———. (1977). *The Restoration of the Self*. New York: International Universities Press.
———. (1978a, 1990, 1991). *The Search for the Self, Vols. 1, 2, 3, and 4*. Ed. P. Ornstein. New York: International Universities Press.

———. (1978b). Reflections on advances in self psychology. *In Search for the Self, Vol. 3*, ed. P. Ornstein. New York: International Universities Press, pp. 261–357. (1990).

———. (1979). The analysis of Mr. Z. In: *Search for the Self, Vol. 4*. Ed. P. Ornstein. New York: International Universities Press, pp. 395–46. (1991).

———. (1980). Selected problems in self-psychological theory. In: *Search for the Self, Vol. 4*. Ed. P. Ornstein. New York: International Universities Press, pp. 489–523. (1991).

———. (1981a). On empathy. In: *Search for the Self, Vol. 4*, ed. P. Ornstein. New York: International Universities Press, pp. 525–35.

———. (1981b). Introspection, empathy, and the circle of mental health. In: *The Search for the Self, Vol. 4*, ed. P. Ornstein. New York: International Universities Press, pp. 537–67.

———. (1981c). Letters 1981. In: *The Search for the Self, Vol. 4*, ed. P. Ornstein. New York: International Universities Press, pp. 684–711.

———. (1981d). "One needs a twinkle of humor as a protection against craziness." Interview with C. Stozier, March 12, 1981. In: *Self Psychologies and the Humanities: Reflections on a New Psychoanalytic Approach*. Ed. C. Strozier, pp. 244–53.

———. (1984). *How Does Analysis Cure?* Chicago: Chicago University Press.

———. (1987). *The Kohut Seminars on Self Psychology and Psychotherapy with Adolescents and Young Adults*, ed. M. Elson. New York: Norton.

———. (1996). *Chicago Institute Lectures*, eds. P. and M. Tolpin. The Analytic Press.

Kohut, H., and Levarie, S. (1950). On the enjoyment of listening to music. In: *The Search for the Self, Vol. 1*, ed. P. Ornstein. New York: International Universities Press, pp. 135–58.

Kohut, H., and Wolf, E. (1978). Disorders of the self and their treatment. In: *Search for the Self, Vol. 3*, ed. P. Ornstein. New York: International Universities Press, pp. 359–85. (1990).

Kris, E. (1952). *Psychoanalytic Exploration in Art*. New York: International Universities Press.

Kristiva, J. (1987). *In the Beginning Was Love*. New York: Columbia University Press.

Krystal, H. (1988). *Integration and Self-healing: Affect-trauma-alexthymia*. Hillsdale, NJ: The Analytic Press.

Kubie, L. (1953). "Say you're sorry." *The Psychoanalytic Study of the Child*, 10:289–99.

———. (1975). The language tools of psychoanalysis: A search for better tools drawn from better models. *International Review of Psycho-Analysis*, 2:11–24.

Kubler-Ross, E. (1969). *On Death and Dying*. New York: Macmillan.

Kuhn, T. (1962). *The Structures of Scientific Revolutions*. Chicago: Chicago Universities Press.

Kupfermann, I., Castellucci, V., Pinsker, H., and Kandel, E. (1970). Neuronal correlates of habituation and dishabituation of the gill-withdrawal reflex in Aplysia. *Science*. 167:1743–1745.

Lacan, J. (1977). *Ecrits:A Selection*, trans. A Sheridan. New York: Norton.

Lachmann, A. (1999). The theme of cuckoldry in Othello. Paper presented at the 22nd Annual Conference of the Psychology of the Self, Toronto, Canada, October.

Lachmann, F. (2000). *Transforming Aggression*. New York: Aronson.

Lakatos, I. (1970). Falsification and the methodology of scientific research programmes. In I. Lakatos and A. Musgrave (eds), *Criticism and the Growth of Knowledge*. Cambridge, England: Cambridge University Press, pp. 91–196.

———. (1974). Popper on demarcation and induction. In P. Schlipp (ed.), *The Philosophy of Karl Popper* pp. 241–73.

Lampl-De Groot, J. (1981). Notes on "multiple personality." *The Psychoanalytic Quarterly*, 50:614–24.

———. (1983). On the process of mourning. *The Psychoanalytic Study of the Child*, 38:9–13.

Langer, S. (1967). *Mind: An Essay on Human Feeling, Vol.1*. Baltimore: John Hopkins University Press.

Laudan, L. (1984). *Science and Values: The Aims of Science and Their Role in Scientific Debate*. Berkley: University of California Press.

Laughlin, R. (2005). *A Different Universe: Reinventing Physics from the Bottom Down*. New York: Basic Books.

LeDoux, J. (1996). *The Emotional Brain: The Mysterious Underpinnings of Life*. New York: Touchstone.

———. (2002). *Synaptic Self: How Our Brains Become Who We Are*. New York: Viking.

LeDoux, J., and Gorman, J. (2001). A call to action: Overcoming anxiety through active coping. *American Journal of Psychiatry*, 158:1953–1955.

Lee, H. (1996). *Virginia Wolf*. London: Chatto and Windus.

Lee, R. (1988). The reverse selfobject experience. *American Journal of Psychotherapy*, 42:416–24.

———. (1993). Perfectionism and self-cohesiveness. Presented to the Canberra Self Psychology Seminar, June 2003.

———. (1994). Cohesive functions of the self. Paper presented to the American Institute of Medical Education conference, Santa Fe, August 1994.

———. (1998). Empathy and affects: An intersubjective view. *Australian Journal of Psychotherapy*, 17:126–49.

———. (1999). An infant's experience as a selfobject. *American Journal of Psychotherapy*, 53:177–187.

———. (2003). The humiliating patient and the humiliated psychotherapist. Presented to the Canberra Self-Psychology Seminar, June 2003; Eric Seal lecture, St. Vincent's Mental Health, Melbourne, August 2007.

———. (2004). Psychotherapeutic Alliances. Presented to Empathink workshop, June 2004.

———. (2005). Psychotherapy supervision: A self-psychology view. Presented to the Canberra Self-Psychology Seminar, June 2005.

Lee, R., and Martin, J. (1991). *Psychotherapy After Kohut: A Textbook in Self Psychology*. Hillsdale, NJ: The Analytic Press.

Lehrman, D. (1970). Semantic and conceptual issues in the nature-nurture problem. In: *Development and the Evolution of Behavior*. Eds. L. Aronson, E. Tobach, D. Lehrman, and J. Rodenblatt. San Francisco: Freeman, pp. 17–52.

Levin, D. (1969). The self: A contribution to its place in theory and technique. *International Journal of Psychoanalysis*, 50: 41–51.

Lichtenberg, J. (1989). *Psychoanalysis and Motivation*. Hillsdale, NJ: The Analytic Press.

Lindner, R. (1955). *The Fifty Minute Hour: A Collection of True Psychoanalytic Tales*. New York: Rinehart. Reprinted (1982).

Liotti, G. (1992). Disorganized/disoriented attachment in the etiology of dissociative disorders. *Dissociation*, 4:196–204.

Llinas, R. (2001). *I of the Vortex: From Neurons to Self*. Cambridge MA: Bradford Press.

Loewald, H. (1960). On the therapeutic action of psychoanalysis. In: *Papers on Psychoanalysis*. New Haven, CT: Yale University Press, pp. 221–56.

———. (1973). On internalization. In: *Papers on Psychoanalysis*. New Haven, CT: Yale University Press, pp. 69–86. (1980).

———. (1980). *Papers on Psychoanalysis*. New Haven, CT: Yale University Press.

Lyons-Ruth, K. (1998). Implicit relational knowing: Its role in development and psychoanalytic treatment. *Infant Mental Health Journal*, 19:282–89.

MacLean, P. (1970). The triune brain, emotion and scientific bias. In: *The Neurosciences: Second Study Program*, ed. F. Schmitt. New York: Rockefeller University Press, pp. 336–49.

Macmurray, J. (1957). *The Self as Agent*. New Jersey: Humanities Press. (1991).

———. (1961). *Persons in Relation*. New Jersey: Humanities Press. (1999).

Main, M. (1996). Introduction to the special section on attachment and psychopathology: 2 Overview of the field of attachment. *Journal of Consulting and Clinical Psychology*, 64:237–43.

———. (1997). Attachment narratives and attachment across the lifespan. Paper presented at the Fall Meeting of the American Psychoanalytic Association, New York.

Main, M., and Goldwyn, R. (1985–1994). Adult attachment scoring and classification system. Unpublished scoring manual, Department of Psychology, University of California, Berkley.

Main, M., and Hesse, E. (1990). Parents' unresolved traumatic experiences are related to infant disorganized attachment status: Is frightened and/or frightening parental behavior the linking mechanism? In: *Attachment in Preschool Years*. Eds. M. Greenberg, D. Cichetti, and E. Cummings. Chicago: Chicago University Press, pp. 161–82.

Main, M., Kaplan, N., and Cassidy, J. (1985). Security in infancy, childhood, and adulthood: A move to the level of representation. In: I. Bretherton and E. Waters, eds., *Growing Points in Attachment Theory and Research*. *Monographs of the Society for Research in Child Development*, 50 (1–2, Serial No. 203), pp. 66–107.

Main, M., and Solomon, M. (1986). Discovery of an insecure disorganized/disoriented attachment pattern. In: *Affective Development in Infancy*. Norwood, NJ: Ablex.

Maltsberger, J., and Buie, D. (1974). Countertransference hate in the treatment of suicidal patients. *Archives of General Psychiatry*, 30:625–33.

———. (1980). The devices of suicide: Revenge, riddance, and rebirth. *International Review of Psychoanalysis*, 7:61–72.

Mandler, J. (1988). How to build a baby: On the development of an accessible representational system. *Cognitive Development*, 3:113–36.

Maroda, K. (1999a). *Seduction, Surrender and Transformation*. Hillsdale, NJ: The Analytic Press.

———. (1999b). Creating an intersubjective context for self-disclosure. *Smith College Studies in Social Work*, 69:475–89.

McGraw, M. (1945). *The Neuromuscular Maturation of the Human Infant*. New York: Columbia University Press.

Meares, R. (1988). On boundary formation. *Progress in Self Psychology: Frontiers in Self Psychology, Vol. 3*, pp. 237–52.

———. (2004). The conversational model: An outline. *American Journal of Psychotherapy*, 58:51–64.

Meares, R., Stevenson, J., and Comerford, A. (1999). Psychotherapy with borderline patients: I. A comparison between treated and untreated cohorts. *Australian and New Zealand Journal of Psychiatry*, 33: 467–72.

Megargee, E., Cook, P., and Mendelsohn, G. (1967). Development and validation of an MMPI scale of assaultiveness in overcontrolled individuals. *Journal of Abnormal Psychology*, 72:519–28.

Meins, E., and Fernyhough, C. (1999). Linguistic acquisitional style and mentalizing development: The role of maternal mind-mindedness. *Cognitive Development*, 14:363–80.

Meins, E., Fernyhough, C., Russell, J., and Clark-Carter, D. (1998). Security of attachment as a predictor of symbolic or mentalizing abilities: A longitudinal study. *Social Development*, 1–24.

Meltzoff, A. (1988). Infant imitation and memory: Nine-month-olds in immediate and deferred tests. *Child Development*, 59:217–25.

———. (1990). Foundations for developing a concept of the self. The role of imitation in relating self to other and the value of social mirroring, social modeling, and self practice in infancy. In: *The Self in Transition*, ed. D. Cicchetti and M. Beeghly. Chicago: Chicago University Press.

Meltzoff, A., and Borton, W. (1979). Intermodal matching by human neonates. *Nature*, 282:403–4.

Meltzoff, A., and Gopnik, A. (1993). The role of imitation in understanding persons and developing a theory of the mind. In: *Understanding Other Minds*, ed. S Baron-Cohen, H. Tager-Flusberg, and D. Cohen. Oxford: Oxford University Press.

Menninger, K. (1963). *The Vital Balance*. New York: Viking.

Mesulam, M. (1998). From sensation to cognition. *Brain*, 121:1013–1052.

Meyers, C., Berman, S., Scheibel, R., and Hayman, A. (1992). Case report: Acquired antisocial personality disorder associated with unilateral left orbital frontal lobe damage. *Journal of Psychiatry and Neuroscience*, 17:121–25.

Miller, G. (1956). The magical number of seven, plus or minus two. *Psychological Review*, 63:81–96.

Mitchell, S., and (1988). *Relational Concepts in Psychoanalysis*. Cambridge, MA: Harvard University Press.

———. (1993). *Hope and Dread in Psychoanalysis*. New York: Basic Books.

Mitchell, S. & Black, M. (1995). *Freud and Beyond: A History of Modern Psychoanalytic Thought*. New York: Basic Books.

MMPI (Minnesota Multiphasic Personality Inventory) *Handbook*,. (1975). Vols. 1 and 2. Minneapolis: University of Minnesota Press.

Moss, D., and Lee, R. (1976). Homogamous and heterogamous marriages. *International Journal of Psychoanalytic Psychotherapy*, 5:395–412.

Muslin, H. (1984). Shakespeare and the psychology of the self: The case of Othello. In: *Kohut's Legacy: Contributions to Self Psycholgy*, ed. P. Stepansky and A. Goldberg. Hillsdale NJ: The Analytic Press.

Nauta, W. (1971). The problem of the frontal lobe: A reinterpretation. *Journal of Psychiatric Research*, 8:167–87.

Nelson, K. (1986). *Event Knowledge: Structure and Function in Development*. Hillsdale, NJ: Lawrence Erlbaum Associates.

———. (1989). *Narratives from the Crib*. Cambridge MA: Harvard University Press.

———. (1993). The psychological and social origins of autobiographical memory. *Psychological Science*, 4:7–14.

Nishitani, N., Schurmann, M., Amunts, K. and Hari, R. (2005). Brocas' region: From action to language. *Physiology*, 20:60–69.

Nyberg, L., and Tulving, E. (1996). PET studies of encoding and retrieval. The HERA model. *Psychonomic Bulletin and Review*, 2:134–47.

O'Conner, T., Bredenkamp, D., Rutter, M., et al. (1999). Attachment disturbances and disorders in children exposed to early severe deprivation. *Infant Mental Health Journal*, 20:10–29.

Orange, D. (1995). *Emotional Understanding: Studies in Psychoanalytic Epistemology*. New York: Guilford.

Orange, D., Atwood, G., and Stolorow, R. (1997). *Working Intersubjectivity: Contextualism in Psychoanalytic Practice*. Hillsdale, NJ: The Analytic Press.

Ornstein, P. (1978). Introduction: The evolution of Heinz Kohut's psychoanalytic psychology of the self. In: *The Search for the Self: Selected Writings of Heinz Kohut: 1950–1978*, ed. P. Ornstein. New York: International Universities Press, pp. 1–106.

Panksepp, J. (1998). *Affective Neuroscience: The Foundations of Human and Animal Emotions*. New York: Oxford University Press.

Panksepp, J., Moskal, J., Panksepp, J. B., and Kroes, R. (2002). Comparative approaches in evolutionary psychology: Molecular neuroscience meets the mind. *Neuroendocrinology Letters*, 23: 105–15.

Papez, J. (1937). A proposed mechanism of emotion. *Archives of General Psychiatry*, 79:217–24.
Passmore, J. (1985). *Recent Philosophers*. La Salle, IL: Open Court. (1992).
Perry, B. (1996). Childhood trauma, the neurobiology of adaptation, and "use-dependent" development of the brain: How "states" become "traits." *Infant Mental Health Journal*, 16:271–91.
Piaget, J. (1951). *Play, Dreams, and Imitations in Childhood*. New York: Norton.
———. (1952). *The Origins of Intelligence in Children*. New York: International Universities Press.
———. (1954). *The Construction of Reality in the Child*. New York: Basic.
———. (1970). *Psychology and Epistemology*. New York: Norton.
Piaget, J., and Inhelder, B. (1969). *The Psychology of the Child*. New York: Basic.
Pillemer, D., and White, S. (1989). Childhood events recalled by children and adults. In: *Advances in Child Development and Behavior, Vol. 21*, ed. H. Reese. New York: Academic Press, pp. 297–340.
Popper, K. (1957). *The Poverty of Historicism*. New York: Harper and Row.
———. (2002). *The Logic of Scientific Discovery*. New York: Routledge (1934).
Post, R. (1992). Transduction of psychosocial stress into the neurobiology of recurrent affective disorder. *American Journal of Psychiatry*, 149: 999–1010.
Potter, M. (1975). Meaning in visual search. *Science*, 187:965–66.
Quine, W. (1953). Two dogmas of empiricism. In: *From a Logical Point of View*. Cambridge, MA, Harvard University Press.
Raine, A., Buchsbaum, M., Stanley, J., Lottenberg, S., Abel, L., and Stoddard, J. (1994). Selective reductions in prefrontal glucose metabolism in murderers. *Biological Psychiatry*, 36:365–73.
Ramachandran, V. (2006). Mirror neurons and imitation learning as the driving force behind "the great leap forward" in human evolution, www.edge.org/3rd_culture/ramachandran/ramachandran_pl.html
Rauch, S., van der Kolk, B., Fisler, R., Alpert, N., Orr, S., Savage, C., Fischman, A., Jenike, M., and Pitman, R. (1996). A symptom provocation study of posttraumatic stress disorder using positron emission tomography and script-driven imagery. *Archives of General Psychiatry*, 53:380–87.
Read, G. (1996). *Clinical Understanding*. Northvale, NJ: Aronson.
Reik, T. (1937). *Surprise and the Psychoanalyst*. New York: Dutton.
Rhodes, R. (1986) *The Making of the Atomic Bomb*. New York: Simon and Schuster.
Richardson, A. (1950). *A Theological Word Book of the Bible*. London: SCM Press.
Riley, J., Greggers, U., Smith, A., Reynolds, D., and Menzel, R. (2005). The flight path of honeybees recruited by the waggle dance. *Nature*, 435:205–7.
Rippa, S. (1971). *Education in a Free Society*. 2nd Edition. New York: David McKay Company.
Rogers, C. (1961). *On Becoming a Person*. Boston: Houghton Mifflin.
Rovee-Collier, C., and Fagen, J. (1981). The retrieval in early memory. In: *Advances in Infancy Research, Vol. 1*, ed. L. Lipsitt. Norwood: NJ: Ablex.

Rovee-Collier, C., and Hayne, H. (1987). Reactivation of infant memory: Implications for cognitive development. In: *Advances in Child Development and Behavior, Vol. 20.*, ed. H. Reese. New York: Academic Press, pp. 185–283.

Rovee-Collier, C., and Lipsitt, L. (1981). Learning, adaptation and memory. In: *Psychobiology of the Human Newborn*, ed. P. Stratton. New York: Wiley.

Rovee-Collier, C., Sullivan, M., Lucas, D., and Fagen, J. (1980). Reactivism of infant memory. *Science*, 208:1159–61.

Sander, L. (1977). Regulation and exchange in the infant-caregiver system: A viewpoint on the ontogeny of structures. In: *Communicative Structures and Psychic Structures*, ed. N. Feedman and S. Grand. New York: Plenum, pp. 13–34.

Sandler, J. (1983). Reflections on some relations between psychoanalytic concepts and psychoanalytic practice. *International Journal of Psycho-Analysis*, 64:35–46.

Schacter, D. (1983). Amnesia observed: Remembering and forgetting in a natural environment. *Journal of Abnormal Psychology*, 92: 236–42.

———. (1987). Memory, amnesia, and frontal lobe dysfunction. *Psychobiology*, 15:21–36.

———. (1996). *Searching for Memory: The Brain and the Mind, and the Past.* New York: Basic Books.

Schafer, R. (1959). Generative empathy in the treatment situation. *Psychoanalytic Quarterly*, 28:342–73.

———. (1968). *Aspects of Internalization.* New York: International Universities Press.

———. (1972) Internalization: Process or fantasy? *The Psychoanalytic Study of the Child*, 27:411–36.

———. Action: Its place in psychoanalytic interpretation and theory. *Annual of Psychoanalysis*, 1: 159–96.

———. (1976). *A New Language for Psychoanalysis.* New Haven, CT: Yale University Press.

Schank, R., and Abelson, R. (1977). *Scripts, Plans, Goals, and Understanding.* Hillsdale, NJ: Erlbaum.

Schlesinger, H. (2005). *Endings and Beginnings: On Terminating Psychotherapy and Psychoanalysis.* Hillsdale, NJ: The Analytic Press.

Schlinger, B., and Arnold, A. (1991). Androgen effects on the development of the zebra finch song system. *Brain Research*, 61:99–105.

Schon, D. (1983). *The Reflective Practitioner: How Professionals Think in Action.* New York: Basic Books.

Schore, A. (1994). *Affect Regulation and the Origin of the Self.* Hillsdale, NJ: Lawrence Erlbaum.

———. (1996). The experience-dependent maturation of a regulatory system in the orbital prefrontal cortex and the origin of developmental psychopathology. *Development and Psychopathology*, 8:59–87.

———. (1997). Early organization of the nonlinear right brain and development of a predisposition to psychiatric disorders. *Development and Psychopathology*, 595–631).

———. (2003). *Affect Regulation and the Repair of the Self.* New York: Norton.

Schwaber, E. (1992). Countertransference: The analyst's retreat from the patient's vantage point. *International. Journal of Psycho-Analysis*, 73:349–36.
Searle, J. (1999). *The Rediscovery of the Mind*. Cambridge, MA: The MIT Press.
Shane, M., Shane, E., and Gales, M. (1997). *Intimate Attachments: Towards a New Self Psychology*. New York: Guilford.
Shin, L., McNally, R., Kosslyn, S., Thompson, W., Rauch, S., Alpert, N., et al. (1999). Regional cerebral blood flow during script-imagery in childhood sexual abuse-related PTSD: A PET investigation. *American Journal of Psychiatry*, 156:575–84.
Siegel, D. (1999). *The Developing Mind*. New York: Guilford.
Skinner, B. (1953). *Science and Behavior*. New York: Macmillan.
Slade, A. (2005). Parental reflective functioning: An introduction. *Attachment and Human Development*, 7:269–81.
Slavin, M., and Kriegman, D. (1992). *The Adaptive Design of the Human Psyche: Psychoanalysis, Evolutionary Biology and the Therapeutic Process*. New York: The Guilford Press.
Solms, M., and Turnbull, O. (2002). *The Brain and the Inner World: An Introduction to the Neuroscience of Subjective Experience*. New York: Other Press.
Spangler, G., and Grossman, K. (1993). Biobehavioral organization in securely and insecurely attached infants. *Child Development*, 64:1439–1450.
Spencer, H. (1867). *First Principles*. Westport, CT: Greenwood Press. (1976).
Spezzano, C. (1993). *Affect in Psychoanalysis: A Clinical Synthesis*. Hillsdale, NJ: The Analytic Press.
Spitz, R. (1945). Hospitalism: An inquiry into the genesis of psychiatric conditions in early childhood. *The PsychoAnalytic Study of the Child, Vol. 1*, pp. 53–74.
———. (1946). Hospitalism: A follow-up report. *The PsychoAnalytic Study of the Child, Vol. 2*, pp. 113–17.
Squire, L. (1992). Memory and hippocampus: A synthesis from findings with rats, monkeys, and humans. *Psychological Review*, 99:195–231.
Sroufe, L., Egeland, B., Carlson, E., and Collins, W. (2005). *The Development of the Person: The Minnesota Study of Risk and Adaptation from Birth to Childhood*. New York: The Guilford Press.
Steinthal, H. (1881). *Einletting in die Psychologie und Sprachwissenschaft*. Translated by W. James, Principles of Psychology, Vol. 2, p. 108. (1890).
Stepansky, P. (1977). *A History of Aggression in Freud*. New York: International Universities Press.
Stern, Daniel. (1974). Mother and infant at play: The dyadic interaction involving facial, vocal, and gaze behaviors. In: M. Lewis and L. Rosenblum, eds. *The Effect of the Infant on Its Caregiver*. New York: Wiley.
———. (1985). *The Interpersonal World of the Infant*. New York: Basic.
Stern, Donnel. (1983). Unformulated experience—from familiar to chaos to creative disorder. *Contemporary Psychoanalysis*, 19:71–99.
———. (1991). A philosophy for the embedded analyst—Gadamer's hermeneutics and the social paradigm of psychoanalysis. *Contemporary Psychoanalysis*, 27:51–80.

———. (1992). Commentary on constructivism in clinical psychoanalysis. *Psychoanalytic Dialogues*, 2:331–63.

Stolorow, R., and Atwood, G. (1979). *Faces in a Cloud: Subjectivity in Personality Theory*. New York: Aronson.

———. (1992). *Contexts of Being: The Intersubjective Foundations of Psychological Life*. Hillsdale, NJ: The Analytic Press.

Stolorow, R., Atwood, G., and Brandchaft, B. (1994). *The Intersubjective Perspective*. Hillsdale NJ: The Analytic Press.

Stolorow, R., Atwood, G., and Orange, D. (2002). *Worlds of Experience: Interweaving Philosophical and Clinical Dimensions in Psychoanalysis*. New York: Basic.

Stolorow, R., Brandchaft, B., and Atwood, G. (1987). *Psychoanalytic Treatment: An Intersubjective Approach*. Hillsdale NJ: The Analytic Press.

Stolorow, R., and Lachmann, F. (1980). *Psychoanalysis of Developmental Arrests*. New York: International Universities Press.

Stone, L. (1961). *The Psychoanalytic Situation*. New York: International Universities Press.

———. (1981). Notes on the noninterpretive elements in the psychoanalytic situation and process. *Journal of the American Psychoanalytic Association*, 29:89–118.

Strozier, C. (2001). *Heinz Kohut:The Making of a Psychoanalyst*. New York: Farrar, Straus and Giroux. (Biography).

Stuss, D., Gallup, G., and Alexander, M. (2001). The frontal lobes are necessary for "theory of mind." *Brain*, 124:279–86.

Sullivan, H. (1953). *The Interpersonal Theory of Psychotherapy*. New York: Norton.

Swales, P. (1986). Freud, his teacher, and the birth of psychoanalysis. In: *Freud Appraisals and Reappraisals*, *Vol. 1*, ed. P. Stepansky. Hillsdale, NJ: The Analytic Press.

Tausk, V. (1933). On the origins of the 'influencing machine' in schizophrenia. *Psychoanalytic Quarterly*, 2:519–56.

Taylor, S., Klein, L., Lewis, B., Gruenewald, R., Gurung, A., and Updegraff, J. (2002). Bio-behavioral responses to stress in females: Tend-and-befriend, not fight-or-flight. *Psychological Review*, 107:411–29.

Teicholtz, J. (1999). *Kohut, Loewald, and the Postmoderns: A Comparitive Study of Self and Relationship*. Hillsdale, NJ: The Analytic Press.

Terman, D. (1980). Object love and psychology of the self. In: *Advances in Self Psychology*, ed. A. Goldberg. New York: International Universities Press.

Terr, L. (1994). *Unchained Memories*. New York: Basic.

Tessler, M. (1986). *Mother-child Talk in a Museum: The Socialization of a Memory*. Unpublished manuscript, City University of New York Graduate Center. New York.

———. (1991). Making memories together: The influence of mother-child encoding on the developmental of autobiographical memory style. Unpublished doctoral dissertation. City University of New York Graduate Center, New York.

Thelen, E., and Smith, L. (1998). *A Dynamic Systems Approach to the Development of Cognition and Action*. Cambridge, MA: The MIT Press.

Tillich, P. (1953). *Systematic Theology, Vol. 1*. London: Nisbert & Co.

Tinbergen, N. (1966). *Animal Behavior*. New York: Time Life.
Titchener, E. (1912). The schema of introspection. *American Journal of Psychology*, 23:485–508.
Tolpin, M. (1971). On the beginnings of a cohesive self. In: *The Psychoanalytic Study of the Child*, 26:316–352. New York: Quadrangle Books.
———. (1974). The daedalus experience: A developmental vicissitude of the grandiose fantasy. *Annual of Psychoanalysis*, 2:213–28.
———. (1978). Self-objects and oedipal objects—a crucial developmental distinction. *Psychoanalytic Study of the Child*, 33:167–84.
———. (1993). The unmirrored self, compensatory structure, and cure: The exemplary case of Anna O. *The Annual of Psychoanalysis*, 21:157–77.
———. (1997). Compensatory structures: Paths to the restoration of the self. *Progress in Self Psychology*, 13:3–19.
———. (2002). Doing psychoanalysis of normal development: Forward edge transferences. In: *Postmodern Self Psychology: Progress in Self Psychology, Vol. 18*. Hillsdale, NJ: The Analytic Press, pp. 167–92.
Tomkins, S. (1962, 1963, 1991, 1992). *Affect, Imagery, Consciousness*, Vols. 1–4. New York: Singer.
Tronick, E., and Cohn, J. (1989). Infant-mother face-to-face interaction: Age and gender differences in co-ordination and occurance in misco-ordination. *Child Development*, 60:85–92.
Tronick, E., Sander, L., Lyons-Ruth, K., Stern, D., Harrison, A., Nahum, J., Bruschweiler-Stern, N., and Morgan, A. (1998). Interventions that effect change in psychotherapy: A model based on infant research. Commentaries by Beebe, B., Modell, A., and Fonagy, P. *Infant Mental Health Journal*, 19:277–353.
Tulving, E. (1985). Memory and consciousness. *Canadian Psychology*, 25:1–12.
———. (1993). What is episodic memory? *Current Directions in Psychological Science*, 2:67–70.
Tulving, E., Kapur, S., Craik, F., Moscovitch, M., and Houle, S. (1994). Neurological of retrieval in episodic memory: Auditory sentence recognition. *Proceedings of the National Academy of Sciences USA*, 91:2012–2015.
Tulving, E., and Schacter, D. (1990). Priming and human memory system. *Science*, 247: 301–5.
Vaillant, G. (2002). *Aging Well*. New York: Little Brown and Company.
Van der Kolk, B. (1996). The body keeps the score: Approaches to the psychobiology of posttraumatic stress disorder. In: *Traumatic Stress: The Effects of Overwhelming Experience on Mind, Body, and Society*, eds. B. van der Kolk, A. McFarlane, and A. Weisaeth. New York: Guildford, pp. 214–41.
———. (2006). Clinical implications of neuroscience research in PTSD. *Annals of the New York Academy of Science*. In press.
Van Ijzendoorn, M. (1995). Adult attachment representations, paternal responsiveness and infant attachment: A meta-analysis on the predictive validity of the Adult Attachment Interview. *Psychological Bulletin*, 117:387–403.

Wallerstein, R. (1986). *Forty-two Lives in Treatment*. New York: Guilford.

Waters, E., Merrick, S., Albersheim, L., Treboux, D., and Crowell, J. (1995). From the strange situation to the Adult Attachment Interview: A 20-year longitudinal study of attachment security in infancy and early adulthood. Presented at the Society for Research in Child Development. Indianapolis.

Watson, J. (1925). *Behaviorism*. New York: Norton Press.

Watzlawick, P. (1984). Foreword. In: *The Invented Reality: How Do We Know What We Believe We Know?* (Contributions to Constructivism), ed. P. Watzlawick. New York: Norton, pp. 9–11.

Weinberg, M., and Tronick, E. (1994). Beyond the face: An empirical study of infant affective configurations of facial, vocal, gestural, and regulatory behaviors. *Child Development*, 65:1503–1515.

Westen, D., and Morrison, K. (2001). A multidimentional meta-analysis of treatments for depression, panic, and generalized anxiety disorder: An empirical examination of the status of empirically supported therapies. *Journal of Consulting and Clinical Psychology*, 69:875–99.

Wheeler, M., Stuss, D., and Tulving, E. (1997). Toward a theory of episodic memory: The frontal lobes and autonoetic consciousness. *Psychological Bulletin*, 121:331–54.

Whelan, P. (1996). Control of locomotion in the decerebrate cat. *Progress in Neurobiology*, 49:481–515.

Williams, B. (1985). *Ethics and Limits of Philosophy*. Cambridge, MA: Harvard University Press.

Williams, M. (1992). Exploitation and inference: Mapping the damage from therapist-patient sexual involvement. *American Psychologist*, 47:412–21.

Winnicott, D. (1945). Primitive emotional development. In: *Through Paediatrics to Psycho-Analysis*. New York: Basic, pp. 145–56.

———. (1953). Transitional objects and transitional phenomenon. In: *Through Paediatrics to Psycho-Analysis*. New York: Basic, pp. 229–42.

———. (1960). True and false self. In: *The Maturational Processes and the Facilitating Environment*. New York: International Universities Press.

———. (1974). *The Maturational Processes and the Facilitating Environment*. Fourth Edition. New York: International Universities Press.

Wise, C. (1983). *Pastoral Psychotherapy*. Northvale, NJ: Aronson.

Wolf, E. (1983). Empathy and countertransference. In: *The Future of Psychoanalysis*, ed. A. Goldberg. New York: International Universities Press, pp. 309–26.

Wolf, E., Gedo, J., and Terman, D. (1972). On the adolescent process as a transformation of the self: Discussion. In: *The Search for the Self, Vol.2*, ed. P. Ornstein. New York: International Universities Press, pp. 659–62.

Wolf, V. (1925). *Mrs. Dalloway*. London: Hogarth Press, (1993, Penguin).

Yerkes, R., and Dodson, J. (1908). The relation of strength of stimulus to rapidity of habit formation. *J Comparative and Neurological Psychology*, 18:459–82.

Young-Bruehl, E. (1988). *Anna Freud: A Biography*. New York: Norton.

Index

About the Authors

Ronald R. Lee was formerly a professor of pastoral psychology at Garrett Theological Seminary in Evanston, Illinois. He now lives near Melbourne, Australia. He lectures in the department of psychiatry at the University of Melbourne and is an honorary consulting psychologist to St. Vincent Hospital's Mental Health Department. He was elected to the International Council of the International Association of Psychoanalytic Self Psychology in 2008.

Angie Rountree, a New Zealander of Maori extraction, is a graduate of the Melbourne College of Contemporary Psychotherapy who conducts psychotherapy in private practice in Melbourne using psychoanalytic self psychology. She teaches in the Empathink Summer Schools.

Sally McMahon, a social worker with private practices in Melbourne and Geelong, conducts psychotherapy using psychoanalytic self psychology. She teaches in the Australian College of Contemporary Somatic Psychotherapy and in Empathink Summer Schools.

www.ingramcontent.com/pod-product-compliance
Ingram Content Group UK Ltd.
Pitfield, Milton Keynes, MK11 3LW, UK
UKHW012036150926
475560UK00001B/43

9 780765 70633